Advance Praise

"As piercing as a crime story, *From Tulips to Bitcoins* guides us through the boom and bust cycles of commodity and crypto markets."

—FRANK MEYER, Journalist, n-tv

"Being a historian, I loved Torsten's insight into some of the most well-known (and less well-known) events that have shaped the commodities sector. I would thoroughly recommend *From Tulips to Bitcoins* to those wanting a better understanding of what makes commodities markets tick."

—ANDREW THAKE, Content Director, Mines and Money

"This book is a real enrichment for private and institutional investors, who are interested in commodities. Torsten Dennin shows a pattern in history and it is wise to read this book very carefully."

—JOCHEN STAIGER, Chief Executive Officer, Swiss Resource Capital

"I have been looking forward to this book! The historical events are intriguing and so fantastically concentrated!"

—THOMAS REHMET, Chief Operating Officer and Founding Partner, Bloxolid

"From economic ups to downs in oil, flowers, food, and metal markets, whether caused by a human error, wars, or a natural disaster, this book drives you through the financial storms of the past 400 years. Despite the stormy weather, there is always someone who wants to catch an opportunity even in the deepest crisis. Some succeed; some obviously fail. *From Tulips to Bitcoins* is a definite must-read."

—DR. ALEXANDER YAKUBCHUK, Chief Operating Officer and Exploration Director, Orsu Metals Corporation

"Torsten is a true student of the market, and his detailed account of major boom and bust cycles over time is a reminder that all of us are still students."

—DANIEL BREEZE, Managing Director and Head of Region, BMO Capital Markets

"The phrase 'boom and bust' is often associated with paper gains and cash losses, but Torsten's book demystifies this phrase. He navigates readers through a thrilling ride, explaining what it actually means and identifying the opportunities it presents."

—GREG HARRIS, Executive Director, CIBC World Markets

"Fantastic read. This will become the definite standard!"

—RONALD-PETER STÖFERLE, Managing Partner and Fund Manager, Incrementum AG

"Success and failure are closely related in commodity and crypto markets. Dennin succeeds in bringing together the economic facts and the persons involved. *From Tulips to Bitcoins* is an exciting read for anyone interested in commodities and cryptos."

—CHRISTIAN ANGERMEYER, Founder, Apeiron Investment Group

"Regardless of whether it's 300 years ago or today, the capital markets continue to attract fortune hunters seeking to ride the big bubbles. Every few years, investors and speculators who should have learned from the past seem to be brutally reeducated. Greed and fear will continue to dominate the investment markets. In *From Tulips to Bitcoin*, Dennin has impressively summarized the big bubbles of the last few centuries. This is an exciting and instructive book for the seasoned investor or anyone who wants to become one."

—HANNES HUSTER, Managing Director, Goldreport

"Torsten provides an informed and interesting perspective on several financial speculations throughout the last few hundred years. This history does not become boring in its repetition."

—MARK BURRIDGE, Managing Partner and Fund Manager, Baker Steel Capital Managers

"Torsten Dennin has written a must-read for anyone interested in commodity and cryptocurrency markets. Read this book—and learn from the past."

—DR. JAN PETER FIRNGES, Berlin Institute of Finance, Innovation and Digitalization e.V.

"The fate of Bitcoin will be known to us only in the future. However, I think that the Internet of Things will not be possible without cryptocurrencies. We cannot foresee if we will have an e-franc or another means of payment; we even do not know today."

—DOLFI MÜLLER, Mayor of Zug, Switzerland (2007–2018)

"An imposing and captivating journey through the history of commodities and their exaggerations. True to this day. Brilliant!"

—BJÖRN JESCH

FROM
TULIPS
TO
BITCOINS

FROM
TULIPS
TO
BITCOINS

A HISTORY OF FORTUNES
MADE AND LOST
IN COMMODITY MARKETS

TORSTEN DENNIN

RIVER GROVE
BOOKS

Published by River Grove Books
Austin, TX
www.rivergrovebooks.com

Distributed by River Grove Books

Design and composition by Greenleaf Book Group
Cover design by Greenleaf Book Group
Cover images by borchee, slubjug, and Vjom. Copyright 2019.
Used under license from iStockPhoto.com.

Publisher's Cataloging-in-Publication data is available.

Print ISBN: 978-1-63299-227-7

eBook ISBN: 978-1-63299-228-4

First Edition

To Alina

"The Wheel of Time turns and, Ages come and pass,
leaving memories that become legend.
Legend fades to myth, and even myth is long forgotten
when the Age that gave it birth comes again."

—**Robert Jordan** (1948–2007), *The Wheel of Time*

"Wall Street people learn nothing and forget everything [. . .]
to give way to hope, fear and greed."

—**Benjamin Graham** (1894–1976)

Contents

21. **Zinc: Flotsam and Jetsam** *(2005)*   129

The city of New Orleans, called The Big Easy, is well known for its jazz, Mardi Gras, and Creole cuisine. Less well known, however, is that about one-quarter of the world's zinc inventories are stored there. Hurricane Katrina's flooding makes the metal inaccessible, and concerns over damage cause the price of zinc to rise to an all-time high.

22. **Natural Gas: Brian Hunter**
    and the Downfall of Amaranth *(2006)*   135

In the aftermath of the closure of MotherRock, an energy-based hedge fund, the bust of Amaranth Advisors shakes the financial industry, as it is the largest hedge fund failure since the collapse of Long-Term Capital Management in 1998. The cause? A failed speculation in US natural gas futures. Brian Hunter, an energy trader at Amaranth, loses 6 billion USD within weeks.

23. **Orange Juice: Collateral Damage** *(2006)*   143

"Think big; think positive. Never show any sign of weakness. Always go for the throat. Buy low; sell high." That's the philosophy of Billy Ray Valentine, played by Eddie Murphy in the 1983 movie *Trading Places*. The film's final showdown has Murphy and Dan Aykroyd cornering the orange juice market. In reality, the price of frozen orange juice concentrate would quadruple between 2004 and 2006 on the New York Mercantile Exchange—a consequence of a record hurricane season.

24. **John Fredriksen: The Sea Wolf** *(2006)*   149

John Fredriksen controls a corporate empire founded on transporting crude oil. Among the pearls of that empire is Marine Harvest, the largest fish-farming company in the world.

25. **Lakshmi Mittal: Feel the Steel** *(2006)*   155

The dynamic growth of the Chinese economy and its hunger for raw materials rouses the suffering steel industry from near death. Through clever takeovers and the reorganization of rundown businesses, Lakshmi Mittal rises from a small entrepreneur in India to the largest steel tycoon in the world, a position he crowns with the acquisition of his main competitor and the world's second-largest steel producer—Arcelor.

42. Crypto Craze: Bitcoins and the Emergence of Cryptocurrencies *(2018)*   261

Bitcoins, the first modern cryptocurrency, emerged in 2009. The value of bitcoins explodes in 2017 from below 1,000 to above 20,000 USD, attracting worldwide attention. This stellar price rise, followed by a crash of almost 80 percent in 2018, makes bitcoins the biggest financial bubble in history, dwarfing even the Dutch tulip mania of the 17th century. Despite the boom and bust, the future looks bright, as underlying blockchain technology reveals its potential and starts to revolutionize daily life.

#Commodities

By Jochen Staiger,
CEO of Swiss Resource Capital

Commodities and futures trading have a long history, dating back to the days before exchanges as a way to insure farmers and producers against unexpected losses. With the establishment of the Chicago Mercantile Exchange in 1898, futures trades became standardized; suddenly this was a secure market and a way to speculate on the prices of soft commodities like wheat or corn without owning or physically needing them. At first the circle of speculative investors was limited, but over time that changed. Today we see hedge funds and even pension funds investing and speculating in commodities like gold, silver, copper, pork bellies, and frozen orange juice. In addition, there are large-scale private investors who think they can outsmart the markets. Times are changing rapidly, and we are now undoubtedly in the early stage of a new commodity and raw materials boom.

On the one hand, the commodity industry itself has changed a lot due to unforeseen taxation, changing governments, customs, and, most important, a new era of e-mobility, which will continue to alter the world of commodities dramatically in the next 20 to 30 years. Take transportation. In the future we will all want to drive in an environmentally "clean" way and will want to feel good about it. That means we need more copper, lithium, cobalt, zinc, nickel, silver, and lead to produce those environmentally desirable cars. In addition, the value of uranium is once again rising, because by 2030 we will need to more than double the energy consumption of 2018 to fuel our mobility. Last but not least, gold remains the ultimate secure commodity in which to place one's wealth. But because mines for all these commodities do not yet exist, a new bull market for them will start soon. We are about to create new bubbles and boom cycles because of that.

Throughout this book, starting with tulip mania and ending with the bitcoin craze, Torsten Dennin explains the different booms and busts in these markets. (Oddly enough, bitcoins are "mined" too, but they have eroded sharply in price as there is no real value behind them, nor are there any physical reserves in the ground.) The story is always the same; only the name of the bubble changes. Torsten explains the pattern, and it is wise to read this book very carefully. Investors need that historical information to better understand commodity markets. Perhaps they can learn something from the past and avoid making the same mistakes again. Also they will come to understand that commodity markets are always in danger of being manipulated, as they are sometimes very small and financial assets are often concentrated in a few hands that can move hundreds of billions.

Oil, tulips, silver, soybeans—markets can be moved by the "phantom of the opera," and Torsten's great contribution is to illuminate the hidden or unknown events affecting the commodity markets. Torsten is one of the few people in the sector who have been intensively involved with this topic since before the beginning of the commodity boom. For more than 16 years, he has dealt extensively with individual commodity markets and their hetero-geneous behaviors in terms of demand, supply, and prices.

I have known Torsten Dennin for more than 10 years, and I see him as one of the few top experts in commodity markets. Through the varied episodes in this book, he draws the reader into the topic of commodities, speculation, booms, and busts in a light and entertaining fashion. With its lessons from historic market events, this book offers true enrichment for private and institutional investors who are involved with commodities.

#Blockchain and Bitcoins

By Thomas Rehmet,
COO of Bloxolid

Since the eruption of the financial crisis in 2008, central banks all over the world have fired up the printing presses and flooded the financial markets with billions of dollars, euro, yen, and so on by means of Quantitative Easing. During this time of abundant liquidity, the raw materials market has increasingly attracted the attention of investors. Not only have institutional investors dealt in commodities, but more and more private investors are also seeking to invest their assets in real values, to protect themselves from the risks of a growing inflation of the fiat currencies. Material value is beating monetary value—those are the right catchwords.

But there were also repeated distortions within the raw materials markets, whether economic, political, or fraudulent events.

At the same time as the start of the financial crisis, on November 1, 2008, the founding document of cryptocurrencies was published, entitled plainly: "Bitcoin: A Peer-to-Peer Electronic Cash System."

That was the starting signal, since blockchain is now regarded as the next revolutionary technology in the whole world.

The most recent cryptocurrency hype in 2017 was the zenith of worldwide attention, while 2018 saw the reality check of hype vs. usability. 2019 will be the year of blockchain innovations. Our mission is to combine real assets such as precious metals with innovative blockchain technology to create a new class of safe and stable assets and currencies.

Bloxolid is establishing ARG3NTUM: the first cryptocurrency fully backed by physical silver and made in Germany.

Torsten Dennin has summarized wonderfully the past four centuries of financial and commodity market history, with their respective highlights. *From Tulips to Bitcoins* does not concentrate merely on the extreme events, but describes in detail all the highs and lows over the course of time, summarized chronologically in 42 chapters. A must-have for every investor. After all:

"Whoever knows the past can understand the present and shape the future."[1]

---

1   Golo Mann (historian 1909-1994).

Introduction

"The price of a commodity will never go to zero . . . you're not buying a piece of paper that says you own an intangible piece of company that can go bankrupt."
—**Jim Rogers**

"On April 20, 2020, WTI settles at $-37.6 a barrel on the New York Mercantile Exchange."
—**Marketwatch**

Commodities came into vogue with the beginning of the new millennium, as investing in crude oil, gold, silver, copper, wheat, corn, or sugar was introduced and marketed massively as an "investment theme" and a "new" asset class by banks and other financial intermediaries. The first investable commodity indices—the S&P Goldman Sachs Commodity Index and the Dow Jones AIG Commodity Index—were developed in the early 1990s, but after the turn of the millennium, every major investment bank offered its own commodity index and index concept. This development opened up a new and attractive asset class for institutional investors and wealthy individuals. We witness today the same development in the cryptocurrency world, making an exotic new asset class investable for the public.

The rapid growth of the Chinese economy is the key parameter of the commodity boom, which has been evident since around the year 2000, when the "workbench of the world" developed a gigantic hunger for raw materials: Imports of iron ore, coal, copper, aluminum and zinc began soaring, and China became the dominant factor in worldwide demand. The dynamic growth of the Chinese economy catapulted commodity prices sky-high. Like a gigantic vacuum cleaner, China swept up the markets for energy, metals, and agricultural goods, and prices kept rising, since supply growth couldn't keep up with rising demand.

At least temporarily, the collapse of Lehman Brothers and the worsening financial crisis caused a break in the skyrocketing prices. Crude oil crashed from its high at 150 USD/barrel during the summer of 2008 to below 40 USD in the spring of 2009 and turned negative during the coronavirus crisis in early 2020. As of today, prices recovered again, to above 80 USD. Industrial metals also benefited from the economic recovery during the coronavirus. In the aftermath of the financial crisis, and amid worries about rising public debt as well as the stability of the financial system, the interest of investors in gold rose substantially. In 2009, with the European debt crisis looming, gold surpassed the level of 1,000 USD for the first time, but it climbed above 2,000 USD in 2020.

Exotic agricultural products such as sugar, coffee, and cocoa were also among the goods that experienced significant price increases in 2009, as the ghost of "agflation" returned and spooked markets. Market recovery after the financial market meltdown of 2008/2009 proved not to be sustainable, however. After April 2011, commodity markets entered a severe five-year bear market. A period of sluggish growth, deleveraging, and a slower economy in China worsened a massive imbalance of demand and supply for raw materials. A supply glut caused crude oil to fall back to 26 USD early in 2016. But since then, commodity markets have turned around. Even a global pandemic caused merely a bump in prices, as recovery of growth and an increase in inflation is driving prices of energy, metals, and agriculture goods.

The Commodity Market and Cryptocurrencies—Some Basics

A commodity is any raw or primary economic good that is standardized. Organized commodity trading in the United States dates back almost 200 years, but commodity trading has a much longer history. It goes back several thousand years to ancient Sumerians, Greeks, and Romans, for example. In comparison to commodity trading, the history of the stock market—where you exchange pieces of ownership in companies—is much younger. In 1602 the Dutch East India Company officially became the world's first publicly traded company on the Amsterdam Stock Exchange in Europe. In the United States, the first major stock exchange was the New York Stock Exchange, created in 1792 on Wall Street in New York City.

Commodities can be categorized into **energy, metals, agriculture, livestock, and meat.** You can also differentiate between **hard commodities** like metals and oil, which are mined, and **soft commodities** that are grown, like wheat, corn, cotton, or sugar.

By far the most important commodity sector is **crude oil** and its products like gasoline, heating oil, jet fuel, or diesel. With the world consuming more than 100 million barrels of crude oil every day, that comes to a market value in excess of 6 billion USD per day, or 2.2 trillion USD per year! About three-quarters of crude oil goes into the transportation sector, fueling cars, trucks, planes, and ships.

Metal markets are usually divided into base and precious metals. By tonnage, **iron ore** is the biggest metal market, with more than 2.2 million tons of iron ore mined globally. Nearly two-thirds of global exports go to China; that's around 1 billion metric tons! At 70 USD per ton, the market value of iron ore, on the other hand, is rather small.

continued

The biggest metal market, in value of US dollars, is **gold**. Around 3,500 tons are mined per year, an equivalent of 140 billion USD. The total aboveground stocks of gold are estimated at around 190,000 tons; that makes gold a physical market of nearly 8 trillion USD. In value terms, **copper, aluminum,** and **zinc** are next, whereas other precious metal markets—silver, platinum, or palladium—are rather small.

In agriculture and livestock, the biggest markets are grains like wheat and corn as well as oil seeds like soybeans, and sugar.

Bitcoins were released as the first cryptocurrency in January 2009. Since then, more than 10,000 alternative coins ("altcoins") have been invented. The website coinmarketcap.com tracks prices of about 2,000 of them on a daily basis. After massive price corrections in 2018, the total market capitalization of all cryptocurrencies dropped below 200 billion USD. Bitcoins remain the dominant cryptocurrency, with a market capitalization of almost 1 trillion USD and a market share of almost 50 percent. The next most traded cryptos are **ethereum, cardano,** and **XRP**. Together these three cryptos amount to a market capitalization of 500 billion USD, less than half of bitcoins.

Organized commodity trading by itself has a longer history than equity markets, a fact often overlooked in the focus on the dramatic price swings over the past decades. For example, the Chicago Board of Trade (CBOT) was founded in 1848 to provide a platform for trading agricultural products such as wheat and corn. But trade and the speculation in commodities is much older than that. Around 4000 BCE, Sumerians used clay tokens to fix a future time, date, and number of animals, such as goats, to be delivered, which resembles modern commodity future contracts. Peasants in ancient Greece sold future deliveries of their olives, and records from ancient Rome show that wheat was bought and sold on the basis of future delivery. Roman traders hedged the prices of North African grains to protect themselves against unexpected price increases.

The history of commodity and crypto trading is colorful and instructive, and my aim with this book is to bring to life the most important episodes from the past up to the present. Some of these are spectacular boom-and-bust stories; others are examples of successful trading. All are worth paying attention to.

The first six chapters cover major events from the 17th to the 19th century. The Dutch tulip mania of the 1600s is considered one of the first documented market crashes in history and is still a topic of university lectures. In the 18th century, rice market fortunes were earned and lost in Japan, and in the process candlestick charts—which are used today in the financial industry—were invented. In the 1800s, J. D. Rockefeller's strategies and the rise of Standard Oil marked the beginning of the oil age. At nearly the same time in the midwestern United States, two men were trying to accumulate a fortune by manipulating wheat markets, while in California the Gold Rush broke out, with momentous consequences.

The episodes of commodity trading in the 20th century read like a "Who's Who" of business history: Aristotle Onassis, Warren Buffett, Bill Gates, and George Soros are just some of the major players. Meanwhile, crude oil was playing an increasingly important role.

The 1970s saw a real boom in commodity markets. After a shortfall in its wheat harvest, the Soviet Union went shopping for US agricultural goods, reinforcing an already positive price trend in wheat, corn, and soybeans. It's no overstatement to say that the rapid rise of crude oil prices during two oil crises in 1973 and 1979 changed the existing world order; the 1990 Gulf War was, in part, an attempt to reverse the clock. During this period the price of oil doubled. Among the collateral damage, the German conglomerate Metallgesellschaft was driven to the brink of insolvency by its crude oil-trading activities.

In the years that followed, a boom in gold, silver, and diamond prices was followed by a crash, and the Hunt brothers lost their oil-based family fortune because of the collapsing silver price. Warren Buffett, Bill Gates, and George Soros later were also involved in the silver market. And in the jungles of Borneo, the biggest gold scam of all time culminated in the bankruptcy of Bre-X. Another huge speculation in 1996 was caused by the Japanese trader Hamanaka in the copper market. That was repeated almost ten years later by Chinese copper trader Liu Qibing, which also signaled the shift of economic forces from Japan to China.

The emerging commodity boom of the new millennium attracted additional speculators and led to other boom-and-bust episodes. The collapse of Amaranth Advisors, which accumulated a loss of 6 billion USD within a few weeks by betting on natural gas, hit news headlines worldwide.

Weather often has played a role. The flooding of New Orleans by Hurricane Katrina led to a price spike in zinc in London, as the majority of zinc warehouses licensed by the London Metal Exchange became inaccessible. An active Atlantic hurricane season in 2006 not only caused oil prices to rise due to damage in the Gulf of Mexico but also pushed the price of orange juice concentrate to new heights.

A "millennium drought" threatened Australia, resulting in record high wheat prices worldwide. A few years later, a drought in India drove the price of sugar to levels that had not been observed for 30 years. Shortly before that, Cyclone Nargis in Asia caused a human catastrophe. Rice had to be rationed, and the rising prices led to unrest in several countries.

These fateful events often contrast with individual speculations, in which huge sums of money were involved. For example, trader Evan Dooley lost more than 100 million USD in wheat futures, just a few weeks after the loss of billions by Jérôme Kerviel, in the proprietary trading of French banking giant Société Générale, made world headlines. In 2011, the heritage of Marc Rich, "The King of Oil," was cashed in: Glencore celebrated its initial public offering, catapulting its CEO Ivan Glasenberg into the list of the top 10 richest people in Switzerland.

As a new decade began, the trendy themes of commodity markets shifted first to rare earths like neodymium and dysprosium, then to "energy metals" like lithium and cobalt, which are essential for energy storage and the electrification of transportation in the future. Since 2009 blockchain and bitcoins have caught the attention of traders. With tradeable bitcoin futures introduced at COMEX in 2017, the cryptocurrency has now become a commodity. With prices starting the year below 1,000 USD, bitcoins rose to 20,000 USD in 2017; then the cryptocurrency crashed by 80 percent in the first weeks of 2018. It took a severe crypto winter before prices recovered: 5,000, 10,000, 50,000 USD. The next target is 100,000 USD. In the history of the biggest financial bubbles of mankind, tulip mania was pushed to second place after 400 years at the top.

The chapters in this book are framed by the biggest and the second biggest financial bubbles in financial history: tulips and bitcoins. In between are the stories of 40 major commodity market events over four centuries. These episodes were accompanied by extreme price fluctuations and individual outcomes, and they demonstrate that each market can be subject to a boom-and-bust cycle due to a change in supply, demand, or other external factors. This holds true for South African–dominated platinum production, sudden frost in coffee or orange harvests, unrest in Côte d'Ivoire that affected the price of cocoa, strikes by Chilean mine workers that pushed copper prices up, and the fluctuation of bitcoin and other cryptocurrency prices because of financial woes.

Commodity and cryptocurrency markets are now at the crossroads of investment mega trends like demographic revolution, climate change, electrification, and digitalization. Investing in commodities, blockchain, and its applications will remain a thrilling ride.

1

Tulip Mania:
The Biggest Bubble in History

1637

In the Netherlands in the 17th century, tulips become a status symbol for the prosperous new upper class. Margin trading of the flower bulbs, which are weighed in gold, turns conservative businessmen into reckless gamblers who risk their homes and fortunes. In 1637 the bubble bursts.

"Like the Great Tulip Mania in Holland in the 1600s and the dot-com mania of early 2000, markets have repeatedly disconnected from reality."
—Tony Crescenzi, Pimco

A t the beginning of the 17th century, the Netherlands were on the threshold of a golden age, a period of economic and cultural prosperity that would last for about a hundred years. The country's religious freedom attracted a great diversity of people who were persecuted elsewhere because of their faith. At this time, the small and recently founded Republic of the Seven United Netherlands was rising to the rank of world power, becoming one of the leading nations in international trade, while the rest of Europe stagnated.

As the Hanseatic League (a dominant mercantile confederation in Europe in the Middle Ages) declined in power, the young maritime nation built colonies and trading posts around the world, including New Amsterdam (today's New York), Dutch India (Indonesia), and outposts in South America and the Caribbean, such as Aruba and the Netherlands Antilles. In 1602 merchants founded the Dutch East India Company (Vereenigde Oostindische Compagnie—VOC), which was endowed with sovereign rights and commercial monopolies by the government. The VOC was the first multinational corporation and one of the largest trading companies of the 17th and 18th centuries. Merchants from Haarlem and Amsterdam experienced an unprecedented economic boom.

The new class of rich merchants eagerly imitated the lifestyle of noble lords and ladies by building large estates with gigantic gardens. Tulips—which had arrived in Leiden from Armenia and Turkey in the 16th century by way of Constantinople, Vienna, and Frankfurt am Main—quickly became a luxury good and a status symbol of the wealthy. Upper-class women wore the exotic flowers as hair ornaments or on their clothes for social occasions.

Tulip Mania on the Silver Screen

Tulip mania is not only an important topic in economics and finance, but it also frequently surfaces in modern pop culture. In the movie *Wall Street: Money Never Sleeps* (2010), Michael Douglas explains to Shia LaBeouf what happened during the Dutch tulip mania, and a painting of tulips in his apartment is a mocking reminder of that bubble.

In 2017 Alison Owen and Harvey Weinstein produced the movie *Tulip Fever*, whose plot is set against the backdrop of the 17th-century tulip wars. In the movie a married noblewoman (Alicia Vikander) switches identities with her maid to escape the wealthy merchant she married, and has an affair with an artist (Dane DeHaan). She and her lover try to raise money by investing what little they have in the high-stakes tulip market.

The supply of tulip bulbs, however, grew very slowly since a bulb produced only two to three offspring every year, and the "mother" bulb actually faded away after a few seasons. Thus the supply lagged behind demand, and prices rose, opening up a lucrative niche for intermediaries. Tulips were now no longer sold by growers to wealthy clients but at auctions. And instead of occurring at organized exchanges, trading initially took place in pubs and inns. Later, groups gathered to form trading clubs, or informal exchanges, and they organized auctions according to fixed rules.

Initially the tulip bulbs were traded only during the planting season. However, as demand rose, traders sold bulbs that were still in the ground: It wasn't the flowers that were sold anymore, but the rights to buy tulip bulbs. By this time, in the 1630s, tulip trading had become a speculative business because no one knew what the flowers would actually look like. Around 400 painters were commissioned to produce pictures that would entice potential buyers.

> Tulips quickly advanced to become a status symbol. Prices skyrocketed, rising to 50 times the original level between 1634 and 1637.

Flower experts tried to satisfy their demanding clients with newer and ever more gorgeous creations characterized by particularly uniform petals and striking color patterns. The appearance of the mosaic virus, a plant infestation transmitted by aphids, actually created an extremely rare specimen, a surprising plant with flamed, two-color petals.

At the height of the boom, tulip contracts changed hands as many as 10 times. Prices skyrocketed and between 1634 and 1637 multiplied by a factor of 50. In individual cases, for example the variety Semper Augustus, buyers paid as much as 10,000 guilders for a single tulip bulb, about 20 times a craftsman's annual salary. In January 1637 alone, prices doubled in a short period of time. An entire house in Amsterdam could be bought for just three tulip bulbs. The speculative bubble reached its climax on February 5, 1637. Traders from all over the region met in Alkmaar, and 99 tulip bulbs changed hands for 90,000 guilders, the equivalent of one million US dollars today. The excess carried the seeds of the tulip's downfall since the crash had already begun two days earlier in Haarlem. There for the first time, at a simple pub auction, no buyer was found. The reaction spread rapidly. Suddenly all market participants wanted to sell, resulting in the collapse of the entire tulip market in the Netherlands.

> In 1637, the bubble burst: Prices fell by 95 percent, and trading ceased.

On February 7, 1637, trading stopped entirely. Prices had fallen by 95 percent, and the number of open contracts referring to tulip bulbs exceeded existing bulb supply by a huge multiple. Both buyers and sellers were hoping for a solution from the Dutch government. In the end, futures trading was prohibited, and buyers and sellers were forced to agree among themselves.

Large parts of the Dutch population had been infected by tulip fever, from nobles and merchants to farmers and casual workers. Most participants, knowing nothing about the market, started their trading with the tulip bulbs and mortgaged their house or farm to increase their initial capital. However, the booming economy in the Netherlands did dampen the negative economic impact of this speculative bubble.

Dutch tulip mania is the first documented market crash in history, and the analysis of the process can be applied to the dot-com bubble of 1998–2001 or any other financial bubble. In the decades following the tulip fever, the flower changed from an upper-class status symbol to a widespread ornamental plant, which it still is today, almost 400 years later. And almost 80 percent of the world's tulip crop still comes from the Netherlands.

Key Takeaways

- During the Dutch economic boom of the Golden Age, during the 17th century, tulips became an exclusive status symbol of the new, wealthy upper class.

- Prices skyrocketed, rising by more than 50 times between 1634 and 1637. Wide segments of the Dutch population were gripped by the speculative fever.

- Before the bust, tulip bulbs traded for as much as the value of a house in Amsterdam. Then, in February 1637, the bubble burst. Prices fell by 95 percent.

- The tulip mania is the first well-documented market crash in history. And for almost four centuries, it was known as the biggest financial bubble in history, much larger than the dot-com crash of 2000.

2

The Dojima Rice Market and the "God of Markets"

1750

In the 18th century, futures contracts on rice are introduced at the Dojima rice market in Japan. The merchant Homma Munehisa earns the nickname "God of Markets" for his market intelligence, and he becomes the richest man in Japan.

> *"After 60 years of working day and night I have gradually acquired a deep understanding of the movements of the rice market."*
> —Homma Munehisa

During Japan's Edo period, which began in 1603, the country enjoyed its longest uninterrupted period of peace, and during this time domestic trade and the agriculture sector strengthened. The Dojima rice market was established in Osaka toward the end of the 17th century, and the city became the center of Japanese rice trading in the hundred years that followed. At the Dojima market, rice was traded for other goods, such as silk or tea. A common currency had not yet been established, but rice was generally accepted as payment (for taxes, for example).

Due to the financial needs of the country's feudal lords, warehouses started to accept warrants, which promised future delivery instead of the actual goods, and many landowners pledged their harvests for years in advance. Soon trading warrants were uncoupled from trades of physical rice at Dojima; a lively trade in so-called rice coupons evolved. Over time the rice coupons surpassed rice production levels by far. In the middle of the 18th century, almost four times the quantity of rice produced was traded in rice coupons.

> **In 1749 around 100,000 bales of rice were traded in Osaka, but at the same time, there were only about 30,000 physical bales of rice in Japan.**

What Is a Rice Coupon?

Rice coupons are a standardized form of a promise for the future delivery of rice, in which the price, quantity, and delivery date are fixed. If the market price is above the agreed price, the buyer makes a profit. If the price of rice is lower than the contract price, the buyer suffers a loss. Rice coupons are the first known standardized commodity futures in the world, and the Dojima rice market can be regarded as the first modern futures exchange, predating the introduction of trading in Amsterdam, London, New York, and Chicago.

In 1750, at the age of 36, Homma Munehisa took over his family's rice-trading company. As the owner of large rice fields in the northwest of Japan, Homma specialized in grain trading. At first he concentrated his activities in Sakata, where his family was located. Later he moved to Osaka.

There Homma began to trade rice coupons, and in order to be informed as quickly as possible about the actual harvest in Sakata, he built up his own communication system, which covered about 600 kilometers. His family's rice fields offered him valuable insider information. But in addition, Homma was probably the first to use analyses of historic price movements. He invented a graph, later known as a candlestick chart, that is still in use today. In contrast to a line chart, the "candles" not only show the opening and closing prices in the course of a day but also track the intraday high and low prices. Homma was convinced that by analyzing historic price movements, it was possible to recognize repetitive patterns that would allow him to make a profit.

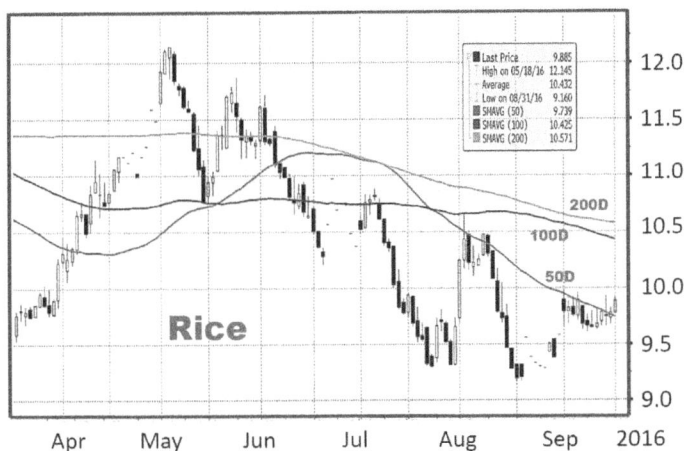

Figure 1. Rice. Candlestick chart in USD/cwt 2016, Chicago Board of Trade (CBOT). Data: Bloomberg, 2019.

The following episode is legendary: Over several days Homma, who seemed to have more background information than his competitors, bought more and more rice from local farmers at the rice exchange in Dojima. Again and again he drew a paper out of his pocket and peered at symbols that remotely looked like candles. On the fourth day, a messenger from the countryside arrived in Osaka with reports of harvest losses because of a storm. The price for rice in Dojima jumped up, but there was hardly any rice for sale.

In just a few days Homma had gotten control of Japan's entire rice market, and he became rich beyond description. After his success at the Dojima exchange, Homma moved to Edo (Tokyo) and continued his ascent, acquiring the nickname "God of Markets." Raised to the aristocracy, he served as a financial advisor to the Japanese government. He died in 1803. It was almost 200 years before his invention, the candlestick chart, was rediscovered and popularized by investors and traders alike.

Key Takeaways

- The trader Homma Munehisa cornered the Japanese rice market in 1750, buying physical supplies of rice and acquiring rice coupons on the basis of his superior market intelligence.

- Earning the nickname "God of Markets," he became the richest man in the country.

- Homma invented candlestick charts, which are still used today in financial and technical analysis.

3

The California Gold Rush

1849

Gold Rush! Some 100,000 adventurers stream into California in 1849 alone, lured by the vision of incredible wealth. The following year, the value of gold production in California exceeds the total federal budget of the United States. Because of this treasure, California becomes the 31st state in the Union in 1850.

"Gold! Gold! Gold from the American River!"
—Samuel Brannan

It's hard to imagine today, but before 1848 California was an inhospitable and remote place, populated mainly by Mexicans, descendants of Spaniards, and Native Americans. Among the few European settlers was the Swiss-German émigré John Augustus Sutter, who had left his wife and children in Switzerland after the bankruptcy of his company and moved to the American West. By this time he owned a large piece of land in the Sacramento Valley, a settlement he called Nueva Helvetica. Sutter built a fort at the confluence of the American and Sacramento Rivers, and on the southern arm of the American River, near the village of Coloma, he started to put up a sawmill. It was there, on the morning of January 24, 1848, that one of the workers, carpenter James Wilson Marshall, found a gold nugget in the riverbed. Sutter and Marshall tried to keep the find secret while they gradually bought up more land. But the news of the spectacular discovery couldn't be concealed for long when Sutter's employees began to pay for goods with the gold they had found.

Things soon got out of control. Samuel Brannan, a Coloma shopkeeper, filled a bottle with gold nuggets and traveled to San Francisco. There he rode through the streets, waving the bottle and shouting, "Gold, gold from the American River," to gain attention for his business, which just happened to include prospecting equipment. The California Gold Rush was on.

In 1848 only 6,000 people came to search for gold. But the following year gold fever truly took hold. As news of the finds spread, adventurers from all over the world hurried to California. Almost 100,000 people traveled to California in search of wealth and fast fortune in the boom year of 1849. They came from Asia as well. More and more Chinese arrived at Gum San, the "mountain of gold," as they called California.

The numbers are staggering. In 1848 California had fewer than 15,000 people. In 1852, four years after the first gold discovery, the population exploded tenfold. San Francisco grew from fewer than 1,000 inhabitants in 1848 to about 25,000 residents in 1850. By 1855 more than 300,000 adventurers were searching for gold, and there were plenty of merchants to service—and take advantage of—them.

The Gold Rush in the Movies

With *No Country for Old Men*, directed by the Coen brothers, and *The Hateful Eight,* by Quentin Tarantino, recent years have seen a comeback of the Western as a movie genre. The concept of a gold rush was a popular theme in these movies in the past. Perhaps the most prominent is *The Gold Rush* (1925), a classic silent movie with Charlie Chaplin in his Little Tramp persona participating in the Klondike Gold Rush.

Re-released in 1942, the movie remains one of Chaplin's most celebrated works. More recent is *Gold*, made in 2013 by Thomas Arslan:
The plot focuses on a small group of German compatriots who head
into the hostile northern interior of British Columbia in the summer
of 1898, at the height of the Klondike Gold Rush, in search of the
precious metal.

Prices for prospecting gear multiplied by 10. In Coloma, Sam Brannan's business took in 150,000 USD per month. Still, the promise of great
wealth kept miners panning for gold in the riverbeds. Success meant they'd
earn about 20 times as much as a worker on the East Coast in one day. In
many cases six months of hard work in the goldfields earned adventurers
the equivalent of six years of "normal" work. Annual gold production in
California rose to 77 tons in 1851.

The value of that amount of gold exceeded the total US gross domestic product at that time. Many miners, though, had a hard time holding
on to their earnings. Far from civilization, merchants charged fantastic
prices for their goods, while saloonkeepers profited greatly on alcohol and
gambling. In truth, the actual winners of the gold rush were businessmen
and merchants like Samuel Brannan. The most famous of these is probably entrepreneur Levi Strauss. Born in Germany, he set up shop in San
Francisco, and when he realized prospectors needed sturdy trousers to
work in, he trimmed tent fabric to meet the demand. Jeans were born.

**Almost 100,000 people came to California
in 1849 alone. By 1855 there would be
more than 300,000 new migrants.**

With its growth in wealth and population, California's political
weight also increased. In 1850 the "Golden State" was incorporated into
the United States. The boom didn't last forever, though. Around 1860 the

easily accessible gold reserves had been depleted, and many cities were abandoned. The population of Columbia, founded just 10 years earlier, dropped from 20,000 people to 500. Boom towns became ghost towns.

The pattern of the California Gold Rush would be repeated in other places over the next half century. Within a decade, the population of Australia multiplied by 10 in the aftermath of the 1851 gold rush on that continent, which evolved from a British convict colony to a more or less civilized state. In 1886 gold was found on the Witwatersrand south of Pretoria in Transvaal, South Africa. In a few years, Transvaal became the largest gold producer in the world. And in 1896, gold was discovered on the Klondike River in Alaska, leading to boom towns such as Dawson City at the confluence of the Klondike and the Yukon Rivers, which grew from 500 to 30,000 inhabitants within two years.

As for California, Sutter's settlement eventually developed into Sacramento, the capital of the state. The huge wave of 19th-century gold seekers is recalled in the name of San Francisco's football team—the 49ers. And what about John Augustus Sutter? He died in poverty in 1880.

Key Takeaways

- The discovery of gold by Swiss-German immigrant John Augustus Sutter and James Wilson Marshall triggered a true global gold rush. More than the prospectors, however, it was the merchants who generally became rich selling equipment and services.

- The California Gold Rush of 1849 kicked off a huge wave of immigration—with 100,000 new arrivals in that year alone.

- The discovery of gold accelerated California's development, leading to statehood in 1850.

- The pattern of gold rush booms was followed in Australia, South Africa, and the Yukon.

4

Wheat:
Old Hutch Makes a Killing

The Chicago Board of Trade is established in 1848, and Benjamin Hutchinson, known as "Old Hutch," later becomes famous by successfully cornering the wheat market. He temporarily controls the whole market and earns millions.

> *"Did you hear what Charlie said?*
> *Charlie said we were philanthropists! Why bless my buttons,*
> *we're gamblers! . . . You're a gambler! and I'm a gambler!"*
> —Benjamin Hutchinson

A Corner in Wheat is a short silent American film, made in 1909, that tells of a greedy tycoon who tries to corner the world market on wheat, destroying the lives of the people who can no longer afford to buy bread. The classic movie, set in the wheat-speculation trading pits of the Chicago Board of Trade building, was adapted from a novel and a short story by Frank Norris, titled *The Pit* and "A Deal in Wheat," respectively. In 1994 *A Corner in Wheat* was selected for preservation in the US National Film Registry by the Library of Congress as being "culturally, historically, or aesthetically significant."

Chicago had become the hub for agricultural products in the American Midwest in the 19th century, as large quantities of grains entered the city and more and more warehouses were built to better coordinate supply and demand. Prices regularly came under pressure, and in 1848 the Chicago Board of Trade (CBOT) was founded.

Benjamin Peters Hutchinson, nicknamed "Old Hutch," is famous for being the first person to corner the wheat market. Born in Massachusetts in 1829, he moved to Chicago at the age of 30, started trading in grain, and became a member of the CBOT.

In 1866 Hutchinson was betting on a poor wheat harvest. From May to June of that year, he grew his position, both in the spot market and in futures contracts. His average realized price was reported to be 88 US cents per bushel. Then, in August, the price began to rise steadily because of below-average harvests in Illinois, Iowa, and other states that delivered grain to Chicago. On August 4, the price of wheat ranged between 90 and 92 US cents per bushel. Short sellers soon realized that there would not be enough wheat to meet their delivery obligations. (The strategy of short sellers is to sell contracts at the beginning of the season; they assume that prices during harvest season will come under pressure, and they'll be able to close their positions with a profit.)

By August 18, Hutchinson's control of the tight physical market had driven wheat prices up to 1.87 USD. He had become a rich man. As a consequence, however, the CBOT declared illegal the practice of acquiring futures contracts and trying to prevent physical delivery at the same time.

What Is a Commodity Futures Exchange?

The Chicago Board of Trade, established in 1848, is one of the oldest organized commodity futures exchanges in the world. The function of every futures exchange is to provide liquidity and a central market-place for buyers and sellers to handle standardized contracts (futures and options) that are subject to physical delivery in the future. At the CBOT, these are mainly agricultural products such as wheat, corn, or pork bellies. In 1864 the CBOT introduced the first standardized exchange-traded futures contracts. In 2007 the CBOT and the Chicago Mercantile Exchange (CME) merged into the CME Group. Ten years later, the CME introduced bitcoin futures in the commodity segment of the exchange.

In 1888 Hutchinson saw another opportunity for lucrative speculation. During the spring, he bought wheat in the spot market and acquired more and more futures contracts for maturity and delivery in September. The storage capacity in the city was around 15 million bushels, and Hutchinson controlled most of the wheat available in Chicago through the spot market.

**On September 22 the wheat price broke
the psychological level of 1 USD.**

As a few years before, his average realized price was below 90 US cents per bushel. But this time Old Hutch was facing a powerful group of short sellers who included John Cudahy, Edwin Pardridge, and Nat Jones; they would challenge him over future deliveries in September.

Until August, the price of wheat remained at around 90 US cents per bushel. But Old Hutch again had the right instincts. Frost destroyed a large part of the local crop. And European demand for wheat imports also grew because of an unexpectedly large crop deficit. The price started to rise, and on September 22 it broke the psychologically important mark of 1 USD.

One day before maturity of the futures contracts, prices climbed to 1.50 USD. Hutchinson set the final settlement price at 2 USD.

On September 27, three days before the contracts for September expired, wheat prices rose to 1.05 USD, then increased further to 1.28 USD. Market participants caught on the wrong side began to panic, and short sellers were forced to cover their positions in what's known as a "short squeeze." With his positions in the physical market, Old Hutch controlled the price. The day before maturity, on September 29, he offered 1.50 USD to the big short sellers and raised the settlement price to 2 USD. Based on his average realized price, Hutchinson must have realized a profit of around 1.5 million USD.

He wasn't done speculating, however. Within the next three years, Hutchinson had given up his profit. Later he lost his entire fortune.

Key Takeaways

- Benjamin Peters Hutchinson, nicknamed "Old Hutch," was a grain trader who bought wheat on the spot market and acquired contracts for future delivery at the Chicago Board of Trade (CBOT). By cornering the wheat market in Chicago in 1866 and 1888, he was able to double his investments within weeks, earning a fortune.

- The CBOT was established in 1848 and is today one of the oldest organized commodity futures exchanges in the world. The exchange later declared illegal the practice of cornering a market by buying harvests physically and financially at the same time.

- The CBOT and the Chicago Mercantile Exchange (CME) merged in 2007 to become the CME Group.

5

Rockefeller and Standard Oil

The US Civil War triggers one of the first oil booms. During this time, John D. Rockefeller founds the Standard Oil Company. Within a few years, through an aggressive business strategy, he dominates the oil market, from production and processing to transport and logistics.

"Competition is a sin."
—John D. Rockefeller

The production of petroleum from coal or crude oil as an inexpensive alternative to whale oil for lamp fuel is commonly regarded as the beginning of the modern petroleum industry. On August 27, 1859, Colonel Edwin Drake discovered a lucrative deposit of crude oil near Titusville, Pennsylvania. The onset of the American Civil War two years later sparked the first oil boom in that state. The price of oil rose to more than 100 USD per barrel (measured in today's prices). Drilling rigs soon spread across farms in northwestern Pennsylvania, as hundreds of small refineries were created near the oil wells and along the transport routes to Pittsburgh and Cleveland, Ohio, cities that were home to major railroad crossroads: The New York Central and Erie Railroad led to Cleveland, while Pittsburgh served as an important east-west junction on the Pennsylvania Railroad. The majority of freight on these railways still consisted of grains and industrial goods, but the volume of oil products was growing rapidly.

In 1863 John Davison Rockefeller, age 24, founded a small oil refinery in Cleveland together with his brother William. The son of penniless German immigrants, John worked as a dishwasher during his school years and graduated as an accountant. Rockefeller's company was successful and prospered, despite fluctuations in the market. The oil boom had led to a spike in production, and the price of the commodity fell from 20 USD per barrel in 1861 to only 10 US cents. In 1866, one year after the end of Civil War, however, the price had risen again to more than 1.50 USD.

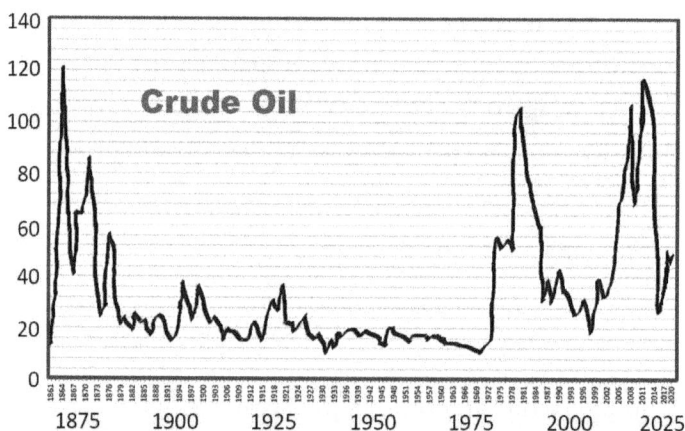

Figure 2. Crude oil prices 1861–2018, in USD/barrel (real prices of 2015). Data: BP Statistical Review of Energy, 2019.

With William, Rockefeller founded a second refinery in 1866, then, in 1870, he reorganized his company, naming it the Standard Oil Company. A year later, Rockefeller and other refinery owners formed an alliance to obtain discounts from railway operators. In addition, this alliance was responsible for railway operators raising prices for competitors, which led to an oil war in 1872.

At the end of that year, Rockefeller took over the presidency of the National Refiners Association, which represented 80 percent of all American refineries. He would continue to aggressively grow Standard Oil, and by 1873 he had managed to acquire or to control almost all refineries in Pennsylvania.

From Crude Oil to the Plastic-Wrapped Cucumber at Your Supermarket

A refinery splits crude oil into its various components, such as light and heavy fuel oil, kerosene, and gasoline. With additional steps, a variety of alkanes and alkenes can also be produced from petroleum. Petroleum remained the most important use of crude oil until the rapid spread of automobiles in the 1920s. Although Henry Ford had intended ethanol to fuel his cars, the Rockefeller family, as founders of the Standard Oil Company, pushed for gasoline to power automobiles and succeeded.

Today, oil is still by far the most important source of energy, at the core of every industrial society, and the base for numerous chemical products, such as fertilizers, plastics, and paints. Although three-quarters of crude oil production is used in transportation, it will take e-mobility further decades at least to challenge the supremacy of crude oil.

Between 1875 and 1878, Rockefeller traveled throughout America to convince the owners of the 15 largest refineries to become part of his Standard Oil Company. Smaller companies had to follow suit or perish: For example, the plant of the Vacuum Oil Company, founded in 1866, went up in flames. Other entrepreneurs sold Rockefeller their companies for well below half of their market value. As early as 1882,

Standard Oil controlled more than 90 percent of the refinery business in the United States.

Next, the company turned to pipeline and distribution networks. Rockefeller built his own sales channels, forcing other trading networks out of the market. In late 1882, the National Petroleum Exchange opened in New York to facilitate the trading of oil futures.

In the end, Standard Oil had a hold over virtually the whole crude oil value chain in the United States—from oil production to processing, transport, and logistics—and began to extend its dominance to the global oil market as well.

Accumulating a fortune of around 900 million USD by 1913, Rockefeller represented the American Dream, the richest man of all time.

By transforming his enterprise, Rockefeller was able to postpone the destruction of his empire. But his aggressive company strategy eventually prompted the first antimonopoly legislation in the United States. In 1911, the Supreme Court ordered the dismantling of Standard Oil. As a result, the company's share price fell like a stone. Rockefeller, nevertheless, was able to buy back large quantities of the stock, which only increased his fortune in the years that followed. World War I, increasing motorization, and advances in the industrialization process all resulted in a rapid increase in the demand for oil.

Eventually Standard Oil was broken up into 34 individual companies, from which today's ExxonMobil and Chevron have emerged. Other sections of the original firm were liquidated over time or were absorbed by other oil and gas companies.

Back in 1913, the total wealth of John D. Rockefeller was estimated at 900 million USD, the equivalent of 300 billion USD today. This is more than twice the private wealth of Jeff Bezos, founder and CEO of

Amazon and, according to *Forbes*, the wealthiest man in the world today (before his divorce).

The son of John D. Rockefeller, Nelson, almost became president of the United States, but instead served as vice president from 1974 to 1977. David Rockefeller, the last grandson of John D. Rockefeller, died in 2017. Even today, the name Rockefeller is a symbol of vast wealth and also of philanthropy.

Key Takeaways

- The American Civil War fueled the first crude oil boom in history. Prices in 1861 soared above 100 USD (in today's currency).

- John D. Rockefeller founded the Standard Oil Company, a corporation that not only came to control the US market for crude oil but also dominated the global market.

- The rise of the automotive industry and industrialization in general propelled all developing countries into the oil age.

- John D. Rockefeller personified the American Dream par excellence, rising from a dishwasher to a multibillionaire. Even in 2019 his surname remains a synonym for immeasurable wealth.

- Though Standard Oil was broken up, successor companies like Exxon-Mobil and Chevron are still operating today.

6

Wheat:
The Great Chicago Fire

1872

The Great Chicago Fire of October 1871 leads to massive destruction in the city and leaves more than 100,000 residents homeless. The storage capacities for wheat are also significantly reduced. Trader John Lyon sees this as an opportunity to earn a fortune.

> *"Being a firefighter is not something you do;*
> *it's something you are."*
> —the TV show *Chicago Fire*

The sun burned hot in the American Midwest during the summer of 1871. In and around Chicago, only 3 centimeters of rain fell between July and October. Water resources were nearing depletion, and small fires sprang up regularly. On October 8, a fire broke out in a barn, initiating a disaster that became known as the "Great Chicago Fire."

Winds from the southwest fanned the flames and set neighboring houses on fire. Traveling quickly, the fire spread toward the city center and crossed the Chicago River. It took two days to get the conflagration under control, and by then an area of more than 8 square kilometers and 17,000 buildings had been destroyed. Every third inhabitant of the city lost his home. The damage has been estimated at more than 200 million USD. In addition to large parts of the city, the fire destroyed 6 out of the 17 warehouses approved by the Chicago Board of Trade (CBOT). The city's total storage capacity decreased from about 8 to 5.5 million bushels. John Lyon, a large-scale wheat trader, saw the opportunity to make a profit. He joined with another trader, Hugh Maher, and CBOT broker P. J. Diamond, to manipulate the wheat market.

What's What with Wheat

Different types of wheat are traded on futures exchanges. In the United States, wheat is traded on the Chicago Board of Trade (CBOT) and the Kansas City Board of Trade (KCBT), with the volume of Chicago Soft Red Winter Wheat (soft wheat) outweighing Kansas Hard Red Winter Wheat (hard wheat). Chicago wheat is mainly grown in an area that extends from Central Texas to the Great Lakes and the Atlantic Ocean. Kansas wheat grows primarily in Kansas, Nebraska, Oklahoma, and parts of Texas.

At CBOT, wheat is traded in US cents per bushel and designated with the abbreviation W plus a letter and number that stands for the current contract month (e.g., W Z9 for wheat delivered in December 2019). A contract refers to 5,000 bushels of wheat, with one bushel corresponding to 27.2 kilograms. Therefore, one contract refers to around 136 metric tons of wheat.

In the spring of 1872, the group began to buy wheat in the spot and futures market. Wheat prices rose continuously through early July, and contracts specifying delivery in August traded between 1.16 and 1.18 USD per bushel. At the beginning of July an average of just 14,000 bushels of wheat a day reached the city; by the end of the month, prices had climbed to 1.35 USD. In response, however, wheat deliveries to Chicago increased.

By the beginning of August, 27,000 bushels a day were coming in. But luck was still with Lyon. Another warehouse burned to the ground, and the city's already stretched storage capacity was reduced by another 300,000 bushels. Rumors about a below-average harvest due to bad weather pushed up prices even more. On August 10 these two factors combined to push wheat contracts for August up to 1.50 USD. On August 15 prices climbed to above 1.60 USD. But then the wheel of fortune started to turn.

As more and more wheat reached the city of Chicago, Lyon was forced to give up.

The high prices incentivized farmers to speed up their harvest: Crops were picked into the night. In the second week of August, about 75,000 bushels of wheat reached Chicago each day; a week later that figure had risen to 172,000 bushels. For the rest of the month, daily deliveries increased to nearly 200,000 bushels.

Wheat that had already been shipped from Chicago to Buffalo returned to the Windy City, because of the high local prices. Newly opened warehouses also added to the storage capacity in the city, bringing it to more than 10 million bushels—two million bushels more than before the Great Fire!

To secure their profits and stabilize prices, Lyon and his partners had to buy all the wheat coming into Chicago. But they were already leveraged by local banks, and the additional funds they needed soon exceeded the group's financial options.

On Monday, August 19, Lyon had to admit defeat. He could no longer afford to buy wheat in the spot market. The price of wheat with delivery in August fell by 25 US cents. The following day prices dropped another 17 US cents. The crash ruined John Lyon, who was unable to meet his margin calls. His attempt at market manipulation ended in financial disaster and bankruptcy.

Key Takeaways

- The Great Chicago Fire of 1871 led to massive destruction and left more than 100,000 people homeless.

- With the number of grain warehouses drastically reduced, a group of speculators around John Lyon saw a big opportunity in the wheat market. Together they tried to corner the wheat market, but rises in price also resulted in increased shipments of wheat to the city. After initially increasing to 1.60 USD, the price of wheat crashed.

- Lyon and his friends were unable to meet their margin calls. Their attempt at cornering the market ended in bankruptcy and financial disaster.

7

Crude Oil:
Ari Onassis's Midas Touch

1956

Aristotle Onassis, an icon of high society, seems to have the Midas touch. Apparently emerging out of nowhere, he builds the world's largest cargo and tanker fleet and earns a fortune with the construction of supertankers and the transport of crude oil. Onassis closes exclusive contracts with the royal Saudi family, and he is one of the winners in the Suez Canal conflict.

> *"The secret of business is to know*
> *something that nobody else knows."*
> —Aristotle Onassis

At the beginning of December 2005 the youngest billionaire in the world, Athina Roussel, age 20, celebrated her wedding to 32-year-old Brazilian equestrian Álvaro Alfonso de Miranda Neto. A thousand bottles of Veuve Clicquot were ordered for the 1,000 guests at the São Paulo nuptials. Athina was the only heiress to the Onassis fortune, the last of her clan. Her grandfather, Aristotle "Ari" Socrates Onassis, would have been almost 100 years old.

A central figure in the high society of the 1950s, '60s, and '70s, Aristotle Onassis earned his fortune by constructing supertankers and transporting crude oil. Like Rockefeller, Onassis became synonymous with wealth and fortune. But his rise to fame was not a straightforward one.

The Onassis family initially became wealthy through the tobacco trade. Based in the city of Smyrna, Ari's father had a fleet of ten ships. Ari himself enjoyed a good education. At 16 he already spoke four languages—Greek, Turkish, English, and Spanish. In 1922, however, when the Turks retook Smyrna (Izmir), which had been under Greek rule since World War I, the family had to flee. They were forced to leave everything behind. Virtually penniless, Onassis migrated to Argentina and earned money by importing tobacco. He also kept himself afloat with occasional jobs.

> **In the 1930s the world economic crisis offered Onassis an attractive business opportunity in the form of large-scale transport of crude oil.**

The economic crisis of the 1930s offered Onassis the opportunity to get into the crude oil transport business on a large scale. There were rumors that the Canadian National Steamship Company was in serious financial difficulties and that several of its freighters were for sale. Onassis took all the money he'd accumulated and purchased six rundown ships for 120,000 USD, one-tenth of their value at the time.

With that bold move, Onassis laid the foundation of his empire. The purchase quickly paid off during the economic recovery that followed. At the beginning of World War II, Onassis's fleet had grown to 46 freighters and tankers, and he leased them to the Allied forces on profitable terms.

Ari and the Women

Aristotle Onassis married into another family of successful Greek shipowners when he wed Athina "Tina" Livanos. They divorced in the 1950s, however, after he began a long relationship with celebrated opera diva Maria Callas, who separated from her husband for Onassis. In 1968 Onassis married Jacqueline Kennedy, widow of President John F. Kennedy. At the time, Onassis was 62 years old; Jackie was 23 years younger. Because of her spending on travel and shopping, Onassis nicknamed her "supertanker," since he said she cost him just as much as a ship.

During the war, Onassis's ships changed their flags to neutral Panama and remained undisturbed by naval battles. As more and more freight ships were lost to the conflict, his own fleet's rates rose higher, creating a gold mine for Onassis. After the war, he expanded the number of his ships into the largest private commercial fleet in the world, and in 1950, he commissioned the biggest tanker in the world, 236 meters long, to be completed at the German Howaldt shipyard.

But it was not until spring 1954 that the 48-year-old Onassis made a definite breakthrough. Through shady contacts and friendships, he struck a lucrative agreement with the royal family of Saudi Arabia. Onassis not only received the exclusive right to transport crude oil for King Saud, but he also was to produce a new supertanker for the country almost every month and would participate in the sale of crude oil. Together Onassis and Saudi Arabia set up the Saudi Arabian Tanker Company, with a goal of having 25 to 30 ships that could transport about 10 percent of the country's crude oil.

By royal decree the Arabian American Oil Company (Aramco) would have had to use Saudi Arabian ships for the tonnage previously shipped in charter ships. Aramco—a joint venture among Standard Oil (New Jersey), Standard Oil of California, Socony Vacuum, and Texas Co.—had had a concession agreement with King Ibn Saud since 1933 and was responsible for nearly 10 percent of the world's oil production. About half of the oil produced in Saudi Arabia went by pipeline to Lebanon; the other half was transported by tankers. Of the tanker market, 40 percent of crude was shipped in Aramco's own tankers; for the remaining 60 percent, the company used charters.

The Suez Canal conflict resulted in enormously profitable opportunities for Onassis.

By breaking into this system, Onassis made some powerful enemies. The United States tried to block the agreement to safeguard its own influence, and Europe—which in the 1950s derived 90 percent of its oil supply from the Middle East, whose largest producer was Saudi Arabia—was also unenthusiastic. The deal with Saudi Arabia ultimately fell through, and without the new freight orders, Onassis's ships sat idle in shipyards around the world. The Greek magnate's empire began to crumble. But he was rescued by the Suez crisis in 1956.

With the growing economic importance of crude oil, European nations increasingly were dependent on the use of the Suez Canal to bring fuel from the producing countries. But the nationalist policies of the new Egyptian president, Gamal Abdel Nasser, were intensifying conflicts with Israel as well as with France and Great Britain, which controlled the canal. Egypt blocked the Gulf of Aqaba and Suez Canal to Israeli shipping; then on July 26, 1956, Nasser nationalized the Suez Canal.

Britain's prime minister, Anthony Eden, responded together with Israel and France with Operation Musketeer. On October 29, Israel invaded the Gaza Strip and the Sinai Peninsula and quickly pushed toward the canal. Two days later Britain and France began bombing Egyptian airports. Although the Egyptian army was quickly beaten and the war was over by December 22, 1956, sunken ships continued to block the Suez passage until April 1957.

The crisis brought salvation to Aristotle Onassis. No other shipowner had the transport capacity to move the oil. With more than 100 idle tankers and virtually no competition, he was able to double his rates, once again earning a fortune. The Six-Day War in 1967 offered a similar opportunity, and later, during the oil crisis in 1973, Onassis's Olympic Maritime Company posted a profit of more than 100 million USD.

Aristotle Onassis earned his fortune through the transport of crude oil. He became a society icon through his extravagant lifestyle and his marriage to Jackie Kennedy.

By then, Onassis's total private wealth was estimated at more than 1 billion USD. Throughout his career he had diversified into other businesses: He bought banks in Geneva, founded Olympic Airways, built the Olympic Tower on Fifth Avenue in New York, and acquired the Greek island of Skorpios. Onassis became enamored of Monaco, which had been a dull, sleepy little place until he transformed it. In Monte Carlo, Onassis bought beautiful hotels and dozens of houses and villas, built public facilities and beach clubs, and renovated the port and the casino. He held legendary gatherings on his yacht, inviting guests who included President John F. Kennedy and his wife, Winston Churchill, Ernest Hemingway, and other members of high society from business, politics, and Hollywood. Onassis even brought together Prince Rainier of Monaco and American actress Grace Kelly, helping establish Monaco as a paradise for the rich and beautiful in Europe.

Key Takeaways

- Aristotle "Ari" Socrates Onassis earned a fortune by transporting crude oil in his huge tanker fleet and through his excellent relationships with the Saudi family.

- He profited massively from the Suez crisis in 1956 and the oil crises of the 1970s.

- Onassis was an icon of the international jet set, thanks to his relationship with opera star Maria Callas, and his second marriage to Jacqueline Kennedy, the widow of John F. Kennedy.

- With his private wealth of more than 1 billion USD, Onassis supported Prince Rainer of Monaco and established the principality as *the* place to be for the rich and beautiful.

8

Soybeans:
Hide and Seek in New Jersey

Soybean oil fuels the US credit crisis of 1963. The attempt to corner the market for soybeans ends in chaos, drives many firms into bankruptcy, and causes a loss of 150 million USD (1.2 billion USD in today's prices). Among the victims are American Express, Bank of America, and Chase Manhattan.

> *"You have caused terrific loss to many of your fellow Americans!"*
> US federal judge Reynier Wortendyke

A t first glance, it seemed like a plot for a Hollywood movie: Workers deceived warehouse inspectors using oil tanks filled with water to hide one of the largest credit frauds in US history. It was all part of an attempt to corner the soybean market, a fragile house of cards whose collapse caused a loss of more than 150 million USD (the equivalent of about 1.2 billion USD today) and whose effects rippled throughout corporate America.

At the center of the debacle were Allied Crude Vegetable Oil, a New Jersey company, and its owner Anthony ("Tino") De Angelis. In the end the unraveling of the scheme was analogous to the bankruptcy of Lehman

Brothers in 2008: On a November evening in 1963, a group of employees of the Wall Street brokerage firm Ira Haupt & Co., including managing partner Morton Kamerman, sat in a conference room and spoke on the phone with Anthony De Angelis. As the conversation heated up, De Angelis accused Kamerman of ruining his company. Kamerman was not responsible for his firm's commodity trading, but he was aware that De Angelis was one of his biggest customers. The Haupt & Co. partners were desperately looking for someone willing to buy soybean oil in large quantities, but they had no success. The next morning Kamerman understood a lot more about his company's commodity business. However, the knowledge went hand in hand with the fact that Haupt & Co. was bankrupt due to the insolvency of Allied Crude.

Some Background About Soybeans

Soybeans, which are predominantly crushed for soybean oil and soybean meal, are produced and exported mainly by the United States "Corn Belt" (Illinois and Iowa), Brazil, and Argentina. Together these countries account for about 80 percent of the world's soybean harvest of around 215 million metric tons. In most of the world's production, the oil is extracted first, and the residual mass is used primarily as a feedstock. Soybeans, soybean meal, and soybean oil are traded on the Chicago Board of Trade (CBOT) with the symbol S, SM, and BO and the respective contract month (for example, S F0 = Soybean January 2020).

Last Price	10.94
High on 04/11/61	13.85
Average	9.38
Low on 11/20/63	7.05
SHAVG (50)	11.52
SHAVG (100)	10.60
SHAVG (200)	9.33

Figure 3. Prices for soybean oil, 1960 – 1964, in US cents/lb, Chicago Board of Trade. Data: Bloomberg, 2019.

Anthony De Angelis had founded Allied Crude Vegetable Oil in 1955 to buy subsidized soybeans from the government, process them for soybean oil, and sell the product abroad. Born in 1915, he was the son of Italian immigrants and grew up in the Bronx in New York. As a commodity trader, he dealt in cotton and soybeans, and between 1958 and 1962, he built a refinery in Bayonne, New Jersey, and leased 139 oil tanks, many as high as a five-story building. American Express Warehousing, a subsidiary of American Express, was paid by Allied Crude for storage, inspection, and certification of the oil volume. In 1962 De Angelis was responsible for about three-quarters of the total soybean and cottonseed oils in the United States. But in order to finance the rapid growth of the company in a highly competitive industry, he increased leverage by taking more and more credit, which was largely collateralized by the oil he produced.

And that is where the fraud began: Allied Crude Vegetable Oil never had as much oil as was necessary to secure its loans. A close investigation by American Express Warehousing would have revealed that De Angelis needed to store more oil than was available in the entire United States, according to the US Department of Agriculture's monthly data. At its peak, De Angelis's credit volume represented more than three times the amount of oil that could be stored in the tanks in Bayonne. But De Angelis was American Express's largest customer. And his employees deceived the inspectors who were sent to check the collateral by pumping oil from tank to tank or filling the tanks mainly with water and only a small amount of oil. In this way the company continued to receive new credit lines.

Instead of expanding operations, however, the company used the credit lines for speculation in soybean futures at Chicago's commodity exchange. De Angelis placed huge bets on rising prices for soybeans; he had to deposit only about 5 percent of the future purchase sum as a margin. Nevertheless, in his attempt to corner the entire market through further positions, De Angelis needed an even higher credit line.

He was already trading in futures contracts with Wall Street brokers Ira Haupt and J. R. Williston & Beane, and they agreed to further credit against stockpiles of the nonexistent oil. Both institutions were financed on the basis of their warrants by commercial banks Chase Manhattan and Continental Illinois.

By mid-1963, De Angelis had accumulated soybean positions equaling about 120 million USD or 1.2 billion pounds. A tick of only 1 US cent in the price of soybeans meant that De Angelis gained or lost 12 million USD. For a while his trades were profitable. In just six weeks in autumn 1963, the price of soybean oil climbed from 9.20 USD per pound to 10.30 USD. But on

> **De Angelis deceived his creditors and caused losses of more than 1 billion USD in today's prices.**

November 15 the market collapsed because of Russian plans to buy more US grain and the negative reaction to this. Allied Crude Vegetable Oil collapsed with it.

Within four hours soybean oil had fallen to 7.60 USD per pound, and the Chicago Board of Trade called for additional margins from Ira Haupt, which the company was unable to provide because its main customer, De Angelis, was not in a position to do so. Even another 30 million USD borrowed by American and British banks was not enough to rescue Ira Haupt. Williston & Beane was also forced to merge with Walston & Co. because of dwindling equity.

The soybean market tumbled and took Allied Crude down with it.

Allied Crude went into bankruptcy, and as creditors reviewed the company's tanks more carefully, they confirmed there were just 100 million pounds of soybean oil there instead of 1.8 billion pounds. This difference was worth about 130 million USD.

Affected by the debacle were banks, brokers, oil traders, and warehouses, huge firms like Bank of America, Chase Manhattan, Continental Illinois, Williston & Beane, Bunge Corp., and Harbor Tank Storage Co., to name just a few. The main loser was the parent company of American Express Warehousing: American Express faced legal suits by 43 companies, to the tune of more than 100 million USD. The share price of American Express dropped by more than 50 percent after the fraud hit the news. The scandal, however, received only limited attention, because two days later President Kennedy was shot in Dallas.

For Ira Haupt & Co., liabilities amounted to almost 40 million USD, which they were not able to meet, affecting more than 20,000 brokerage customers. Even worse than these financial claims was the damage to the reputation of the US economy. As for Anthony De Angelis, in 1965 he was sentenced to 10 years' imprisonment for fraud.

Key Takeaways

- In 1963 Anthony ("Tino") De Angelis and his company Allied Crude Vegetable Oil were at the epicenter of one of the biggest corporate credit crises before the collapse of Lehman Brothers in 2008.

- By cheating on inventories and in a bold pattern of fraud, Allied Crude received immense credit lines for its business and heavily speculated on the rise of soybean and soybean oil futures in Chicago. Eventually the market for soybeans crashed in November 1963 and took Allied Crude Vegetable Oil with it.

- Affected by the fraud were several banks, brokers, oil traders, and warehouse companies, including prominent names like American Express, Bank of America, and Chase Manhattan.

- The huge scandal, however, was overshadowed by the assassination of President John F. Kennedy two days later.

9

Wheat:
The Russian Bear Is Hungry

The Soviet Union starts to buy American wheat in huge quantities, and local prices triple. Consequently, Richard Dennis establishes a groundbreaking career in commodity trading.

"If you live among wolves you have to act like a wolf."
—Nikita Khrushchev

In the history of capital markets, 1972 is known as the year of "The Great Russian Grain Robbery." Because of harvest shortages, Soviet commissioners were traveling all over the United States, buying as much wheat as they could. Their actions affected not only the grain market but also the career of a young commodity trader named Richard Dennis.

At the beginning of the 1970s, the United States was beginning to abolish the gold standard, and as a result the US currency subsequently weakened. At the same time, wheat was trading close to 1 USD—historically low levels. That was not a surprise, since wheat production was massively subsidized by the government. But the weakening dollar gradually made American products, including many agricultural goods, more com-petitive. As a result, exports rose, and hand in hand with export volume, prices began to rise as well: That included grain prices, which were slowly awakening from their slumber.

In the history of capital markets, 1972 is known as the year of "The Great Russian Grain Robbery."

Weather is always a key factor for agricultural prices, and after years of good harvests, the world's grain production started to decline in 1972. Poor weather conditions were responsible for lower yields in important producer nations like the United States, Canada, Australia, and the Soviet Union. In comparison to 1970–1971, wheat stocks in 1973–1974 fell by 93 percent in Australia, 64 percent in Canada, and 59 percent in the United States. Inventories approached critically low levels.

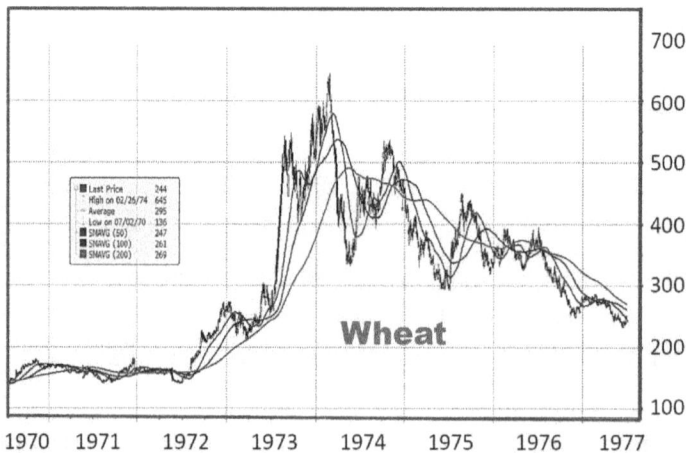

Figure 4. Wheat prices, 1970–1977, in US cents/bushel, Chicago Board of Trade. Data: Bloomberg, 2019.

In July and August 1972, the Soviets bought nearly 12 million metric tons of US wheat—approximately 30 percent of the country's production—amounting to a net value of about 700 million USD. Because farmers were already facing problems meeting demand, prices increased sharply, from below 2 USD at the beginning of the decade to more than 6 USD in February 1974. Corn spiked at the same time, from less than 1.5 USD to nearly 4 USD, while soybean prices more than tripled, reaching their highest level of more than 12 USD in June 1973.

Weather Woes

The harvest of Kansas wheat (Hard Red Winter Wheat), which is mainly exported, can be threatened by climatic fluctuations three times during the year: in late autumn, when it is too hot and dry or too cold and humid for germination; during winter, when sudden temperature changes threaten growth; and finally, in spring, when rain prevents pollination. For these reasons crop quality, quantity, and price are all subject to huge fluctuations.

The rapid price spike favored young Richard Dennis, who had studied in Chicago and at Tulane University in Louisiana and had worked as a student at the Chicago Mercantile Exchange (CME) in 1966 at the age of 17. He began speculating with 2,000 USD in initial capital from his family, first with small contracts on the MidAmerica Exchange, and later on the CME.

In 1972 the 23-year-old Dennis recognized the new agricultural market trend. He bet on rising wheat prices and won. A year later, in 1973, his initial capital increased to 100,000 USD as he took advantage of a trend-following system, aggressively increased his positions, and remained invested. In 1974 he made a profit of 500,000 USD on soybeans alone, and by the end of the year, he'd become a millionaire at the age of 25.

The Soviet shopping spree of 1972 was repeated in 1977 after another bad harvest in Eastern Europe.

Three years later history repeated itself. In 1977 Soviet president Brezhnev announced a national wheat harvest of less than 200 million tons, which took the markets by surprise as the US Department of Agriculture and US intelligence both were forecasting a good harvest.

By this time Soviets had already bought 18 to 20 million tons of wheat from the United States, Canada, Australia, and India. Although worldwide production of wheat was around 600 million metric tons, according to data from the Food and Agriculture Organization (FAO), only a small fraction of that quantity was globally traded. Because large amounts are consumed by the producer countries themselves, world market prices can fluctuate dramatically based on relatively small changes in global trading.

Meanwhile, Dennis's career continued to soar. At the beginning of the 1980s, his capital rose to around 200 million USD. At 35 he was known as the "Prince of the Pit" and was one of the most recognized commodity traders in the world.

In 1983 and 1984 Dennis recruited and trained 21 men and two women in commodity trading. The group later became known as "Turtle Traders," thanks to an often-quoted comment by Dennis, who said, "You can breed traders like turtles in a laboratory." Five years later the group had earned him a profit of 175 million USD.

Key Takeaways

- After a bad harvest, agents of the Soviet Union quickly and secretly purchased 30 percent of the total US wheat crop. Therefore, 1972 became famous as the year of the "Great Russian Grain Robbery."

- Grain shortages and the Soviet actions caused a spike in prices: Wheat prices that traded at 2 USD in 1970 shot up above 6 USD in February 1974, a threefold increase within 24 months. Corn also rose from 1.50 USD to nearly 4 USD, while soybean prices surpassed 12 USD during the summer of 1973.

- Richard Dennis, age 23, recognized the new trend in agricultural markets and bet on rising wheat prices. He became a millionaire two years later, After a decade he was making a profit of 200 million USD, earning the nickname "Prince of the Pit."

10

The End of the Gold Standard

1973

Gold and silver have been recognized as legal currencies for centuries, but in the late 19th century silver gradually loses this function. Gold keeps its currency status until the fall of the Bretton Woods system in 1973. The current levels of sovereign debt are causing many investors to reconsider an investment in precious metals.

"Gold and silver, like other commodities, have an intrinsic value, which is not arbitrary, but is dependent on their scarcity, the quantity of labour bestowed in procuring them, and the value of the capital employed in the mines which produce them."
—David Ricardo

"You have to choose . . . between trusting to the natural stability of gold and the natural stability of the honesty and intelligence of the members of the government. And, with due respect to these gentlemen, I advise you, as long as the capitalist system lasts, to vote for gold."
—George Bernard Shaw

"Only gold is money. Everything else is credit."
—J. P. Morgan

I n June 2011 the US Mint announced a 30 percent increase in silver coin sales compared to the previous month. With more than 3.6 million silver eagles sold, the US Mint reached its limit of production, so great was the interest of investors in silver coins. Similar figures were reported by the Royal Canadian Mint, the Australian Mint in Perth, and also by the Vienna-based Mint Austria, producer of the Vienna Philharmonic Coin. In March 2011 newspaper headlines proclaimed that the state of Utah was considering once again accepting gold and silver as legal currencies. Utah was not an isolated case in the United States; Colorado, Georgia, Carolina, Tennessee, Vermont, and Washington were also looking to return to the stable value of gold.

What seems curious at first glance made many investors thoughtful. After all, the use of a paper currency without a tie to precious metals like gold or silver is a relatively recent experiment. Only in the early 1970s, when President Nixon abolished gold convertibility in 1971, and with the collapse of the Bretton Woods system of fixed exchange rates and the convertibility of all currencies into gold in 1973, was the gold standard abolished and replaced by fiat money.

Fiat money is a currency without intrinsic value that has been established as money, often by government regulation. Thus, the fiat money experiment has been tested in international financial markets for less than 50 years.

**The international monetary system—
detached from gold and silver—has existed
in this form for less than 50 years.**

The gold standard was the prevailing monetary system until World War I. Under a pure gold standard, the money supply equals the gold possession of a country. In the wake of the Great Depression in 1929 and the subsequent banking crisis in 1931, however, the gold standard came increasingly under pressure. In Britain, the suspension of sterling's gold convertibility in September 1931 (the Sterling Crisis) heralded the collapse of the international gold standard. The United States also began to break away from the gold standard as it gradually devalued the US dollar. In 1933 President Franklin D. Roosevelt declared private gold ownership illegal so the government could print more paper money as a way to overcome the Great Depression.

Gold or Silver?

In the historical context, the gold standard was just a short transitional period for global financial markets. For many centuries silver was the dominant currency. Most countries used a silver standard or a bimetallic standard. Similar to the gold standard, under a silver standard the total amount of money in circulation is hedged by silver, while a bimetallic standard additionally prescribes a fixed exchange ratio between silver and gold. For many years in the United States, that was 1:16. The gold-silver ratio indicates how many units of silver are needed to buy one unit of gold.

After both the silver and gold standards ended, the range of this ratio has fluctuated between 1:10 and 1:100. At the beginning of the 1980s, the ratio dropped below 1:20. In the early 1990s, it peaked at just under 1:100. In the years 2009 and 2010, the price of silver rose much more sharply than the price of gold. While 80 ounces of silver had to be paid for 1 troy ounce of gold by the end of 2008, it was just 40 ounces in mid-2011 and fell further to 1:50 by the beginning of 2019. Considering the natural resources and the amount of each metal mined annually, it would imply a long-term ratio of 1:10.

After World War II the world's economic and political center shifted toward the United States. The Bretton Woods system reorganized the international monetary system, and the US dollar, backed by gold, became the new global reserve currency.

Figure 5. Gold-silver ratio, 1973–2013. Data: Bloomberg, 2019.

All central banks were obligated to other central banks to exchange currency for gold at a fixed rate of 35 USD per ounce. But since the 1960s, US gold reserves have been shrinking, due to increasing account deficits. Social welfare entitlements and the growing financial burden of the Vietnam War accelerated the US current account deficit, raised inflation, and lowered international confidence in the US dollar. For the first time in 1970, the US money supply exceeded the amount of gold reserves. A year later, in August, President Nixon stopped the conversion of US dollars to gold (an event known as "Nixon shock"), but it was not until 1973 that the Bretton Woods system was officially overruled and replaced by a system of floating exchange rates. After that, the gold standard faded into history.

Today, central banks and supranational organizations like the International Monetary Fund (IMF) hold 33,000 metric tons of gold, almost 20 percent of all known aboveground stocks of the precious metal.

Silver Gives Way to Gold

Silver gradually lost its official payment function in the late 19th century due to several factors. On the one hand, the United Kingdom, as a leading economic nation, was able to prevail with its gold standard against the French-dominated Latin coinage based on the silver standard. On the other hand, gold discoveries in California and Australia led to a tenfold increase in worldwide gold production and thus to lower gold prices. This made the gold standard more attractive. In 1871 Germany also switched to the gold standard. The transition from the silver or bimetallic standard to a pure gold standard led to an oversupply of silver and weighed on the price of silver for several decades.

However, attention again has been focused on the solvency of many countries, including the United States, Japan, and some European economies. Measures taken to combat the financial and economic crisis that started in spring 2007 with the US real estate crash caused the national debt and the money supply to explode.

Global debt accelerated to 320 trillion USD, whereas global GDP only rose to 80 trillion USD, and the dollar's purchasing power declined by more than 90 percent since 1971. In addition to some European countries—Portugal, Ireland, Greece, and Spain (known as "PIGS countries")—the United States was also temporarily threatened by a downgrade of its creditworthiness

A sovereign crisis and a lack of trust are attracting investors to gold, silver, and cryptocurrencies.

by international rating agencies. In the face of all this, it is not surprising that gold and silver bullion and coins, even if they are no longer legal tender, are popular with investors, and that bitcoins have emerged as an alternative currency. Gold-backed cryptocurrencies offer another alternative to fiat money. It seems like the gold standard is rising from its ashes through private initiatives instead of by government institutions.

Key Takeaways

- In 1933 President Franklin D. Roosevelt issued Executive Order 6102, which declared private possession of gold bars and coins illegal and punishable by up to 10 years in prison. All private gold holdings had to be turned over to the Federal Reserve in exchange for paper money at 20.67 USD per troy ounce. This prohibition against gold ownership wasn't lifted until 1975 by President Gerald Ford.

- After World War II, the US dollar was declared the world reserve currency, pegged to gold at a fixed exchange ratio. All other currencies were then pegged to the US dollar (the "Gold Standard").

- As US debt spiraled out of control, President Nixon ended the convertibility of US dollars into gold in 1971 (the "Nixon Shock").

- With the end of the Bretton Woods system in 1973, one of the greatest economic experiments began: a system of free and floating exchange rates for currencies that are not backed by any collateral other than the faith in national governments.

11

The 1970s—Oil Crisis!

During the 1970s the world must cope with global oil crises in 1973 and 1979. The Middle East uses crude oil as a political weapon, and the industrialized nations— previously unconcerned about their rising energy addiction and the security of the supply—face economic chaos.

"Peak oil is the point in time when the maximum rate of global petroleum extraction is reached, after which the rate of production enters terminal decline."
—"Peak Oil," **Wikipedia**

"Just like global warming, the rationale for peak oil sounds great, it makes sense, but there is just one small problem, the facts don't support it . . . it is a myth."
—seekingalpha.com

O n Sunday, November 25, 1973, highways in Germany were emptied by a driving ban! The same day almost no cars moved in Denmark, the Netherlands, Luxembourg, or Switzerland. A week earlier, on November 19, Germany had introduced a general "Sunday driving ban" for four weeks, combined with a speed limit of 100 km/h on motorways and 80 km/h on ordinary roads. This was noteworthy: Germany—home to Mercedes, BMW, and Audi—is one of the few countries in the world today that does not have a general speed limit on its highways. Germans generally are in love with their cars! But the ban was the reaction of the German government to a sudden spike in energy prices caused by an oil crisis.

The crisis was due to a conflict in the Middle East, between the Arab countries and Israel, that had been intensifying since the beginning of the 1970s. During the Six-Day War in 1967, Israel had conquered the Golan Heights and the Sinai Peninsula and occupied the Gaza Strip, the West Bank, and East Jerusalem. The Arab countries called for an immediate withdrawal from the occupied territories, and international pressure on Israel increased. But warnings about possible retaliation were ignored, as was the Egyptian offer of a peace treaty if the Sinai Peninsula were to be returned. On October 6, 1973, during the Jewish holy day of Yom Kippur, Egypt and Syria together attacked Israel.

At first Syria achieved some success in the Golan Heights, and Egypt was prevailing on the Sinai Peninsula. However, the United States supported Israel with substantial military resources, and the small country finally changed the course of the war. Subsequently, the Arab countries pursued a different option.

On October 17, 1973, OPEC decided to limit the supply of crude oil as a political weapon.

On October 17, 1973, all Arabian crude oil–producing nations retaliated by reducing oil supply by 5 percent compared to September 1973 levels. They also imposed a complete supply boycott for crude oil against the United States and the Netherlands, which were considered Israel's close allies. The league of exporting countries then announced that they would continue to restrict oil production until all occupied areas were "liberated" and the rights of Palestinian people were restored. The first oil crisis had begun.

What Is OPEC?

The Organization of the Petroleum Exporting Countries (OPEC) was established in 1960 in Baghdad by five founding members: Iraq, Iran, Kuwait, Saudi Arabia, and Venezuela. The development of new oil fields and a global oversupply had resulted in steady price declines in the 1950s. In response OPEC's objective was to establish a common crude oil production level by joint agreement of all OPEC member countries, so that the world market price for crude oil stayed within a defined target corridor. OPEC has also been a driving force to break the power of the "seven sisters," a group of Western oil companies. As of March 2019 the cartel consisted of 14 members—Algeria, Angola, Ecuador, Equatorial Guinea, Gabon, Iran, Iraq, Kuwait, Libya, Nigeria, Republic of the Congo, Saudi Arabia, Venezuela, and the United Arab Emirates, representing about 44 percent of global oil production and about 80 percent of the world's "proven" oil reserves. Saudi Arabia is by far the largest crude oil producer among all OPEC members, responsible for about 12 million barrels per day in 2018. According to figures from the Energy Information Administration (EIA), the largest non-OPEC producing countries include Russia, the United States, China, Mexico, Canada, Norway, and Brazil.

Up to this point, Western industrialized countries had been living with the illusion that global energy reserves were inexhaustible and that they needn't be concerned with the security of the supply. Their addiction to crude oil kept rising, so the sudden embargo triggered an economic shock in many industrialized countries. Germany, for instance, sourced more than 50 percent of its energy demand from imported oil, about three-quarters of which came from the Middle East. It turned out that even with reduced consumption, reserves would have lasted only for three months, which caused people to panic. To limit the use of oil and reduce the degree of dependence, European countries began implementing energy-saving measures. They intensified negotiations with alternative crude oil suppliers, started to develop domestic sources of oil as well as alternative energy sources, and implemented strategic oil reserves.

Economic Ripples

In Germany and other industrialized countries, the first oil price shock triggered stagflation, which is economic stagnation combined with rising prices (inflation). Rising energy prices fueled an inflation spiral and at the same time slowed economic growth: Gross domestic output shrank from 5.3 percent in 1972 to 0.4 percent in 1974 and −1.8 percent in 1975. Many industries recorded a massive decline in production; construction fell 16 percent, and the automotive industry declined 18 percent. The stock market value of German companies dropped drastically and recorded a loss at the end of September 1974 of almost 40 percent, compared to July 1972. Unemployment rose from almost-full employment to 2.6 percent in 1974 and 4.8 percent in 1975.

The impact of the cuts in the crude oil supply was visible immediately: Prices started to rise. At the end of 1972, US crude oil was trading at 3.50 USD per barrel; in September 1973 it rose to 4.30 USD, and at the end of 1973 oil prices traded above 10 USD. Sales in OPEC countries grew from about 14 billion USD in 1972 to more than 90 billion USD in 1974.

> **During the first oil crisis in 1973**
> **oil prices spiked from 3.50 USD**
> **to more than 10 USD.**

Using oil as a weapon brought quick political results: On November 5, 1973, the European foreign ministers called for Israel to evacuate the areas it had occupied since 1967. OPEC responded by gradually loosening the supply restrictions.

But the world had changed. Even after the initial relaxation, prices for crude oil remained high. In 1974 alone, the value of German oil imports increased by more than 150 percent compared to the previous year.

> **With the second oil crisis in 1979, oil prices**
> **jumped from under 15 USD to almost 40.**

Over the following years, crude oil prices stagnated, but they started to rise rapidly again in 1979–1980. After the Iranian Revolution and Iraq's attack on neighboring Iran, industrialized countries once more became concerned about oil supply security. At the beginning of 1979, crude oil was trading at less than 15 USD per barrel. Within 12 months, prices had risen to nearly 40 USD, causing a second oil crisis. As a side effect, both oil crises marked the most prosperous years in the Soviet Union after discovery of oil in western Siberia and the rise of non-OPEC Western offshore oil production.

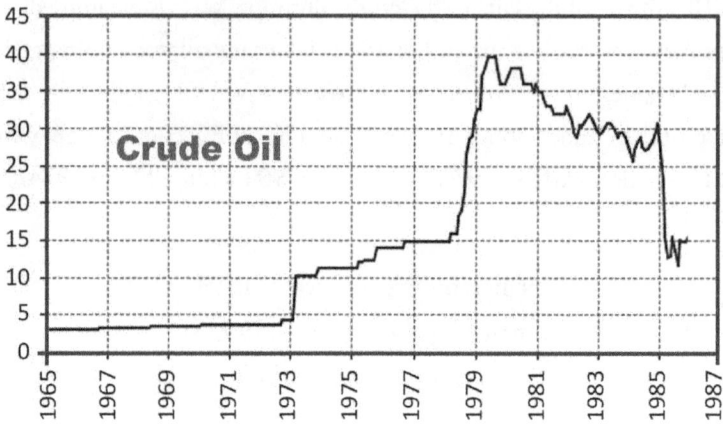

Figure 6. Crude oil prices, 1965–1986, in USD/barrel.
Data: Datastream, 2019.

OPEC raised their basket price—an average of the prices of petroleum blends that are produced by OPEC members—to 24 USD per barrel; Libya, Algeria, and Iraq even asked 30 USD for their crude oil. In 1980 OPEC's prices reached their peak when Libya demanded 41 USD, Saudi Arabia 32 USD, and the other countries 36 USD per barrel. In the following year, however, sales volume declined due to weaker economic development in the Western industrialized countries.

As investments in alternative energy sources bore fruit, global crude oil consumption between 1978 and 1983 dropped by 11 percent. OPEC's global market share of crude oil production fell back to 40 percent and continued to decline because of a lack of cartel discipline. US president Ronald Reagan made an agreement with Saudi Arabia to increase oil production in the 1980s, putting crude oil prices into a slide until the late 1990s. In the late 1980s, oil prices briefly dropped below 10 USD per barrel, bringing the Soviet Union to the brick of insolvency. OPEC's market share fell during that time to 30 percent of world production.

Key Takeaways

- In 1973, because of tension in the Mideast, the Organization of the Petroleum Exporting Countries (OPEC) used its oil exports to Western industrialized countries as a political weapon and limited the supply, precipitating the first oil crisis. Crude oil prices soared from 3.50 USD at the end of 1972 to more than 10 USD just 12 months later.

- The oil crisis came as a shock to most involved nations, strongly affecting economic growth and leading to rising unemployment.

- During the second oil crisis, in 1979, oil prices jumped from less than 15 USD to almost 40.

12

Diamonds:
The Crash of the World's
Hardest Currency

Despite the need for individual valuation, diamonds have shown a positive and stable price trend over a long period of time. In 1979, however, monopolist De Beers loses control of the diamond market; "investment diamonds" drop by 90 percent in value.

> *"Diamonds are a girl's best friend."*
> —Marilyn Monroe,
> as Lorelei Lee in *Gentlemen Prefer Blondes*

Precious stones such as diamonds, rubies, sapphires, emeralds, and opals are mainly known for their use in jewelry. Of these, diamonds are by far the largest market segment, and many individual gemstones—for example, the Blue Hope, the Cullinan, the Millennium Star, the Excelsior, the Koh-i-Noor, and the Orlov—have famous histories.

> Global production of rough diamonds
> generally ranges between 20 and 25
> metric tons per year. This represents
> 100 to 130 million carats and is worth
> approximately 10 billion USD.

Only about 20 percent of all diamonds are used in the jewelry industry, however. Industrial diamonds make up a huge market, and within this segment of smaller stones, artificially produced (industrial) diamonds also play an important role. The largest diamond production sites are in Russia, Australia, Canada, and Africa—in particular South Africa, Namibia, Botswana, Sierra Leone, and the Democratic Republic of the Congo.

The Four Cs in Diamonds

Unlike other commodities, diamonds do not have a standardized fixed value per unit weight. A diamond's value is determined by various criteria, of which the "4 Cs" are the best known: color, clarity, cut, and carat. Sometimes, a fifth "C" is included. It stands for certification, which confirms the physical characteristics of a particular stone as certified by an official institution.

Color grading depends on how close a stone is to colorless. The classification begins at D—which corresponds to very fine white or almost colorless diamonds—and continues through E, F, G, H (simple white), and so on. Colored diamonds (e.g., yellow, red, blue, or green) are particularly rare, so these so-called *fancy diamonds* are very precious.

The clarity (purity) of a diamond is determined by the degree of inclusions in the stone. The higher the clarity, the rarer it is. The scale begins with IF (internally flawless) and continues through small to clear and coarse inclusions. Cut refers to the angles and proportions of a diamond. The most popular is the brilliant cut. Finally, traditionally a diamond's weight is given in carats (1 ct = 0.2 gram).

The largest diamond exchanges are located in Antwerp, Amsterdam, New York, Ramat Gan (Israel), Johannesburg, and London. Antwerp is the most important market; 85 percent of rough diamonds and about half of global cut stones are traded in the Diamond Quarter of that Belgian city.

The value chain begins with mining and includes purchasing agents, processing, wholesalers, traders, intermediaries, jewelers, and other retailers, but a valuation is not simply a linear correlation to size: Larger stones are much rarer and thus exponentially more precious. In addition, prices fluctuate from one size class to the next. For example, the price can vary by more than 1,000 USD from a 0.49-carat diamond to a 0.5-carat diamond, though the difference is only 100 mg or less. In December 2018 prices for 1-carat diamonds ranged from 500 USD to 10,000 USD, depending on the degree of purity and colorlessness.

By far the most important player in the diamond industry—analogous to OPEC in the global oil market— is De Beers. The South African company, part of the Anglo American mining group, is the largest diamond producer and trader in the world.

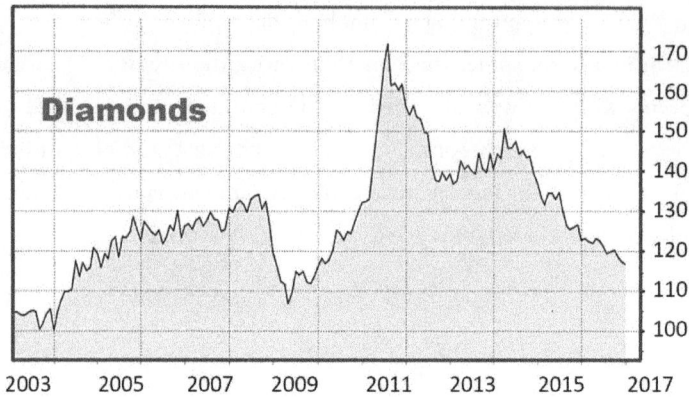

Figure 7. Diamond prices, 2003–2016. Prices indexed over different sizes and qualities. Data: PolishedPrices.com, Bloomberg, 2019.

De Beers has long dominated the global diamond market, similar to the way OPEC dominates global oil.

De Beers controls about 30 percent of the world's diamond production, and its influence in marketing and sales is even stronger. The company determines the volume and quality of rough diamonds that traders are able to buy. The Diamond Trading Company (DTC), which is controlled by De Beers, buys most of the world's raw diamond production, allocates production quotas to mining companies, and manages sales through the Central Selling Organization (CSO), which is also an extended arm of the DTC. The CSO regularly organizes "sights" in London where about 150 authorized sightholders are offered compilations of rough diamonds for sale.

For years the De Beers Syndicate guaranteed stable prices. At the end of the 1970s, however, the company lost control of the diamond market.

A De Beers Primer

De Beers, the largest diamond producer and trader in the world, has been active in the diamond market for more than 100 years. The company's name goes back to the first mine in Kimberley, which was located on the farm of brothers Johannes Nicolaas and Diederik Arnoldus de Beer. After diamonds were found there in 1871, a group of adventurers transformed the remote place into the world capital of diamonds. British businessman Cecil Rhodes gradually bought up all the mining licenses and founded De Beers in 1888. Today, the company is 45 percent owned by the Anglo American Corporation, with 40 percent owned by the Oppenheimer family.

Ernest Oppenheimer was born in Friedberg, Germany, near Frankfurt am Main, in 1880, and at age 32 he was pulling the political strings in Kimberley. In 1916, Oppenheimer founded Anglo American, which quickly became one of the most successful mining companies in the world. In 1926, he took over the majority of De Beers.

De Beers's entire production was always bought by the London Diamond Syndicate, which was established in 1890. The syndicate was the cornerstone of the Diamond Corporation, precursor to the Central Selling Organization (CSO). In the 1930s, during the Great Depression, Oppenheimer bought up massive quantities of diamonds in order to stabilize prices. Since then, De Beers and CSO have formed an exclusive diamond cartel.

During that decade the US dollar depreciated significantly against other currencies, due to rising inflation in the United States and a search by investors for nontraditional investment opportunities. Interest in diamonds as a "hard" currency and a stable store for wealth increased, leading to greater demand for high-quality stones. De Beers, however, only moderately expanded the supply at the time, which resulted in further price increases that, in turn, attracted more and more potential investors.

Diamond hysteria took hold. In 1979, the value of investment diamonds doubled, and prices for a 1-carat diamond of the best quality increased tenfold.

Meanwhile, in Israel, rough diamonds were also becoming a favorite investment. In order to support Tel Aviv as an emerging center of diamond processing, the government granted large loans to banks under favorable conditions. As a result, a number of diamond investment companies were set up, which were able to sell diamonds directly to private investors.

The hysteria over investment diamonds fueled a vicious circle. In 1979 the average price for diamonds doubled. Prices for a 1-carat, best-quality diamond multiplied by 10 and for a while traded at around 60,000 USD!

De Beers attempted to gradually cool the market by expanding the supply, but the strategy was unsuccessful. The result was complete market chaos. The inevitable bust finally began in Japan, where it was common practice to accept diamonds as collateral for loans. When the first bank considered the market overheated and stopped accepting diamonds as collateral, the house of cards collapsed. The first drop in prices kicked off a race to sell stones. As speculators disposed of their stock, more and more borrowers fell below their collateral limits and were forced to raise money. Diamonds flooded the market, which was already oversaturated by De Beers's efforts to cool it down. Even a cessation of sales and a buyback of diamonds by the cartel didn't help. Prices crashed, and investors' net wealth decreased, a downtrend accelerated by global recession.

Within a year, the prices of investment diamonds fell from 60,000 to 6,000 USD.

Within 12 months, the price of investment diamonds fell from 60,000 to 6,000 USD, approximately the level before the hysteria started. After that diamond prices recovered slowly, although in the early 1980s, the CSO withdrew diamonds worth more than 6 billion USD from the market, while De Beers cut mining quotas and closed one of its mines in South Africa. De Beers took similar actions to stabilize the price of diamonds after the global financial crisis in 2009, which had lessened the demand for luxury goods.

Key Takeaways

- South African company De Beers, today part of the Anglo American mining group, has long dominated international diamond production and sales.

- In 1979 the company lost control of the diamond market after a market frenzy, during which average diamond prices doubled within a year, and prices for a 1-carat best-quality diamond rose tenfold, only to crash by 90 percent after the bubble burst.

13

"Silver Thursday" and the Downfall of the Hunt Brothers

1980

Brothers Nelson Bunker Hunt and William Herbert Hunt try to corner the silver market in 1980 and fail in a big way. On March 27, 1980, known as "Silver Thursday," the metal loses one-third of its value in a single day.

> *"The U.S. government has a technology, called a printing press,*
> *that allows it to produce as many U.S. dollars as it wishes."*
> —**Ben Bernanke,** Chairman of the Federal Reserve, 2006–2014

The Hunt clan is one of the most glamorous families in the United States. They have a colorful history. In the 1920s Haroldson Lafayette Hunt (1889–1974), adventurer and professional poker player, won a drilling license in El Dorado, Arkansas, during a round of poker. Hunt, also known as "Arkansas Slim," struck oil with his initial drilling exploration. With the first profits from El Dorado, he purchased additional drilling licenses in Kilgore, Texas, and discovered the world's biggest known oil field to that date. In 1936 he founded the Hunt Oil Company, which became the largest independent oil producer in the United States. *Fortune* magazine estimated his net wealth at between 400 and 700 million USD in 1957, placing Hunt among the top 10 richest

Americans. The Hunts also possessed large segments of Libyan oil fields until Muammar Gaddafi expropriated them in the early 1970s.

H. L. Hunt's private life was equally notorious: He had six children with his first wife, Lyda Bunker, including Nelson Bunker, Lamar, and William Herbert. Later, he started an affair with Frania Tye, whom he married and with whom he had four children before the couple separated in 1942. Hunt had another four children with one of his secretaries, Ruth Ray, whom he finally married in 1957.

Unlike the Rockefellers, whose surname has always been associated with wealth, crude oil, and the Standard Oil Company, the name Hunt is forever tied to the largest failed speculation in silver.

A Precious Metal Primer—A Recap

The two most significant factors in the past 50 years for precious metals have been the prohibition of private gold holdings in the United States and the collapse of the Bretton Woods system, which was created in 1944. In 1933 President Franklin D. Roosevelt declared private possession of gold of more than 100 USD illegal, and the ban remained in place for more than 40 years. With the Nixon Shock of 1971, the United States declared an end to the official convertibility of the US dollar into gold, due to massive increases of government debt, expansion of the money supply, and rising inflation. In 1973 the Bretton Woods system—the international currency system that established the US dollar as the leading currency, backed by gold ("the Gold Standard")—fell apart. With the abolition of the silver and gold standards, both metals lost their economic importance, and large quantities became available on the market. As a result, silver fell to 2 USD per troy ounce. But this price level also has had a lasting negative effect on silver production, as only a few countries are able to produce it at this low price level.

The Hunt brothers' speculation, which culminated in the collapse of the silver market in 1980, became a legend in commodity trading.

William Herbert and Nelson Bunker Hunt were the first big investors to recognize the rare opportunities offered by the silver market in the 1970s: There was constant industrial demand, low incentives for subsidies due to low prices, and a small market of available silver.

Nelson Bunker had made no secret of his aversion to "paper money" after the gold standard was abandoned. "Every moron could buy a printing press, and everything might be better than paper money," he said. To preserve the family fortune, the Hunt brothers focused their investments on real estate and the silver market.

Between 1970 and 1973 Nelson Bunker and William Herbert bought about 200,000 troy ounces of silver. Within these three years, the price of silver doubled from 1.5 USD to 3 USD per troy ounce.

Encouraged by this success, the brothers expanded their activities to futures exchanges and acquired, at the beginning of 1974, futures contracts representing 55 million ounces of silver. Then they waited for physical delivery. Physical delivery was as unusual at that time as it is nowadays, and with constant purchases on the spot markets, the Hunts generated an artificial shortage of silver. Keeping in mind how the United States had appropriated private gold holdings 40 years before, they had the bulk of the precious metal delivered to banks in Zurich and London, where they thought their silver stocks would be safe from US authorities.

In spring 1974 the price of silver rose to more than 6 USD. Rumors spread that the Hunts—who by now possessed about 10 percent of the world's silver supply—were targeting a dominant market position. Before 1978 another 20 million ounces of silver were delivered to Nelson Bunker and William Herbert, who tried to convince more investors to partner with them. Together with two Saudi sheikhs, they founded the International Metal Investment Group, and by 1979 they had acquired additional futures contracts for more than 40 million ounces of silver at the Commodity Exchange (COMEX) and the Chicago Board of Trade (CBOT).

Over almost a decade, the Hunts and their partners had amassed some 150 million ounces of silver, about 5,000 tons.

This was equivalent to half of US silver reserves, about 15 percent of the world's total. In addition, the Hunt brothers possessed around 200 million ounces of silver in the form of exchange-traded futures contracts. Global demand for silver rose to around 450 million ounces, while output remained below 250 million ounces, due to the low price level of just a few years earlier.

In the meantime, the price of silver had risen to 8 USD, then it doubled to 16 USD in just two months, due to a growing physical shortage of silver. The CBOT and COMEX combined were able to deliver only 120 million ounces of silver, since the Hunts' strategy concerning physical delivery was now being imitated by an increasing number of market participants.

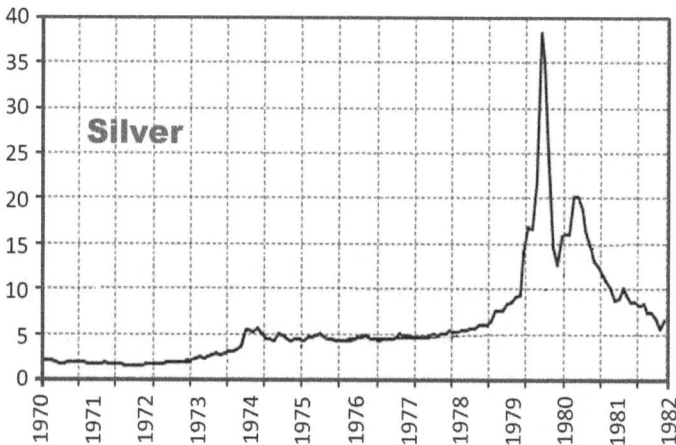

Figure 8. Silver prices, 1970–1982, in USD/troy ounce. Data: Bloomberg, 2019.

At the end of 1979, the CBOT announced that no investor would be allowed to hold more than three million silver contracts. All contracts above that limit had to be liquidated. Nelson Bunker interpreted this as a sign of an imminent scarcity; he continued to buy silver, while Lamar joined him and invested 300 million USD. At that point Nelson Bunker held 40 million ounces of silver abroad and—together with the partners of the International Metal Investment Group—an additional 90 million ounces of silver. The International Metal Group in turn held futures contracts for an additional 90 million ounces, with a delivery date of March 1980.

At the end of 1979 the price of silver rose to 34.50 USD; in the middle of January 1980 the price jumped above 50 USD (about 120 USD in today's prices). The Hunt family's silver stocks surpassed 4.5 billion USD in value!

The wheel of fortune was about to turn, however. Once COMEX accepted only liquidation orders, prices started to fall. The US Federal Reserve System increased interest rates, and the stronger US dollar began to negatively affect prices for gold and silver. By mid-March 1980, silver prices had fallen to 21 USD. The crash was accelerated by panic selling on the part of smaller speculators who had followed the Hunts' example. Others cashed in private silver stocks of jewelry and coins because of the record prices, further increasing physical supply of the metal.

As March 1980 came to an end, the Hunts could no longer meet

On "Silver Thursday," March 27, 1980, silver opened at 15.80 USD per troy ounce and closed at 10.80 USD. It was a daily loss of more than 30 percent!

---

the margin requirements of their futures positions and were forced to sell more than 100 million USD worth of silver. On March 27, 1980, silver opened at 15.80 USD and closed at 10.80 USD. The day went down in history as "Silver Thursday."

For the Hunts, whose volume-weighted average entry price in silver futures was 35 USD, this meant a debt of 1.5 billion dollars!

Many investors, including COMEX officials who held short positions, significantly reinforced the downward spiral in silver prices. Although the metal recovered to about 17 USD by the mid-1980s, the Hunts had to file for bankruptcy and were accused of conspiracy to manipulate the market.

The downfall of the Hunts was caused by extensive leverage. Otherwise they would have been able to weather the crash in silver prices without having to liquidate massive positions in the market. In the media the Hunts became a symbol of market manipulation, and their speculation and the collapse of silver prices, which caused huge losses for private investors, weighed down the reputation of the silver market for decades.

Key Takeaways

- Haroldson Lafayette Hunt, known as "Arkansas Slim," founded the family fortune on oil. Subsequently the Hunts were among the top 10 wealthiest families in the United States.

- Brothers Nelson Bunker and William Herbert Hunt tried to preserve the family wealth by investing in silver. They attempted to corner the silver market by buying the metal physically and building up large futures contract positions.

- The price of silver skyrocketed from below 2 USD per troy ounce to above 50 in January 1980. By then, the Hunt family fortune surpassed 4.5 billion USD. But on March 27, 1980—"Silver Thursday"—silver crashed 30 percent. The Hunts had to file for bankruptcy and were accused of conspiracy to manipulate the silver market.

14

Crude Oil:
No Blood for Oil?

1990

Power politics in the Middle East: Kuwait is invaded by Iraq, but Iraq faces a coalition of Western countries led by the United States and has to back down. In retreat, Iraqi troops set the Kuwaiti oil fields on fire. Within three months the price of oil more than doubles, from below 20 to more than 40 USD.

"Once [Saddam Hussein] acquired Kuwait . . . he was clearly in a position to be able to dictate the future of worldwide energy policy, and that gave him a stranglehold on our economy and on that of most of the other nations of the world as well."
—Richard "Dick" Cheney,
US Secretary of Defense, 1990

During the Iran-Iraq War of the 1980s, Iraq had enjoyed good relations with the United States and Europe. The Western countries supported Iraq, especially militarily, in order to counteract the Khomeini regime in Tehran and the further spread of Islamic and Soviet influence.

In 1980 Iraq was producing about six million barrels of crude oil per day, and Iran about five million barrels, most of which came from the oil-rich southwestern province of Khuzestan. Combined, crude oil production in the two countries accounted for about 20 percent of the world's daily consumption. But the eight-year war, which killed a million people on both sides, greatly affected the economy of Iraq, whose main funding came from the Arab states, in particular Saudi Arabia and Kuwait. After the war, the country was heavily in debt to them.

In addition, Iraq had always denied the legitimacy of Kuwait's independence, considering it part of Iraqi territory. Conflicts had been smoldering around the border since its independence from the United Kingdom in 1961. Meanwhile Iraq was working to cancel or renegotiate its debt burden with Saudi Arabia and Kuwait and also trying to lower its debt by reducing crude oil production (thus leading to higher prices and higher profits). But Kuwait counteracted that move by increasing its quota and lowering its export price to increase its own market share.

On July 17, 1990, Iraq accused its neighbors and the United Arab Emirates of producing far more oil than was agreed within OPEC, thereby pushing prices down and resulting in losses of 14 billion USD to Iraq alone. Iraq also accused its neighbors of stealing oil from Iraqi oil fields along their common border.

Negotiations to ease tensions between Iraq and Kuwait failed on July 31, and Iraq deployed its forces along Kuwait's border. During a meeting with Iraqi president Saddam Hussein, the US ambassador affirmed that the United States would not take any position in domestic Arab disputes or concerning the border conflict between Iraq and Kuwait. There were no specific defense or security agreements between the United States and

Kuwait either. The Iraqi president interpreted this as a toleration of further action: On August 2, 1990, 100,000 Iraqi soldiers marched into Kuwait. The Gulf War had begun.

A Quick Primer to Three Persian Gulf Wars

The Iran-Iraq War (1980–1988) was originally referred to as *the* Gulf War until the Persian Gulf War of 1990–1991 (the Iraq-Kuwait conflict), after which the latter was known as the First Gulf War. Consequently, the Iraq War of 2003–2011 has been called the Second Gulf War.

In September 1980 Iraq, headed by Saddam Hussein, invaded Iran, triggering an eight-year war that destabilized the region and devastated both countries. The United States supported Iraq during that war, because America was nervous about the potential spread of the Islamic Iranian Revolution by Ayatollah Khomeini, and Iraq longed to replace Iran as the dominant Persian Gulf state.

The Gulf War of 1990 was waged by coalition forces from 35 nations led by the United States against Iraq, still headed by Saddam Hussein, in response to Iraq's invasion and annexation of Kuwait. By that annexation, Iraq doubled its known oil reserves to 20 percent of global reserves, and was threatening Saudi Arabia, which controlled another 25 percent of global crude oil reserves, a situation that the United States could not tolerate.

But it took another Gulf War to overthrow the government of Saddam Hussein. In 2003 a United States–led coalition invaded Iraq on the pretext that Iraq had weapons of mass destruction.

Today Iran and Saudi Arabia are fighting for regional hegemony in a renewed cold war that is also an Islamic conflict of Sunni against Shiite. The Sunni-Shia conflict has been 1,400 years in the making.

continued

The arguments are complicated but essentially boil down to who is the rightful leader of Muslims following the prophet Mohammed after his death. With as much as 90 percent, the majority of the world's Muslims are Sunni. Iran, Iraq, Azerbaijan, and Bahrain, however, have a majority Shia population.

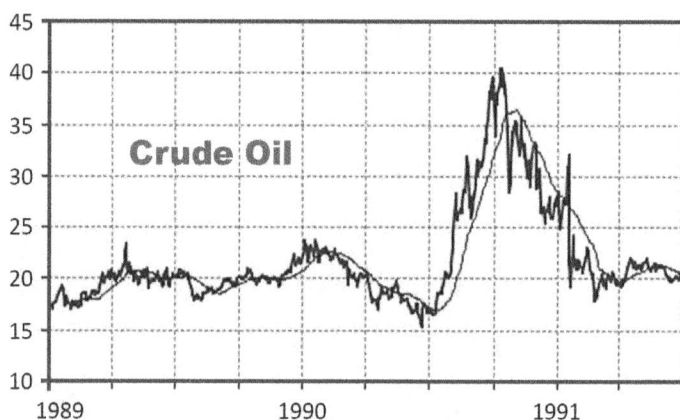

Figure 9. Crude oil prices, 1989–1991, in USD/barrel. Data: Bloomberg, 2019.

The effect on oil prices was obvious. Oil prices marked a low in June 1990 of around 15 USD per barrel, having bounced between 15 and 25 USD in the previous months. At the end of July, on the eve of the war, the price of crude oil was already back at 20 USD. On August 3, West Texas Intermediate (WTI, a trading benchmark for crude oil) was just below 25 USD. Crude closed the month above 30 USD, then, at the end of September, oil traded at 40 USD for the first time. In October 1990 the price of crude oil marked a new high—more than 40 USD per barrel.

Together, Iraq and Kuwait accounted for about 20 percent of the world's oil reserves.

Strategically, Kuwait was extremely valuable to Iraq. Although it is only 20,000 square kilometers, Kuwait has a 500-kilometer coastline, far exceeding the 60-kilometer coastline of much larger Iraq, whose area is almost 450,000 square kilometers. During the invasion, Iraq captured gold worth more than 500 million USD and, more importantly, gained access to Kuwaiti oil resources.

Saddam Hussein had counted on the United States not to interfere in internal Arab affairs, but he now faced a completely different reaction from President George H. W. Bush. It seemed that US interests not only concerned Kuwaiti oil fields; they touched indirectly on Iraqi oil fields as well. Iraq controlled 10 percent of the world's oil reserves; the annexation of Kuwait added another 10 percent.

Moreover, as US Secretary of Defense (and later CEO of Halliburton, a major oil company) Richard "Dick" Cheney noted a few weeks after the Iraqi invasion, "Iraqi troops are only a few hundred kilometers away from another 25 percent of the world's oil reserves in eastern Saudi Arabia."

Just a few hours after the beginning of the invasion, the UN Secu-

The invasion of Iraq began with Operations Desert Shield and Desert Storm. Oil prices spiked from 15 USD to more than 40 USD per barrel in October 1990.

rity Council adopted Resolution 660, which called for the withdrawal of the Iraqi troops. Within a week, the Security Council had imposed an economic and financial ban against Iraq (Resolution 661), which was designed to put an end to Iraqi crude oil exports. Meanwhile, the United States formed a military alliance of 34 countries against Iraq under the leadership of General Norman Schwarzkopf. Of the more than 900,000 soldiers deployed, about 75 percent were American troops. On August 8, two US Navy aircraft carriers arrived in the region, and President Bush initiated Operation Desert Shield to protect Saudi Arabia from an invasion.

By Resolution 662, the UN Security Council declared the annexation of Kuwait by Iraq void and called for the restoration of its sovereignty. On August 25, the UN Security Council sanctioned the coalition's embargo under Operation Desert Shield. By then 70 warships were deployed in the Gulf region.

In occupied Kuwait arrests, abductions, torture, and executions were the order of the day, and the Iraqi government used foreign hostages as human shields. On September 5 Saddam Hussein invoked holy war against the United States in the Persian Gulf and called for the fall of the Saudi Arabian king Fahd. The Kuwaiti royal family had already fled.

On November 29 the UN Security Council presented Iraq with an ultimatum for withdrawal from Kuwait by January 15, 1991. The US Congress approved military measures on January 12, and five days later, in the early morning hours, coalition forces began a massive air strike against Iraq. Within the first 24 hours of Operation Desert Storm, there were approximately 1,300 attacks.

It took another Gulf War, in 2003, to overthrow the regime of Saddam Hussein.

After a further ultimatum expired, the United States initiated a ground war on February 24. Two days later, the war was essentially over, as Iraqi troops officially began a withdrawal from Kuwait. In doing so, however, they set fire to Kuwaiti oil fields and opened the locking bars of many oil terminals to let the oil flow out into the sea. According to Kuwait, about 950 fields were set on fire or were mined by the Iraqi forces. In addition, oil production was interrupted until summer 1991. Only after the last fires were extinguished in November of that year did production increase again.

Despite the war, American and British aims to eliminate the military power of Iraq, and its claims to supremacy in the region, remained unfulfilled. It took another Gulf War in 2003 to overthrow the regime of Saddam Hussein.

Key Takeaways

- The president of Iraq, Saddam Hussein, aspired to hegemony in the Middle East, the most oil-rich region of the world, but he failed to overthrow Iran during eight years of war in the 1980s.

- Kuwait, despite its small geographic size, was of strategic importance to Iraq, because of its oil resources and its coastal access and harbor.

- The Gulf War of 1990–1991 began with the invasion of Kuwait by Iraq and ended because of the intervention of the United States with Operations Desert Shield and Desert Storm. As a consequence of supply insecurity and burning oil fields, oil prices shot up from 15 USD to more than 40 USD.

- After 9/11, Saddam Hussein was accused of possessing weapons of mass destruction; his regime in Iraq was finally overthrown in 2003.

15

The Doom of
German Metallgesellschaft

1993

Crude oil futures take Metallgesellschaft to the brink of insolvency and almost lead to the largest collapse of a company in Germany since World War II. CEO Heinz Schimmelbusch is responsible for a loss of more than 1 billion USD in 1993.

> *"We're back, we've made it."*
> —Kajo Neukirchen, CEO of MG

He was one of the stars of the German business scene: In 1989 Heinz Schimmelbusch became the youngest CEO in German history, the head of German Metallgesellschaft (MG), a huge industrial conglomerate founded in 1881 with a focus on mining and commodity trading. With Schimmelbusch's arrival, a new wind was blowing through the company. Its traditional dependence on the metal business, which accounted for almost two-thirds of group sales and profit, was about to be reduced. The new growth areas would be engineering, environmental technology, and financial services.

Schimmelbusch went on a shopping spree, acquiring Feldmühle Nobel, Dynamit Nobel, Buderus, and Cerasiv and creating an empire, valued at 15 billion USD, that included more than 250 subsidiaries. In 1991 *Manager Magazine* named him "Manager of the Year." But four years after Schimmelbusch joined MG, his realm would end in disaster.

The subsidiary of the MG Group in the United States was engaged in risky bets on crude oil prices.

Under Schimmelbusch the MG Group was not only getting bigger but also more complicated to manage. At the beginning of the 1990s, the German economy cooled down. There was pressure from cheap Eastern European competitors, the car industry weakened, and Metallgesellschaft's high debt levels began to drag on the company. But the firm's Sword of Damocles was actually hovering above its subsidiary in the United States.

Metallgesellschaft Refining and Marketing (MGRM) in New York sold fuel oil, gasoline, and diesel to large customers at long-term fixed rates; the company dealt in contracts of five- to ten-year maturity that promised delivery of a certain quantity of oil at a fixed price every month. MGRM's customers were hedging against rising crude oil prices. However, MGRM did not have oil through its own sources or inventories. It had to buy the oil itself.

Understanding the Oil Market

From 1984 to 1992, the oil market was dominated by what traders refer to as "backwardation." This means that price of crude oil to be delivered in the future will be traded at a discount to the current (cash) price. For the buyer of oil contracts this means, in addition to interest gained on the capital invested, there's a gain from the difference between the future price and the spot price. Thus, MGRM's rollover hedging strategy generated a continuous profit in addition to its hedging fees.

Due to the volatile price of crude oil, MGRM was facing a market price risk of more than 600 million USD, which corresponded to one-tenth of the balance sheet of the parent company. This market price risk was hedged by futures.

The company entered into a growing volume of crude oil futures whose sizes would be adjusted just before maturity to the contract volume of its customers and which would be rolled forward into the next contract month.

A massive price decline in crude oil flipped the future term structure from backwardation into contango, which resulted in massive losses in MGRM's hedging strategy.

However, in 1993, these conditions changed as a massive decline in crude oil prices reversed the future term structure from backwardation to "contango," in which future prices are higher than current ones. While the current oil price was below 18.50 USD per barrel, prices for a year ahead were more than 1 USD per barrel higher. The monthly gain for MGRM was converting into a widening loss. And there was another factor neglected by MGRM: rising cash-flow risks during contract maturity.

While its delivery obligations matched delivery requirements at maturity, MGRM was now faced with increasing margin payments in the future. This had a direct impact on the balance sheet for MGRM, since realized losses would not be offset by potential future profits.

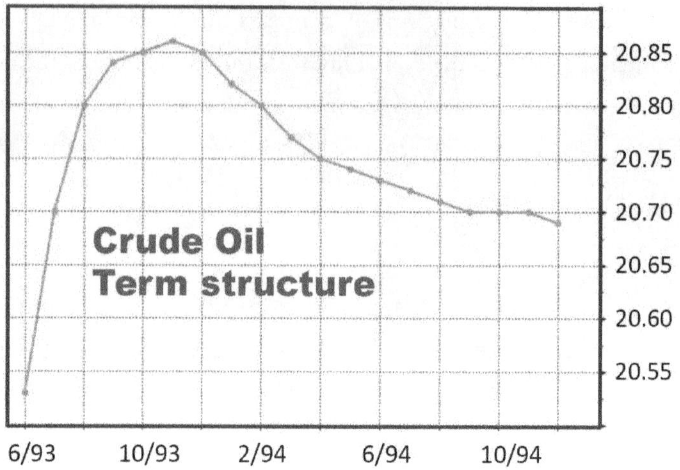

Figure 10. Crude oil future term structure in 1993/1994, in USD/barrel. Data: Bloomberg, 2019.

The situation continued to worsen as MGRM suffered from liquidity problems and poor credit ratings. In the context of declining oil prices, MGRM was caught in a vicious circle.

Local management staked everything on a single throw of the dice and continued to carry out additional contracts with customers. At the low point of the crisis, MGRM alone was responsible for between 10 and 20 percent of all outstanding one-month-forward transactions in crude oil.

By terminating all crude oil futures positions, the MG Group realized a loss of more than 1 billion USD.

Meanwhile, German Metallgesellschaft's fortunes had also been plunging. As a result of the economic slowdown and a high debt burden, the company could only pay a dividend in 1991–1992 by writing down hidden reserves. The following year the deficit had climbed to almost 350 million Deutschmarks, about 200 million USD. Then the bad news from the United States hit. Under pressure from creditors, MGRM was forced to file for bankruptcy with a loss of 1.5 billion USD. That brought the entire group to the brink of insolvency.

In February 1993 Schimmelbusch launched an extensive divestment program to redeem 600 million USD. But the US subsidiary's losses continued to grow and soon exceeded 1 billion USD. Schimmelbusch now had to ask for additional funding by the company's major shareholders, Deutsche Bank and Dresdner Bank. Startled by the imminent loss, Ronaldo Schmitz, a member of Deutsche Bank's executive board and chairman of MG's supervisory board, pulled the trigger. The MG Group realized losses of more than 1 billion USD as a result of the termination of all crude oil contracts, and the group's total liabilities grew to almost 5 billion USD.

On December 17, 1993, Schimmelbusch and CFO Meinhard Forster were dismissed by the supervisory board without notice, and Kajo Neukirchen was hired by Schmitz to save the company. With a bailout of 2 billion USD, rigorous cost savings, and the dismissal of 7,500 employees, Neukirchen restructured the MG Group, which now focused on trading, plant construction, chemicals, and construction technology. In February 2000 the company was renamed MG Technologies, and it became the GEA Group in 2005. The MG Group had met an inglorious end.

Key Takeaways

- CEO Heinz Schimmelbusch became the youngest CEO in Germany when he headed German Metallgesellschaft (MG Group), a large and venerable industrial conglomerate. *Manager Magazine* named him "Manager of the Year" in 1991.

- MGRM—the company's crude oil refining and marketing subsidiary— followed practices that would adversely affect the entire conglomerate.

- MGRM was selling petroleum products at a fixed price to customers, hedging its exposure on the futures market. During normal market conditions, the backwardation term structure of crude oil provided a comfortable markup.

- Things changed when crude oil dropped from more than 40 USD in 1991 to below 20 USD in 1993, and the term structure flipped into contango. Losses mounted to a total of more than 1 billion USD and brought the MG Group to the brink of bankruptcy.

16

Silver:
Three Wise Kings

Warren Buffett, Bill Gates, and George Soros show their interest in the silver market in the 1990s—investing in Apex Silver Mines, Pan American Silver, and physical silver. It is silver versus silver mining. Who would lead and who would lag?

"The financial markets generally are unpredictable."
—George Soros

At the beginning of May 2006, Bolivia's leftist president Evo Morales practiced a little saber rattling as he threatened to nationalize the country's domestic mining industry. A lot of silver was at stake, given Bolivia's two important mines, San Cristóbal (part of Apex Silver Mines) and San Bartolomé (Coeur d'Alene Mines). (Morales had already implemented nationalization of the natural gas industry a week earlier.) In reaction, the stock prices of Apex Silver fell dramatically. From a price of 26 USD in April, the stock plunged to below 13 USD by June. It was a demonstration of how risky investments in mineral resources can be because of politics.

Some Facts About Silver

Silver is about 20 times more common than gold, with the most significant deposits found in North and South America. According to industry figures, there are only 25 relevant silver mines worldwide, and half of their sales are generated by precious metal production. The overwhelming share of global silver production is coupled to the extraction of other metals, especially lead, zinc, copper, or gold. According to the Silver Institute, industrial applications account for about 50 percent of total demand, followed by jewelry and photography.

For standardized silver trading on commodity exchanges, the ticker XAG stands for the price of a troy ounce of silver in USD. The center of physical silver trade is the London Bullion Market, and the London Bullion Market Association (LBMA) fixes an official price once a day. COMEX, part of the New York Mercantile Exchange, is the largest trading place for futures and options on silver. There silver futures are traded under the symbol SI, followed by the contract month and year (e.g., SIH0, Silver March 2020 Futures).

It's not always clear, however, where the best investments lie. In the mid- and late 1990s, Warren Buffett, George Soros, and Bill Gates all entered the silver market as major professional investors, and their actions attracted attention within the international financial community. Like the three kings in the Bible, these men inspired private and institutional investors to follow their lead. However, though Soros, Buffett, and Gates all invested in silver, they used different instruments—physical silver and equity investments in silver-mining companies.

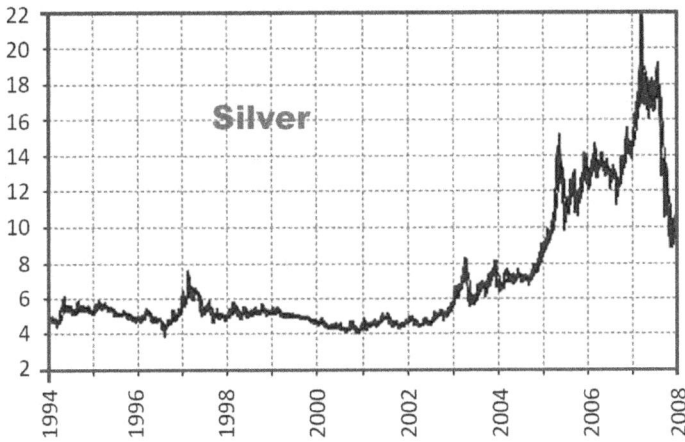

Figure 11. Silver prices, 1994–2008, in USD/ troy ounce. Data: Bloomberg, 2019.

George Soros, born in Hungary in 1930, is known for the success of his Quantum Fund—a hedge fund founded by him and Jim Rogers—and for his bets in 1992 against the pound sterling, which forced the Bank of England to depreciate its currency. Today his net worth is estimated by Forbes to be around 14 billion USD. At the end of 1994, Soros invested in Apex Silver Mines and, together with his brother Paul, temporarily held more than 20 percent of the company. Founded in 1993, Apex owned 65 percent of San Cristóbal, a silver-zinc-lead mine in southwestern Bolivia that was estimated to contain 450 million ounces of silver. Apex also was active in Argentina, Bolivia, Mexico, and Peru.

Warren Buffett, also born in 1930, is the third-richest man in the world, with an estimated net private wealth of about 47 billion USD. As CEO of Berkshire Hathaway, an investment holding company he

In the mid- and late 1990s, Warren Buffett, George Soros, and Bill Gates all got involved in the silver market.

founded, he has demonstrated outstanding investment success over decades. The annual general meetings of the firm are reported to be a "Woodstock for investors," with more than 20,000 people following every statement by the "Oracle of Omaha," as Buffett is known.

William "Bill" Henry Gates III, born in 1955, founded the Microsoft Corporation together with Paul Allen in 1975 and has a fortune of 53 billion USD, which made him the second-richest man in the world before he began to donate large amounts to charitable causes. In 1999 Gates got involved in Pan American Silver as the third big investor in the silver market after Soros and Buffett.

Buffett tried a different strategy. In 1998, before official publication of its annual financial statements, Berkshire Hathaway announced that the company had acquired a total of 130 million troy ounces of silver between July 25, 1997, and January 12, 1998. That was about 4,000 metric tons of silver, which accounted for about 20 percent of the global annual mine production. For Berkshire Hathaway, however, this represented a mere 2 percent of its total invested capital.

The investment in the physical metal surprised the international financial community, as Buffett had always been known for his value-oriented equity investment style. In this case his rationale was based on the discrepancy between supply and demand in the metal over the previous few years and a significant decline in inventories. The increase in silver price that followed proved him right. His investment was very profitable.

As for Bill Gates, it became public in September 1999 that through Cascade Investment LLC he had purchased more than three million shares of Pan American Silver at an average price of about 5.25 USD. This represented 10 percent of the company, which was founded in 1994 and which now had a portfolio of silver-mining projects in Mexico, Peru, Bolivia, and Argentina.

Looking at the price performance of silver versus share price performance of Apex Silver and Pan American Silver since 1997, an interesting picture emerges.

Figure 12. Silver, Pan American Silver, and Apex Silver, 1998–2009. Performance indexed 1998. Data: Bloomberg, 2019.

By the end of 2008, silver was performing the best, followed by the share price of Pan American Silver. Although Apex Silver shares first traded in line with silver and with Pan American Silver, it later crashed: It fell 90 percent between its IPO in 1997 and the end of 2008. Bankruptcy followed. What had happened?

When Bolivian president Morales threatened mining companies with nationalization, investors panicked.

President Morales's threat to nationalize Bolivian mining projects unsettled investors. Actually, in place of a direct nationalization, the tax burden in Bolivia was heavily increased. Nevertheless, Apex Silver was forced to a sell part of its flagship asset to Sumitomo. Developing the San Cristóbal Mine became more and more expensive, as the cost of energy exploded. In order to obtain credit, Apex Silver had to sell futures in high quantities of silver, zinc, and lead. As commodity prices rose, these hedges led to increasing losses, and in January 2009 the company announced bankruptcy.

So which investment was better? The share price of both Apex Silver and Pan American Silver temporarily outperformed silver, because annual production and the value of total mineral resources in the ground had a leverage effect. But leverage is the price investors pay for entrepreneurial and market risk. And when compared to Apex Silver, an investment in physical silver proved to be the much safer bet.

Key Takeaways

- Warren Buffett, Bill Gates, and George Soros became interested in the opportunities offered by the silver market in the 1990s.

- Over a decade, the price of silver climbed from below 4 USD to more than 8 USD in 1997. It reached 22 USD in 2008.

- Silver mining companies seemed to offer a much higher return than a direct investment in silver, but this higher expected return came with a price.

- Because of the rising silver price, Bolivian president Evo Morales threatened to nationalize his country's domestic mining industry. Shares of Apex Silver crashed by more than 90 percent from its IPO in 1997, followed by bankruptcy.

17

Copper: "Mr. Five Percent" Moves the Market

1996

The star trader of Sumitomo, Yasuo Hamanaka, lives two lives in Tokyo, manipulating the copper market and creating record earnings for his superiors but also carrying on risky private trades. In the end, Sumitomo endures a record loss of 2.6 billion USD, and Hamanaka is sentenced to eight years in prison.

"Who is Mr. Copper?"

Investopedia

For years Yasuo Hamanaka was the head trader at Sumitomo Trading in Tokyo, the commodity trading subsidiary of Japanese conglomerate Sumitomo. In insider circles he was known by his nicknames—"Copper Fingers" or "Mr. Five Percent," because he controlled as much as 5 percent of the global copper market. He earned huge profits for his company. However, on June 5, 1996, Hamanaka revealed that he'd lost 1.6 billion USD of his company's money. Since then, the Sumitomo scandal has been considered one of the biggest financial frauds in recent history.

Some Copper Basics

The global production of copper, which is used mainly in construction and electrical and mechanical engineering, is around 20 million metric tons. Chile is the largest producer, with about one-third of the world's output, followed by Indonesia, the United States, and Australia. Copper can be recycled and reprocessed almost without loss of quality, and along with aluminum, it is the most frequently traded industrial metal. The two most important exchanges are the London Metal Exchange (LME) and the New York Mercantile Exchange (NYMEX). At LME copper trades in US dollars per ton; at NYMEX, in US cents per pound. In the United States, the ticker symbol is HG, followed by the contract month and year (e.g., HGZ9, for copper with delivery in December 2019). Currently copper costs 2.80 USD per pound, or 5,600 USD per ton.

In 1985 Yasuo Hamanaka, a 37-year-old expert in copper trading on the commodity futures markets, was hired by the Sumitomo Corporation in Tokyo. His department suffered a considerable loss in the mid-1980s, but the head of trading, and later Hamanaka himself, managed to conceal it with secret trades. Contrary to company tradition in which a trader changed position after a certain period of time, Hamanaka remained at his post for 11 years, because he generated such high profits.

> The Japanese trader Yasuo Hamanaka was a
> dominant factor in global copper.
> But he lost his bet against China.

Any allegations about market manipulation and fraud from the LME went unheeded, while Hamanaka's influential comments about rising copper demand and the occurrence of an artificial shortage were often published in the financial press. Even as Sumitomo's star trader was making a modest impression, however, he was actually living a double life, professionally and privately. During the day he officially traded for Sumitomo; secretly at night he traded for himself on the LME and NYMEX. He lived with his family of four in a small house in Kawasaki, an unattractive Tokyo suburb, and drove a small car. But he enjoyed expensive trips with a lover from the Ginza entertainment district and—of course—had a Swiss bank account.

Beginning in 1993, Hamanaka recognized that the Chinese economy was developing an enormous demand for copper due to its fast industrialization, and he bet that prices would rise. However, the Chinese put the market under pressure by talking down the price. Hamanaka's losses started to pile up. He faked balance sheets, trading reports, and his superiors' signatures in order to obtain additional credit lines to increase his positions and move the market in the "right" direction. But the Chinese seemed in no hurry to buy. By the end of 1995 and the beginning of 1996, the situation was slowly becoming critical. Now mentally unstable, Hamanaka was drinking heavily.

In June 1996, the star trader had no choice but to admit the extent of his losses: Uncovered futures positions came to 1.8 billion USD. Shocked, Sumitomo dismissed Hamanaka, and in a panic it liquidated all positions. This caused another 800 million USD in losses for the

By liquidating copper futures positions it could not cover, the Sumitomo Corporation faced a loss of 2.6 billion USD.

company, as the price of copper dropped by 27 percent in a single day due to the sheer volume of the sales orders. In the end, the Sumitomo Corporation realized a loss of 2.6 billion USD, the biggest ever for a single company in the international financial markets.

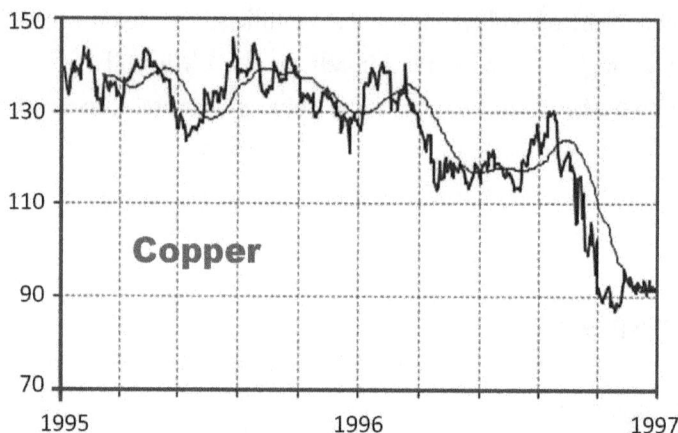

Figure 13. Copper in US cents/lb, 1995–1997. Data: Bloomberg, 2019.

Afterward, reporters wondered how a single trader could have concealed such an unprecedented loss from his superiors. Obviously, internal audits, risk management, and supervision at Sumitomo had failed because, despite the immense transaction volume, none of Hamanaka's superiors knew about his deals in detail. As for Hamanaka himself, the public considered him a criminal offender. He admitted his guilt in court and was sentenced to eight years' imprisonment in 1998.

Key Takeaways

- Yasuo Hamanaka began trading copper for the Japanese conglomerate Sumitomo in 1985. Because of the size of his orders, and his control of up to 5 percent of the global copper market, Hamanaka earned the nicknames "Copper Fingers" and "Mr. Five Percent."

- After 1993, Hamanaka bet on rising copper prices caused by increasing Chinese demand, but when prices continued to fall, he lost money. Hoping that prices would recover, Hamanaka continued to hide his cumulative losses through secret trades.

- In 1996, however, Hamanaka was forced to reveal a loss of 1.8 billion USD. Shocked, his superiors ordered all positions to be sold immediately, which caused a 27 percent drop in copper prices in a single day and resulted in an additional loss for Sumitomo of 800 million USD.

- The Sumitomo copper scandal in Japan of 1996 was one of the biggest financial frauds in history; a single person caused a loss of 2.6 billion USD.

18

Gold:
Welcome to the Jungle

1997

In the jungle of Borneo, the Canadian firm Bre-X supposedly finds a gold deposit with a total estimated value of more than 200 billion USD. Large mining companies and Indonesian president Suharto all want a piece of the pie, but in March 1997 the discovery turns out to be the largest gold fraud of all time.

"Geologically, it's the most brilliant thing I've ever seen in my life! It's so big, it's scary. It's f***ing scary!"
—**John Felderhof,** Bre-X

"This can't be a scam! Do some more tests! Figure it out! I know it's there, okay?"
—**Peter Munk,** Barrick Gold

St. Paul is a remote community with roughly 5,000 inhabitants northeast of Alberta, Canada. Its only tourist attraction has been a landing platform for UFOs that was erected on June 3, 1967. In the middle of the 1990s, however, the tiny town became the focus of international media: Every 50th resident was a shareholder of the mining company Bre-X, whose value had increased 500-fold within just three years. As a result, the number of millionaires in St. Paul had suddenly shot up dramatically. At the center of attention was John Kutyn, an employee of the local savings bank, who had sold everything, including his car and his motorcycle, to invest in Bre-X early on.

St. Paul, a small Canadian community of 5,000, recorded a sudden surge in resident millionaires.

Kutyn spread the news about the gold discovery of the century among his neighbors and customers. He would be one of the few who managed to exit the company before it collapsed. A wealthy man, he went on to settle in New Zealand.

Where's the Gold?

Based on industry estimates of the World Gold Council, around 190,000 metric tons of gold have been produced throughout history, of which one-fifth is stored in central bank vaults. The main gold-producing countries are China, Australia, Russia, the United States, and Canada, followed by Peru, Indonesia, South Africa, Mexico, and Ghana. Together, these 10 countries account for around 75 percent of global mine production. Former number-one gold producer South Africa now barely makes the top 10. Though it dominated gold mining for more than 30 years, the country's production peaked in the 1970s.

The center of global gold trading is the London Bullion Market, and most of the demand comes from the jewelry industry, followed by investors and industrial applications. The largest gold-producing companies in terms of volume are Barrick Gold, Newmont Mining, and Goldcorp.

In the 1980s Canada had witnessed a boom in exploration companies, which searched the world for crude oil, gold, and other commodities. Among them was Bre-X, founded by former stockbroker David Walsh late in the decade. From an initial 0.30 Canadian dollar (CAD), the value of Bre-X shares fell to a few cents in 1993. But that would change after Walsh and a geologist named Felderhof bought exploration rights for Busang in the jungle of Borneo, Indonesia. Together with his colleague Mike de Guzman, Felderhof had explored Busang for another company in the mid-1980s, and the two men had found small traces of gold. On May 6, 1993, Bre-X announced that it had acquired a license for Busang. At that point the share price was around 0.50 CAD. But drilling samples validated gold levels of more than 6 grams per ton of rock. Since 3 grams are considered an excellent result, this caused a sensation.

Was Busang home to the biggest gold treasure of all time?

It wasn't long before analysts picked up the Bre-X story. In March 1994 the stock rose to 2.40 CAD. By September, after a year of exploration and testing, the management of Bre-X estimated that Busang's ore resources were between 3 and 6 million ounces of gold. As Bre-X's drill results got better and better, gold experts and analysts published ever more optimistic forecasts.

In November 1995 Busang's gold resources were estimated at more than 30 million ounces, and toward the end of the year the stock price of Bre-X shares climbed above 50 CAD! At the annual general shareholders' meeting in May 1996, the company was valued at 200 CAD per share, which then split by 1:10. The estimates kept rising: Bre-X reported more than 39 million ounces of gold in June 1996, 47 million ounces in July, 57 million ounces in December, and 71 million ounces in February 1997. Shortly afterward, Felderhof publicly speculated about resources of more than 100 million ounces. This would have made Busang the richest gold deposit of all time. Market rumors even doubled the estimate: Some 200 million ounces, about 6,000 tons, were supposed to lie hidden in the jungle of Borneo!

Though the company had not produced a single ounce of gold, Bre-X shares rose 500-fold.

At the beginning of September 1996, the stock reached its highest price—28 CAD (which corresponded to a price of 280 CAD before the stock split) and a market capitalization of more than 4 billion USD. In just three years the value of Bre-X shares had increased by more than 500 times, even though not a single ounce of gold had been commercially produced!

In the meantime, the industry's big names—Placer Dome, Newmont Mining, Barrick Gold, and Freeport-McMoRan—were also taking part in the race for Busang. Indonesian president Haji Muhammed Suharto wanted his share of the treasure, too. In December 1996 the Indonesian government, Bre-X, and Barrick Gold agreed to divide Busang among themselves. The following February, Freeport joined the group.

But then things began to fall apart. On March 19, 1997, Mike de Guzman committed suicide by jumping from a helicopter. During the due-diligence process, independent drill holes had revealed only negligible amounts of gold. A week later, lab results showed that Bre-X had manipulated the initial samples. It was a personal disgrace for Peter Munk, the head of Barrick Gold, and the news caused investors to panic. The share price of Bre-X collapsed, and the stock was suspended from trading. Later Bre-X had to declare bankruptcy, and the stock became worthless.

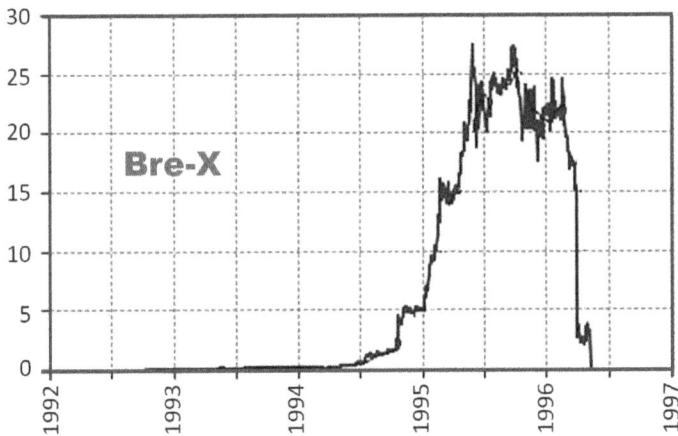

Figure 14. Share price of Bre-X, 1992–1997, in Canadian dollars (CAD). Data: Bloomberg, 2019.

The Bre-X fraud remains one of the biggest capital market scandals in Canada and the biggest mining scandal ever recorded, causing serious lingering damage to the reputation of the Canadian stock market. Major investors who were hurt included the Ontario Municipal Employees Retirement Board, the Quebec Public Sector Pension Fund, and the Ontario Teachers Pension Plan. In addition, many small investors, including some 200 residents of St. Paul, saw their money vanish into thin air.

Bre-X crashed. The stock was worthless.

Not everyone suffered. David Walsh capitalized 35 million USD by selling Bre-X shares before the collapse and moved to the Bahamas. John Felderhof was able to sell nearly 3 million Bre-X shares, with a total value of almost 85 million CAD, between April and September 1996. He found a new home in the Cayman Islands. The Bre-X scandal was finally settled in 2002. However, legal disputes continue today.

Key Takeaways

- The Bre-X scandal remains the biggest corporate mining scandal in Canada to date.

- In 1993 David Walsh and John Felderhof claimed to find the gold deposit of the century in Borneo. Their company, Bre-X, rose from a penny stock, trading below 30 Canadian cents, to 4 billion USD in market capitalization. From mid-1993 to mid-1996, the value of Bre-X shares increased by a multiple of 500. Indonesian president Haji Muhammed Suharto and large multinational gold companies all wanted a piece of the pie.

- But in March 1997 the discovery was unmasked as the largest gold fraud of all time. Lab results confirmed that the company had manipulated its gold samples. Bre-X declared bankruptcy; its stock was worthless.

19

Palladium:
More Expensive Than Gold

In 2001 palladium becomes the first of the four traded precious metals—gold, silver, platinum, and palladium—whose price breaks the psychological mark of 1,000 USD per ounce. That represents a tenfold increase in just four years. The reason lies in continuing delivery delays by the most important producer: Russia.

> *"The actual level of Russian stockpiles of palladium is a closely guarded state secret."*
> —United Nations Conference on
> Trade and Development

Russia is the epicenter of the global palladium market, due to its high share of world annual production and its strategic inventories, which were built up through overproduction in the 1970s and 1980s. Since palladium is mainly a by-product of the production of other metals such as platinum or nickel, the production of palladium continues even when the supply of the metal is sufficient and prices are low.

Russia dominated global palladium production and held significant inventories.

The majority of palladium comes from Russia—and from a single spot, the Norilsk nickel deposit in northern Siberia. If supplies of Norilsk nickel are unable to keep pace with demand, stocks held by the Russian precious metals authority Gokhran, which is under the supervision of the Ministry of Finance, and the Russian Central Bank, fill the gap.

A Palladium Primer

Together with platinum, ruthenium, rhodium, osmium, and iridium, palladium is part of the platinum group of metals (PGM). More than 50 percent of the market for the metal depends on automobile catalysts and other industrial processes, though palladium is also used in jewelry. On average over the past five years, just over 50 percent of the annually mined palladium has come from Russia. Other important producer countries are South Africa, which accounts for just under one-third of global production, and the United States, with 15 percent of the global supply. With an annual production volume of around 220 metric tons, the market for palladium is significantly smaller than, for example, gold or silver. (For comparison, around 3,000 metric tons of gold and 24,000 of silver are produced each year.)

The London Bullion Market Association's (LBMA) twice-daily price fixing is the most internationally recognized price reference, and futures in palladium are traded in the United States (NYMEX) and Japan (TOCOM).

Figure 15. Palladium in USD/ounce, 1998–2004. Data: Bloomberg, 2019.

In the late 1990s the development of automobile catalysts made palladium an important industrial metal, and it was increasingly used instead of platinum because of the relatively low price at the time. But lack of deliveries from Russia started to drive the price up.

In 1997 palladium deliveries from Russia halted for seven months. The next year deliveries stopped again. Moreover, analysts began to question the actual physical availability of the metal. It seemed that a large share of the palladium inventory had been collateralized by Western banks for credits in the aftermath of the Russian Financial Crisis of 1997.

> **The price of palladium rose from 120 USD to more than 1,000 USD, making the metal more valuable than gold, silver, and platinum.**

The price of palladium rose from 120 USD per ounce in early 1997 to more than 200 USD in 1998. In April of that year, the price of the metal surpassed the gold price for the first time since 1971, due to continued supply disruptions in Russia. And the prices for palladium continued to climb: to 400 USD, then to 600 USD. In February 2000 the price of palladium skyrocketed to more than 800 USD, while the price of gold averaged just under 300 USD during that period. It seemed as though the price would consolidate, but instead it rose again to 1,000 USD.

At the beginning of 2001, palladium broke through the psychological barrier of 1,000 USD, the first of the four traded precious metals—the others are gold, silver, and platinum—to do so. The shortage pushed the price up to almost 1,100 USD at the end of January 2001. The value of palladium had increased almost tenfold in just four years!

It didn't last. Subsequently, the value of palladium fell as low as 200 USD, after Russia announced long-term supply contracts with Japan, which were expected to start in January 2001. Then, during the commodity boom in the first decade of the new millennium, the price of palladium once again reached 600 USD before consolidating. Still this represented only a triple rise, compared with a multiple of 10 in 2001.

In 2015 a major emissions scandal in the car industry ("Dieselgate") fueled another palladium rally. In September of that year, the US Environment Protection Agency (EPA) issued a notice of violation of the Clean Air Act to the Volkswagen Group. The German car manufacturer had intentionally manipulated data and software in its diesel engines to meet emissions limits. The scandal spread to other manufacturers and raised awareness of the higher levels of pollution emitted by diesel-powered vehicles. The price of palladium, which was used in catalysts for gasoline cars, more than doubled, from less than 500 USD in mid-2015 to more than 1,100 USD at the end of 2018. At the beginning of 2019, Palladium was trading at 1,320 USD, once again higher than gold. Investors are wondering how long the rally will last this time . . .

Key Takeaways

- More than 90 percent of palladium reserves are found in Russia and South Africa. The metal (together with platinum) is predominantly used in automobile catalyst systems and related industrial applications.

- In January 2001 palladium prices rose to 1,100 USD, 10 times the value of four years before.

- Palladium became more valuable than gold, silver, or platinum, as Russia, the biggest producer and exporter of the metal, withheld shipments.

- Dieselgate, the global diesel-related emissions scandal, fueled a new rally in palladium, whose prices have more than doubled again since 2015.

20

Copper:
Liu Qibing Disappears
Without a Trace

2005

A trader for the Chinese State Reserve Bureau shorts 200,000 tons of copper and hopes for falling prices. However, when copper prices climb to new records, he disappears and his employer pretends never to have heard of him. What sounds like the plot of a thriller shocks metal traders all over the world.

> *"It's one thing to have a rogue trader on your staff—that happens. But I'd be amazed if China wanted a reputation as a rogue nation in these markets, where it has become such an important player."*
> —Anonymous trader

Most people even have trouble pronouncing the name Liu Qibing, but in November 2005 the Chinese copper trader was the number-one topic of conversation on the commodity futures exchanges in London, New York, and Shanghai. Rumors were circulating about a massive, speculative short position in the copper market: Liu Qibing, in his capacity as a trader for the Chinese State Reserve Bureau (SRB), was said to have shorted futures contracts on the London Metal Exchange (LME) amounting to 100,000 to 200,000 tons.

Unlike Yasuo Hamanaka in Japan almost ten years earlier, Liu Qibing was speculating on *falling* copper prices. However, prices continued to rise, and the talk of a massive short position temporarily drove London's three-month-forward copper contracts to a record high of nearly 4,200 USD per metric ton.

Starting at 1,500 USD, the copper price bounced up to 9,000 USD per ton.

Copper prices had started to climb since the turn of the millennium. In December 2003 the price of copper broke the 2,000 USD per ton mark for the first time, while the average price of previous years was only slightly above 1,500 USD. Just a few months later, the price breached the 4,000 USD level. The trigger for this development lay in the growing demand of the Chinese economy, which required more and more of the red metal for its infrastructure and housing industry. Although the OECD countries (members of the Organisation for Economic Co-operation and Development) collectively consumed about 80 percent of the world's copper output at that time, China's growth was more dynamic. Copper consumption in OECD countries increased on average by 2.5 percent per year over the previous five years. However, China's demand grew by about 15 percent per year over the same period, while supply growth proved inflexible. At peak times China's demand growth accounted for more than 80 percent of global demand growth.

China was sucking global copper markets dry.

At that time China alone accounted for a quarter of the world's copper consumption. Meanwhile, the prices for industrial metals continued to rise, because producers were slow to respond with an increased supply.

There were several reasons for their reluctance: First, the development of new mines usually takes several years until the first ton of copper can be produced. Second, many producers didn't trust the high price level to last and therefore delayed long-term investment projects. By 2004, however, the extension of existing projects and the activation of new mines were entering a decisive phase. Experts—including the world's largest copper producer, Chilean Codelco, and the Chinese State Reserve Bureau— expected the supply to increase at the end of 2005, and the rise in copper prices should have come to an end. As it turned out, that was a misperception for which China paid dearly.

Contrary to expectations, almost all major producers had problems with production. Costs increased; high oil prices, strikes, and even earthquakes all had a lasting effect. The projected additional supply in the copper market was lagging, and demand, continually fueled by China's dynamic economic growth, was jumping ahead. As a consequence, the price rose steadily. The rumors surrounding Liu's positions created additional momentum, as copper inventories on commodity futures exchanges in London, New York, and Shanghai reached their lowest levels in 30 years.

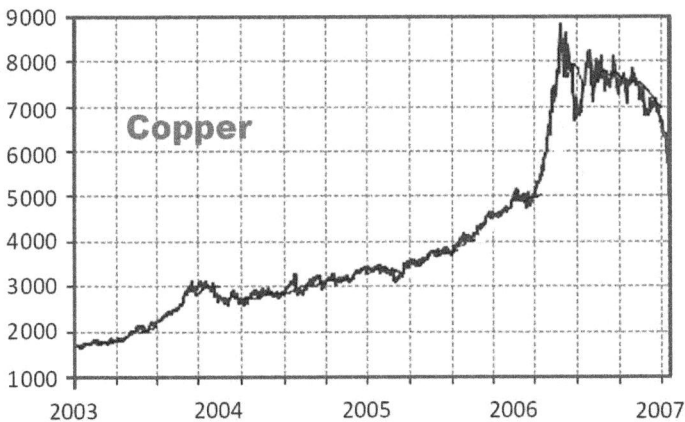

Figure 16. Copper prices in USD/ton, 2003–2007, London Metal Exchange (LME). Data: Bloomberg, 2019.

The newspaper *China Daily* reported that 130,000 metric tons of copper were sold by Liu Qibing for the SRB at an average price of 3,300 USD per ton. As the price of copper rose above 4,000 USD, Liu broke off contacts with other traders in London and China and disappeared. His cell phone remained silent, the door of his apartment on the 10th floor of a Beijing building never opened, and he was absent from his job in Shanghai.

> **The Chinese trader broke off all contacts, never answered his cell phone, and his employer denied his existence.**

At first Liu's employer denied he existed. Later, the SRB claimed that the trader was acting solely on his own behalf. The SRB, which was founded in 1953, was supposed to stabilize prices and secure supplies through commodity trading, not earn profits through speculation. Industry experts considered the 36-year-old trader, who was under house arrest according to Chinese sources, more a pawn than a perpetrator.

Liu, the son of a farming family from Hubei Province, had been with the SRB since 1990 and had been trained for futures and options trading at the London Metal Exchange (LME). Between 2002 and 2004, Liu is said to have generated more than 300 million USD in risky copper trades for the SRB. Now, the Chinese state was facing losses of hundreds of millions of dollars. In response, the government in Beijing tried to push down the world market price through copper auctions. In a first tranche, 50,000 tons were sold. Another tranche of a similar size was to follow, and the leadership in Beijing spread the word that the country had 1.3 million tons of copper in reserve. However, market participants estimated that the amount of copper available was just half that. The Chinese government's actions were unsuccessful, as more and more market participants took counter-positions to force China to make physical delivery of the metal in late December.

Hedge funds—called "crocodiles" in China—particularly saw an opportunity to generate short-term profits. The copper price climbed above 5,000 USD in January 2006, to 6,000 USD in early April, and to 7,000 USD at the end of that month. It rose to the dizzying heights of nearly 8,800 USD a ton in May, before normalizing again over the coming months.

Key Takeaways

- Like the Japanese trader Yasuo Hamanaka almost 10 years before, Chinese trader Liu Qibing was caught on the wrong side of the copper market. He speculated on falling prices and lost a great deal.

- Liu was working for the Chinese State Reserve Bureau (SRB), which handled the Chinese economy's rising demand for the commodity. Market intelligence estimated Liu's short position at about 100,000 to 200,000 tons of copper.

- Copper prices climbed from 1,500 USD per ton in 2003 to almost 9,000 USD in 2006, and Liu, labeled as a rogue trader, vanished.

21

Zinc:
Flotsam and Jetsam

2005

The city of New Orleans, called The Big Easy, is well known for its jazz, Mardi Gras, and Creole cuisine. Less well known, however, is that about one-quarter of the world's zinc inventories are stored there. Hurricane Katrina's flooding makes the metal inaccessible, and concerns over damage cause the price of zinc to rise to an all-time high.

"It's totally wiped out . . . it's devastating."
—President George W. Bush

Zinc, which is traded on the London Metal Exchange (LME) in US dollars per metric ton, is the third-largest metal market, after copper and aluminum. But in the first years of the new millennium, zinc and lead were considered the ugly sisters of copper and aluminum, because of years of low prices and low margins for mining companies. Global supply was stagnating.

What Happens at the LME?

At the London Metal Exchange (LME), copper, aluminum, zinc, lead, nickel, and tin, as well as molybdenum, cobalt, and steel are traded. To capture the opportunities of electrification and electronic vehicles, LME plans to introduce lithium, manganese, and graphite futures contracts in the near future. Trading takes place in two rounds, in the morning and afternoon, in an open ring ("open pit") during which the daily official trading price is determined. In 2012 the 137-year-old LME agreed to a 1 billion GBP takeover from the Hong Kong Exchange and Clearing (HKEx) after a nine-month auction battle that included ICE, CME, and Nasdaq. With an annual turnover of more than 12 trillion USD, the London Metal Exchange is the world's largest trading place for metals, followed by metal exchanges in Singapore and New York.

LME forward contracts are physically deliverable, and inventories of corresponding metals are stocked in LME-approved warehouses. Delivery takes place against LME delivery notes, which provide the owner with the right to a specified quantity of metal at a designated storage location. Currently, there are more than 400 warehouses in 32 locations, from the United States and Europe to the Middle East and Asia.

Even as interest in industrial metals increased in 2003 as a result of the rapid growth of the Chinese economy, zinc's price rise lagged behind those of other industrial metals. Nevertheless, China played a major role in the metal's shortage: In 2004 the country became a net importer of zinc, bringing in about 67,000 tons in the first seven months of 2005, after only 15,000 tons were imported in the entire previous year. The International Lead & Zinc Study Group forecast a market deficit of 200,000 metric tons by the end of 2005, though there had been an excess of 50,000 tons in the first five months.

Even though global inventories continued to decline, many producing companies remained skeptical about increasing the supply. "At this point, nobody in our business is rushing to build new zinc mines," explained Greig Gailey, managing director of Zinifex, the world's third-largest producer of zinc (after Xstrata and Teck Cominco), in 2005. "We're certainly not, nor are Teck Cominco or Falconbridge."

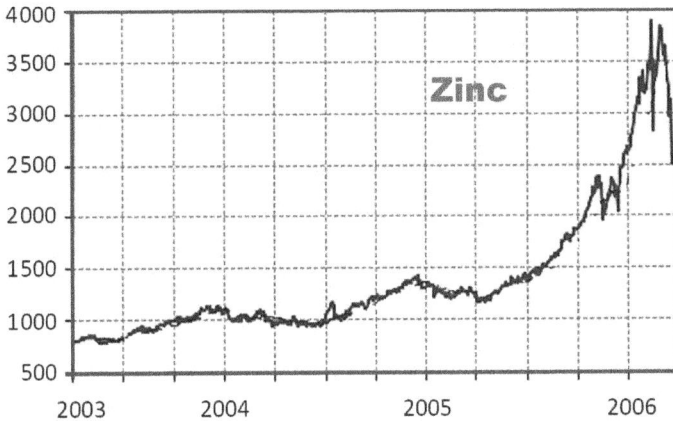

Figure 17. Zinc prices in USD/ton, 2003–2006, London Metal Exchange (LME). Data: Bloomberg, 2019.

By this time the price of zinc was hovering around 1,200 USD per metric ton. It had broken through 1,000 USD at the beginning of 2004, after moving in a narrow range between 750 and 850 USD over the two previous years.

About 25 percent of global zinc inventories were concentrated in warehouses in and around New Orleans.

In a nutshell, that was the situation until August 2005. Then Katrina hit New Orleans like an atomic bomb. The Level 5 hurricane caused devastating damage in the southeastern United States but particularly affected the city, whose urban area was almost completely below sea level.

Twenty-four official LME warehouses had been sited in and around the city at the Mississippi Delta, due to its geographical location and attractive economic conditions. In addition to 250,000 tons of zinc, there were also 1,200 tons of aluminum and 900 tons of copper locked away. Global zinc inventories were estimated by the International Lead & Zinc Study Group to be just over 1 million metric tons at that point—the equivalent to a 35-day global supply. The inventories in New Orleans therefore accounted for around a quarter of global stocks and about half of the zinc traded at the LME. Due to the flood damage in New Orleans, however, access to the zinc was suddenly severely limited.

Stephen Briggs, a metal analyst at Société Générale, summarized the situation: "We have a potentially serious development . . . the market is assuming that the metal is damaged and will be inaccessible for a lengthy period of time."

Who Needs Zinc?

Zinc is mainly used as corrosion protection for other metals or metallic alloys such as iron or steel, and most of the demand for it is based on infrastructure, construction, and transport. Zinc is commonly produced as a co-product with lead, and worldwide mined production is around 11 million metric tons. The largest producer countries are China, Australia, Peru, the United States, Australia, and Canada; the latter two are also the largest exporters of the metal. Unlike the more concentrated markets for copper or nickel, the 10 largest companies produce less than 50 percent of the world's zinc.

Consumers assumed the worst. On September 2, zinc prices rose to a five-month high, as speculators foresaw delays in the delivery of zinc from the New Orleans warehouses. On September 6, the LME decided to temporarily suspend the supply of zinc from its stocks, though it had confirmed delivery of the metal just a week before. Accordingly, the price of zinc in London increased exponentially to 1,454 USD per metric ton, the highest since 1997. Two days later the LME's CEO, Simon Heale, confirmed that suspension of deliveries could last until 2006 because of lack of access to the port of New Orleans.

At the end of the year, zinc prices broke through 1,900 USD and, just under two weeks later, reached 2,400 USD in London. But that was only the beginning: The worsening situation eventually drove the value of the metal to 4,000 USD in the first half of 2006 and marked a new high of just under 4,600 USD per ton in November of that year.

By 2007 the scare was over: Beginning in August, the price dropped continuously over the next 12 months, from 3,500 USD to less than 1,500 USD.

Key Takeaways

- Only market insiders were aware that warehouses in the city of New Orleans held around a quarter of global zinc stocks and about half of the zinc traded at the London Metal Exchange, the biggest physical metal market in the world.

- In August 2005 Hurricane Katrina devastated New Orleans, causing extensive flooding in the area and making zinc inventories inaccessible.

- As a consequence of this shortage of material, the price for zinc climbed from nearly 1,200 USD per ton during summer 2005 to a record of 4,600 USD in November 2006.

22

Natural Gas:
Brian Hunter and
the Downfall of Amaranth

In the aftermath of the closure of MotherRock, an energy-based hedge fund, the bust of Amaranth Advisors shakes the financial industry, as it is the largest hedge fund failure since the collapse of Long-Term Capital Management in 1998. The cause? A failed speculation in US natural gas futures. Brian Hunter, an energy trader at Amaranth, loses 6 billion USD within weeks.

"The market can stay irrational
longer than you can stay solvent."
—John Maynard Keynes

T he news shook financial markets like an earthquake in September 2006: Amaranth Advisors, a 10 billion USD American hedge fund, erased around two-thirds of its capital in two weeks by betting on natural gas and was about to close. Only a few weeks before, MotherRock, another hedge fund that specialized in natural gas futures, had collapsed as well. Some of the causes for these events date back to previous years. Following the record hurricane seasons of 2004 and 2005, many hedge funds had become interested in the energy markets. Hurricanes Ivan, Katrina, Rita, and Wilma had all damaged crude oil and natural gas production facilities in the Gulf of Mexico, resulting in a significantly reduced supply.

Weather and hedge fund speculation drove up natural gas prices from 6 to above 15 USD.

These extreme weather events, as well as relatively constant demand during the winter months, led to increasing price volatility and, in some cases, substantial price spikes for energy, especially natural gas. While the price of gas traded between 6 and 7 USD during 2004 and the first half of 2005, the hurricane season drove up gas prices to more than 15 USD in December. Production disruptions dragged on for months, but the warm winter, the absence of major storms, and a greater number of imports dampened the effect on the price level of natural gas in 2006.

Compared to their all-time high that year, benchmark natural gas prices in New York lost around two-thirds of their value. In September natural gas was trading near 4 USD. The huge fluctuations in price made natural gas interesting for short-term-oriented traders, but natural gas's future contract curve offered an even more interesting investment opportunity. Speculation on the change of price differences between different contract maturities is a popular trading strategy, especially by hedge funds: Traders enter long and short positions in the same commodity simultaneously, and the trade is based on an expansion or narrowing of the price differences, that is, a change in the steepness of the term structure.

Some Thoughts on Natural Gas

Natural gas is one of the most important sources of energy in the United States, with a market share of almost 25 percent. Home heating, electricity generation, and other industrial applications together make up nearly 80 percent of its use. But the need for heat, which accounts for 20 percent of total demand, is very seasonal: There's high demand in the winter months, less during the summer.

Natural gas production in the United States is focused in Texas, the Gulf of Mexico, Oklahoma, New Mexico, Wyoming, and Louisiana. Texas and the Gulf region together contribute more than 50 percent of domestic output. Another 15-plus percent of total US natural gas consumption is imported from Canada or imported in the form of liquefied natural gas (LNG).

Natural gas is traded on NYMEX under the symbol NG and the current contract month in USD per 10,000 MMBtu (1 MMBtu equals 26.4 cubic meters of gas, based on an energy content of 40 megajoules/m^3).

In 2006 the two top hedge fund investors in the US natural gas market were Brian Hunter, head of energy trading at Amaranth Advisors, a fund worth 9 billion USD, and Robert "Bo" Collins, chief executive of MotherRock, which oversaw about 400 million USD. The Mother Rock Energy Master Fund, which launched in December 2004, returned 20 percent to its investors in 2005.

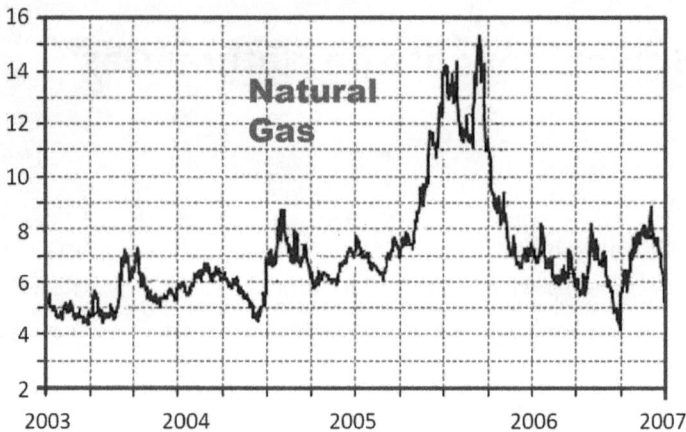

Figure 18. Natural gas prices in USD/MMBtu, 2003 to 2007, New York Mercantile Exchange. Data: Bloomberg, 2019.

Some investors at the time were aware that Collins and Hunter held opposing positions in March–April and October–January natural gas contracts. In July 2006 the price difference between the gas futures for March and April 2007 reached 2.60 USD. Hunter's investment decisions assumed that the difference would increase due to the upcoming cold season. In contrast, MotherRock was betting on a correction in the price spread.

Who Is Brian Hunter?

Born in 1975, Brian Hunter is a Canadian mathematician and hedge fund manager. From 2001 to 2004, he worked at Deutsche Bank in New York. There, in 2001 and 2002, he achieved a profit of 17 and 52 million USD by trading natural gas futures. However, after losses of more than 50 million USD in just one week, Hunter was released from his job. He moved on to Amaranth.

Hunter became a legend on Wall Street by earning more than 1 billion USD speculating on natural gas prices after Hurricanes Katrina and Rita. By August 2006 he had achieved a profit of about 2 billion USD. Within a week, however, he had lost three times that, causing serious problems for Amaranth. After his separation from the company, Hunter went on to found a new hedge fund in 2007.

Amaranth, with about 360 employees, had begun as a company that focused on convertible arbitrage. As those profit opportunities dwindled, it moved on to the energy sector. The firm dominated US natural gas trading on financial markets such as the NYMEX and the Intercontinental Exchange (ICE), as it bought and sold thousands of contracts, sometimes even tens of thousands, on a daily basis. Amaranth held about 100,000 natural gas contracts in one month, which accounted for about 5 percent of the total annual gas consumption of the United States. On the New York Stock Exchange alone, Amaranth controlled 40 percent of all outstanding contracts for the 2006–2007 winter season (October–March) and more than three-quarters of all outstanding November futures contracts.

Amaranth Advisors and MotherRock had opposite guesses on which way the market would move.

In June and July 2006, erratic natural gas price movements caused massive losses in the MotherRock Energy Master Fund. Earlier, the US Department of Commerce had reported a 12 percent increase in gas inventories. As a result, the gas price dropped by 12 percent within a week. The redemption of shares by investors aggravated MotherRock's distress, which increased its losses to more than 200 million USD. However, the hedge fund's high losses were not primarily due to a "normal" price decline. A subsequent Senate investigation confirmed that the sheer volume of Amaranth purchases of March contracts and sales of April contracts had distorted the price spread of natural gas, which moved up by more than 70 percent by July 31, 2006. MotherRock's position worsened to the point where the fund was unable to meet its margin requirements. The fund collapsed, and positions were wound up in August 2006. Brian Hunter had triumphed, but his victory would be short lived.

In late summer, natural gas prices began a downward spiral. The price of natural gas on the NYMEX, with delivery in October, dropped from 8.45 USD in July to below 4.80 USD in September, the lowest price of the previous two and a half years. The difference between futures contracts maturing in March 2007 and April 2007 moved from a high of nearly 2.50 USD in June to below 50 US cents in September—a plunge of around 75 percent!

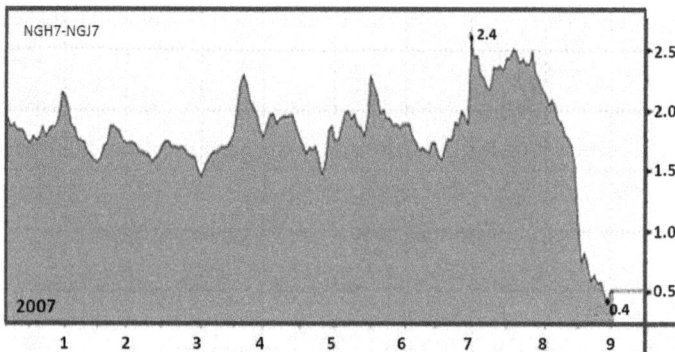

Figure 19. Price spread between natural gas March and April 2007 delivery, in USD/MMBtu, New York Mercantile Exchange. Data: Bloomberg, 2019.

At the end of August, Amaranth held approximately 100,000 contracts in both the September and October futures on the long and short sides. Taken together, these represented enormous positions, because the movement of only 1 US cent on 100,000 contracts meant a change in value of about 10 million USD. The sheer size of the trades caused significant price movements in natural gas and its future term structure, that is, the price relationship of the different maturities.

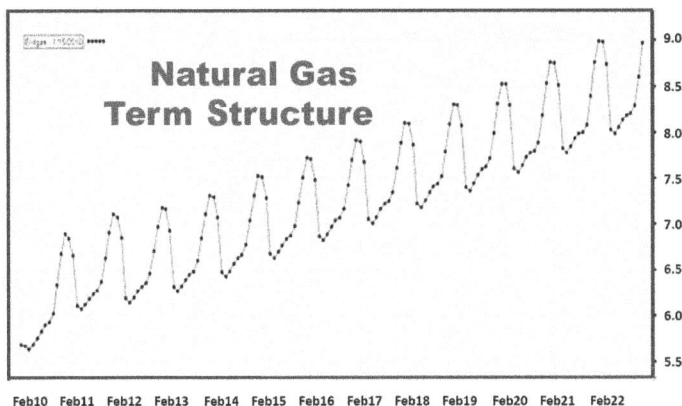

Figure 20. Future Term Structure of natural gas in USD/MMBtu, 2010, New York Mercantile Exchange. Data: Bloomberg, 2019.

The total positions of the fund added up to approximately 18 billion USD. The 60-cent increase in September contracts and the associated drop in the October–September price spread meant a huge loss for Amaranth.

On August 29 the profit-and-loss calculation showed a one-day depreciation of natural gas valuation of just under 600 million USD. The next day's margin obligations would be even worse: They rose to 944 million USD, due to further price depreciation. Two days later Amaranth's margin commitments were in excess of 2.5 billion USD. A week later, on September 8, the hedge fund's obligations exceeded 3 billion USD.

Amaranth's total positions added up to 18 billion USD. In September the fund's margin commitments rose to more than 3 billion USD.

With the price volatility of energy markets remaining high, and because of the cumulative losses, concerns were mounting at Morgan Stanley (one of Amaranth's important investors, along with Credit Suisse and Deutsche Bank), which forced the fund to return money.

Funds under management at Amaranth fell from 9 to 4.5 billion USD in just a week. Founder Nicholas Maounis told his investors in a letter that the company would drastically reduce its positions due to the price fluctuations in the US gas market, and that investors could anticipate losses of 35 percent by the end of the year, even though four weeks earlier the fund had posted a 26 percent profit.

Amaranth got its name from the Greek word for "imperishable," but it was now painfully clear that the firm's profits were anything but. In addition to individual investors, injured parties included umbrella hedge funds of Credit Suisse, Morgan Stanley, and Deutsche Bank. On July 25, 2007, the Commodity Futures Trading Commission condemned Amaranth and Brian Hunter for attempted price manipulation of the natural gas market. Hunter, who had left Amaranth, had already established a new hedge fund—Solengo Capital Advisors.

When Amaranth collapsed in September 2006, investors were told redemptions would be temporarily suspended. Ten years after the blowup, in 2016, Amaranth investors were still waiting to get their money back.

Key Takeaways

- Energy markets were a hot topic in 2005–2006. The price of natural gas climbed from 6 to more than 15 USD, but in late summer the market turned sour and a downward spiral began. In September 2006 natural gas fell below 5 USD.

- Brian Hunter built a position of 18 billion USD in natural gas. By August 2006 his trades had earned him 2 billion USD. But then the market turned against him. Within weeks he had lost 6 billion USD, and Amaranth Advisors collapsed in September 2006.

- The demise of Amaranth Advisors shook the financial industry. It was the biggest hedge fund collapse since the downfall of Long-Term Capital Management in 1998 and investors haven't been paid back yet.

23

Orange Juice: Collateral Damage

"Think big; think positive. Never show any sign of weakness. Always go for the throat. Buy low; sell high." That's the philosophy of Billy Ray Valentine, played by Eddie Murphy in the 1983 movie *Trading Places*. The film's final showdown has Murphy and Dan Aykroyd cornering the orange juice market. In reality, the price of frozen orange juice concentrate would quadruple between 2004 and 2006 on the New York Mercantile Exchange—a consequence of a record hurricane season.

> *"My God! The Dukes are going to corner the entire frozen orange juice market!"*
> —Dan Aykroyd,
> as Louis Winthorpe III in *Trading Places*

The blockbuster movie *Trading Places*, from 1983, stars Eddie Murphy and Dan Aykroyd and culminates in a chaotic scene at the New York commodity exchange over trades of orange juice that hinge on data from the US Department of Agriculture. This was not really farfetched, as trading in orange juice, or more precisely frozen orange juice concentrate, on the New York Mercantile Exchange (NYMEX) is dominated by the effects of weather. Hurricanes, frosts, or droughts in Florida and the region around São Paulo, Brazil—the main places where oranges are grown—can lead to major price fluctuations that vary with the seasons and also affect other agricultural commodities: High prices are due to risk premiums in May (frost in Brazil) and November (hurricane season in Florida), and lows are more common in February and September. Even light storms can lead to a loss of fruit.

Some Juicy Facts

Oranges are cultivated in almost all parts of the world with tropical or subtropical climates, but two countries dominate orange juice production. More than 50 percent of the world's harvest comes from Brazil (the São Paulo region) and Florida in the United States. At harvest, oranges are typically packaged in boxes of 90 pounds or 40.8 kilograms. Processing fruit into concentrate offers advantages, compared to oranges and orange juice, when it comes to storage, shelf life, and transportation.

Orange juice is traded in the form of frozen concentrated orange juice futures in New York. A futures contract refers to 15,000 pounds of concentrate, the equivalent of 2,300 to 2,500 boxes of oranges. Under normal conditions, an orange harvest in Florida provides about 200 million boxes, worth about 1.2 billion USD.

The hurricane seasons of 2004 and 2005
were the most active since weather records
were kept in the United States.

Heavy storms can destroy entire plantations and, at worst, result in lower harvests for several years, because new crops do not bear fruit for three to four years and are most productive only after about eight years. Storms can also make a difference in the spread of pests and diseases, which can greatly impact harvests on monoculture plantations. The years 2004 to 2006 created a "perfect storm" for the price of orange juice, overshadowing even the price spike of crude oil during the 2005 hurricane season.

Storms to Remember

The Atlantic hurricane season typically lasts from June 1 to November 30, and an average season sees just six hurricanes. There are exceptions: The year 2004 was one of the most active and costly hurricane seasons since records began. Winds and floods were responsible for at least 3,000 deaths and property damage of approximately 50 billion USD. The most significant storms—Charley, Frances, Ivan, and Jeanne—all crossed the United States. And all four hit Florida.

But the hurricane season of 2005 stands out even more. It emerged as *the* most active hurricane season since weather records began, with 28 storms, including 13 hurricanes, of which 4 were Category 5 storms! Category 5 on the Saffir-Simpson scale means a hurricane with wind speeds in excess of 251 km/h. The storms in 2005 cost some 2,300 lives and caused damages amounting to 130 billion USD. Hurricanes Dennis, Emily, Katrina, Rita, and Wilma were responsible for the worst of the devastation that year. Katrina caused massive damage in the southeastern United States in August 2005, hitting the city of New Orleans particularly hard. However, Wilma broke all records and is now considered the strongest storm in history.

Florida's orange industry generally has suffered from subsidized over-production. As a result, in times of good harvests income levels are low. The orange harvest in 2004 was very productive, and consequently in May 2004 the price of orange juice was about 35 percent lower than in the previous year. The US Department of Agriculture was estimating a harvest of 245 million cases in 2004, which would have been well above the crop level of the previous year (203 million cases) and would even have topped the record harvest of the 1997–1998 season (244 million cases). In addition, the Atkins diet, which advocated avoiding carbohydrates (including the sugar in orange juice), was particularly popular in the United States at the time and causing noticeably lower demand. At the end of May 2004, orange juice was trading at only 0.54 USD/lb in New York.

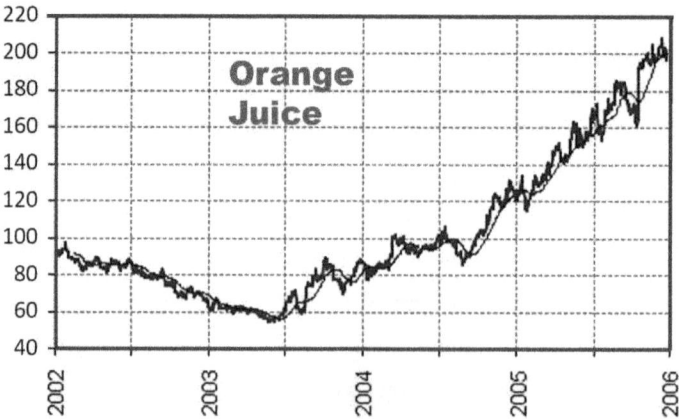

Figure 21. Frozen orange juice concentrate prices in US cents/lb, 2002–2006. Data: Bloomberg, 2019.

But then parameters started to change. The Atkins diet lost popularity, and demand began to pick up. And four hurricanes in 2004–2005—Charley, Frances, Jeanne, and Wilma—would affect the supply of Florida oranges. According to the Florida Citrus Mutual industry association, Hurricane

Wilma alone caused a crop loss of around 35 million boxes, or about 17 percent of unharvested fruit.

From a base of 0.55 USD, the price for frozen orange juice concentrate rose to more than 2 USD. A quadruple increase!

In 2005 the US Department of Agriculture predicted a harvest of only 135 million boxes, that is, a decline of almost 10 percent compared to the already-below-average harvest of the previous year. Market observers expected the lowest harvest level in the previous 17 years due to storm damage and pest infestation. Starting at just under 0.55 USD in May 2004, the price of orange juice concentrate in New York continued to rise, quadrupling within two and a half years.

The prices for orange juice rose to levels unmatched since 1990.

In October 2005 the price rose above 1 USD, breaking a psychological barrier, and the upward momentum continued. Orange juice rose to levels that had not been reached since January 1990, when the price topped 2 USD after a severe frost. In December 2006 the price of orange juice was again trading above 2 USD.

The orange crop in 2005–2006 began to recover slightly in both the United States and Brazil compared to the previous year. But the supply remained about 30 percent below the 2003–2004 level. Finally, in 2007, the price for orange juice fell back to between 1.20 and 1.40 USD, and in 2008, the price normalized to levels below 1 USD again.

Key Takeaways

- Prices of agricultural commodities are very sensitive to extreme weather. As a consequence of a record Atlantic hurricane season, the price of frozen orange juice concentrate quadrupled between 2004 and 2006.

- In October 2005 prices surpassed 1 USD and continued to climb. In December 2006, the price of orange juice traded above 2 USD, a level that had not been reached since January 1990.

- A notable fictional cornering of the market for frozen orange juice concentrate—whose plot hinged on weather information from the US Department of Agriculture's *Crop Report*—took place in the movie *Trading Places* (1983), starring Eddie Murphy and Dan Aykroyd.

24

John Fredriksen:
The Sea Wolf

2006

John Fredriksen controls a corporate empire founded on transporting crude oil. Among the pearls of that empire is Marine Harvest, the largest fish-farming company in the world.

> *"You stand on dead men's legs. You've never had any*
> *of your own. You couldn't walk alone between*
> *two sunrises and hustle the meat for your belly . . ."*
> —Jack London, *The Sea Wolf*

A comparison with socialite Paris Hilton is inevitable: The twin sisters Kathrine and Cecilie, 26, are young, beautiful, and rich. In the list of *Forbes* magazine's "Hottest Billionaire Heiresses," the twins are next to Ivanka Trump and Holly Branson. The sisters have so far kept their names out of scandals, but they are already following in the business footsteps of their father, John Fredriksen. *Forbes* rates the private wealth of the 74-year-old Norwegian shipowner—by far the richest Norwegian—at more than 8 billion USD. Due to high taxes in Norway, however, Fredriksen lives in London and holds Cypriot citizenship.

Fredriksen, born May 11, 1944, near Oslo, became rich in the crude oil business, as have many before him. He was already working in the shipping business when he set up his own company during the oil crises of the 1970s and built up a tanker fleet, today one of the largest in the world. He earned money on risky ventures during the Iran-Iraq War in the 1980s and delivered crude oil to the apartheid regime in South Africa.

Today Frederiksen heads a huge corporate empire, directly or through its investment firms. He is the largest shareholder of the Bermuda-registered shipping company Frontline, which controls a fleet of Liquefied Natural Gas (LNG) tankers with Golar LNG, and is involved in the oil rig operator SeaDrill and the shipping companies Golden Ocean Group and Overseas Shipholding Group. In Germany, Fredriksen is known as a major share-holder of the TUI Group and an advocate of selling the container shipping division Hapag-Lloyd, in order to promote the consolidation of the industry. Prior to 2010 John Fredriksen held the largest stake in TUI Travel and had a significant influence upon its direction and strategy. The Norwegian had already made a name for himself in the world of fish farming and today controls the largest fish-farming company in the world—Marine Harvest.

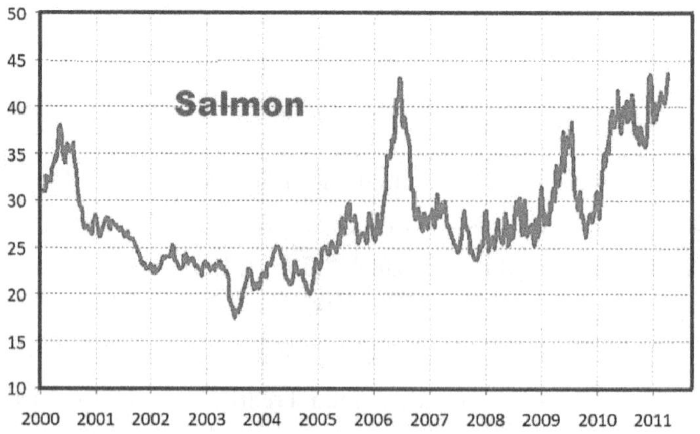

Figure 22. Norwegian salmon prices in NOK/kg, 2000–2011.
Data: Bloomberg, 2019.

In the 1971 German TV adaptation of Jack London's famous adventure novel *The Sea Wolf*, Raimund Harmstorf, in his role as Wolf Larsen, crushes a raw potato to illustrate his worldview—eat, or be eaten. It's an apt metaphor for the dealings of John Fredriksen, the Norwegian Sea Wolf.

In the first years of the new millennium, the Norwegian fish-farming industry was experiencing financial difficulties due to low prices for fish. In particular, the company Pan Fish, founded in 1992, had been struggling since 2000.

What's the Catch?

By far the world's largest fishing nations are China, Peru, India, and Japan. In Europe, Norway, Denmark, and Spain haul in the largest harvests. The value of world exports of fish and fishery products in 2015 reached 96 billion USD. Aquaculture deals with the controlled cultivation of fish, mussels, crabs, and algae, and there's a rapidly growing global market for these products: According to figures from the UN's Food and Agriculture Organization (FAO), slightly more than a third of the almost 150 million metric tons of fish caught come from aquaculture—and the number is rising. The Organisation for Economic Co-operation and Development (OECD) and FAO estimate that by 2020 the proportion of farmed fish will account for almost 50 percent of the total fishery.

Farmed fish have the advantage of lower prices, and some argue that fish farms can also counteract the overfishing of the oceans; according to FAO estimates, more than 70 percent of the fishing grounds are already considered "overfished." However, others point out some

continued

disadvantages: Aquaculture's carnivorous fish, such as salmon and trout, consume many times the body weight of wild-caught fish; and there are particularly negative consequences to keeping fish in unnaturally large and dense pens, especially in countries with low ecological standards, such as in Southeast Asia or South America, because of overfertilization or the use of antibiotics.

Fredricksen controlled an almost 50 percent stake in Pan Fish through his investment company Greenwich Holding and the two vehicles Geveran Trading and Westborough Holdings. In June 2005, he bid successfully for the remaining shares of the company. In the second quarter of 2005, Fredriksen also acquired 24 percent of Fjord Seafood through Geveran Trading. His shares would soon amount to nearly 50 percent of the company. Then, in October 2005, Fjord Seafood made an offer to the state fish-farming company Cermaq, but the bid failed due to opposition from the Norwegian government.

Fredricksen made his next big move in March 2006: Nutreco, today the largest manufacturer of fish feed worldwide, sold 75 percent of Marine Harvest—which had been involved in Chilean fish farming since the mid-1970s—to Geveran Trading for nearly 900 million euros. The remaining 25 percent was acquired by the Norwegian firm Stolt-Nielsen.

On December 29, 2006, Pan Fish, Fjord Seafood, and Marine Harvest merged to form the new Marine Harvest Group. What was by far the largest fish-farming corporation in the world was now under the control of John Fredriksen.

Key Takeaways

- John Fredriksen, a modern version of Jack London's Sea Wolf, made his fortune in the crude oil market, then became active in oil drilling, the transport of crude oil, shipping, and liquified natural gas. Today he controls an extensive corporate empire.

- During the first years of the new millennium, the Norwegian fish-farming industry experienced severe financial difficulties due to low salmon prices.

- By active industry consolidation over two years, Fredriksen built the Marine Harvest Group in 2006. Today it's the world leader in fish farming and aquaculture.

25

Lakshmi Mittal: Feel the Steel

(2006)

The dynamic growth of the Chinese economy and its hunger for raw materials rouses the suffering steel industry from near death. Through clever takeovers and the reorganization of rundown businesses, Lakshmi Mittal rises from a small entrepreneur in India to the largest steel tycoon in the world, a position he crowns with the acquisition of his main competitor and the world's second-largest steel producer—Arcelor.

> *"I want to be the Ford of Steel."*
> —Lakshmi Mittal

> *"Aim for the highest."*
> —Andrew Carnegie

It was a dream wedding, with a setting akin to the court of ancient maharajahs in India or a tale from *1001 Nights*. On June 22, 2004, fireworks illuminated the night sky in Paris, Bollywood stars Aishwarya Rai and Shah Rukh Khan entertained the guests, pop star Kylie Minogue performed, and more than 5,000 bottles of Mouton-Rothschild

1986 were served. The evening festivities were the main attraction of the six-day celebration of the wedding of 23-year-old Vanisha Mittal and London investment banker and founder of Swordfish Investments Amit Bhatia, age 25. Twelve Boeing jets had been chartered to bring more than 1,500 guests from India to France, where they visited the Jardin des Tuileries, Versailles, and the Château de Vaux-le-Vicomte. The silver-wrapped wedding invitations included five-star accommodations at the Hotel Le Grand and the InterContinental, whose 600 rooms had been fully booked. Presents for the guests featured designer handbags filled with jewelry. It is estimated that the cost of this extravaganza was around 60 million USD. The check was signed by the proud bride's father, Lakshmi Mittal.

Who is this tycoon who could arrange a fairytale wedding for his daughter and that same year acquire a princely residence in London's posh Kensington district from the chief executive of the Formula One Group, Bernie Ecclestone, for the equivalent of around 130 million USD?

Lakshmi Mittal's father had run a small steel plant in the Rajasthan province of India. The family later moved to Calcutta, where the father took over a major factory and where Lakshmi learned the steel business from scratch.

After studying business administration in Calcutta, in 1976 Lakshmi was put in charge of modernizing a rundown steelwork in Indonesia that the family had previously acquired for 1.5 million USD. That pattern would continue throughout the Indian mogul's life, as he bought money-losing or underutilized steel producers and restructured their business through cost reductions, sales orientation, layoffs, and closures. When a steel industry

> Lakshmi Mittal
> forged the world's
> largest steel company.

boom was triggered by rapid economic growth in China, Lakshmi Mittal would become one of the richest men in the world in just a few years.

Gradually he added larger and larger acquisition targets. In 1989 Mittal bought a derelict steel plant in Trinidad and Tobago and renovated it. He had a major success in Mexico in 1992: The state had invested 2.2 billion USD in state-of-the-art steel-production equipment, but the end of the oil boom was forcing the government to sell. Mexican president Carlos Salinas awarded the Indian entrepreneur the contract for just 220 million USD, of which Mittal only had to raise 25 million in cash. He then renamed the company Ispat Mexicana. (*Ispat* is Hindi for "steel.")

The year 1995 marked another turning point for the businessman. After the collapse of the Soviet Union, the giant Karmetwerk, which included coal mines, was up for privatization in Kazakhstan. Although Western corporations did not dare invest, Mittal paid 400 million USD, dismissed a third of the workforce, and made the company profitable within a year. Mittal also bought Sidex in Romania after that company was privatized, though it was a controversial deal because of a letter of recommendation written by British prime minister Tony Blair to Romanian president Adrian Năstase after Mittal's donation to Blair's party ("Mittalgate").

Mittal Steel was created
in the spring of 2005.

In October 2004 Mittal announced the merger of privately held LNM Holding and publicly listed Ispat International with the American International Steel Group (ISG). (ISG arose from the assets of LTV Steel and the assets of former industrial titans Acme Steel and Bethlehem Steel.) In the spring of 2005, the deal—worth 4.5 billion USD—was concluded. Mittal Steel, based in the Netherlands, was born.

Steel Ups and Downs

Carnegie and Vanderbilt in USA, or Thyssen and Krupp in Germany—these family names ring a bell in the history of the steel industry. Compared to other industries, the steel industry today is highly fragmented; the 10 largest steelmakers produce less than a third of the world's supply, compared to a market share of more than 90 percent by the world's 10 largest carmakers. ArcelorMittal is the industry leader. Nippon Steel, Baoshan Iron & Steel, POSCO, and JFE Steel follow at some distance.

The 1990s were dark years for steel producers from Western countries. Specifically, the US steel industry slipped into a severe crisis due to overcapacity and cheap imports, and since the late 1990s, more than 30 companies have had to apply for bankruptcy and creditor protection. The situation changed dramatically with the rapid growth of the Chinese economy. The Chinese demand for steel increased from around 15 percent of the world's market in 2000 to almost 50 percent a decade later. This unbalanced the markets for raw materials like iron ore and metallurgical coal and caused prices for crude steel to rise significantly. At the beginning of the millennium, the price for a metric ton of steel was around 200 USD; by 2008, it had risen to 1,100 USD.

Mittal had created the world's largest steel producer, with more than 70 million tons of production capacity. About 90 percent of the company was owned by the family. But Mittal, who wanted to outdo magnates like Andrew Carnegie and Bethlehem Steel's Charles Schwab, was not yet satisfied.

In October of the same year, Mittal Steel acquired Ukrainian steel producer Kryvorizhstal at an auction for 4.8 billion USD, after the Ukrainian president decided against a consortium headed by the son-in-law of the former Ukrainian president. But behind the scenes a much larger deal was looming that would profoundly change the steel industry.

Figure 23. Steel prices in USD/ton, 2000–2010. Data: Bloomberg, 2019.

In January 27, 2006, Mittal announced a takeover bid to the shareholders of Arcelor, which was the industry's second-biggest company. He offered a premium of 27 percent on the closing price of the previous day, a purchase price of nearly 20 billion USD. Arcelor itself had been created by the merger of French, Spanish, Luxembourg, and Belgian steelworks, and in 2005 it had produced almost 50 million metric tons of crude steel. The attempt at the hostile takeover provoked Arcelor's corporate leadership; the governments of Luxembourg, France, and Belgium also opposed the merger.

"L'India"—the Indian—"does not fit in with our great culture," said Guy Dollé, the French head of Arcelor. And, in fact, the takeover battle turned into a war of cultures, during which Arcelor sought to save itself through a merger with Russian steelmaker Severstal. It played out like high-stakes poker. In the course of a month, Arcelor rejected two offers from Mittal as too low. Then, in June 2006, the Arcelor board of directors called for a marathon nine-hour negotiation. For almost 34 billion USD, a further premium of 15 percent on the stock closing price of the previous day—about 45 percent above the original offer—Arcelor finally agreed to the sale.

With the merger of Arcelor and Mittal, the world's largest steel producer was created, with a combined production volume of just under 120 million tons of crude steel, a global market share of around 12 percent, 60 billion USD in sales, and more than 320,000 employees. Number two in the industry, Nippon Steel, had less than one-third of ArcelorMittal's production capacity.

With the acquisition of Arcelor, the Mittal family reduced its stake in the new company to around 45 percent. Nevertheless, with estimated private assets of around 25 billion USD, Lakshmi Mittal is considered the fifth richest person in the world.

Key Takeaways

- The awakening of the Chinese economy, with its dynamic growth and enormous lust for resources, shook up a moribund global steel industry. Between 2000 and 2008, global steel prices increased more than fivefold. One entrepreneur noticed this industry trend faster than others.

- Lakshmi Mittal became the "man of steel." The Indian tycoon created Mittal Steel in 2005 by buying ISG and the remaining assets of former US industry giants Acme Steel and Bethlehem Steel. But that was not enough. After a bidding frenzy, in summer 2006 Mittal bought Arcelor and forged the world's biggest steel company, ArcelorMittal.

- After the transaction was complete, Lakshmi Mittal was considered the fifth richest person in the world, with estimated private assets topping 25 billion USD.

26

Crude Oil:
The Return of
the "Seven Sisters"

(2007)

An exclusive club of companies controls oil production and worldwide reserves. But its influence diminishes with the founding of the Organization of the Petroleum Exporting Countries (OPEC) and the rise of state oil companies outside the Western world.

> *"There is no business like oil business ."*
> —C. C. Pocock, Chairman of Shell

In 2007 the *Financial Times* created the term the "New Seven Sisters" to describe the world's seven most influential energy companies outside the Organisation for Economic Co-operation and Development (OECD). The original Seven Sisters, a term coined in the 1950s, referred to a consortium of predominantly successor companies to the Standard Oil Company: Standard Oil of New Jersey, Standard Oil Company of New York, Standard Oil of California, Gulf Oil, Texaco, Royal Dutch Shell, and the Anglo-Persian Oil Company.

For a long time, the Seven Sisters were regarded as the dominant force in the oil business, since, thanks to a framework agreement with the Iranian government, they held a demand cartel over oil producers in the Third World. Producer countries were forced to sell the majority of their production on the basis of long-term contracts and fixed prices to the oligopoly, which also controlled trade and distribution.

The Seven Sisters were able to set the rules, because until the 1970s the group controlled about 85 percent of global oil reserves. However, early in that decade, more and more important producer countries began to nationalize their oil industry: Algeria was the first country to do so, in 1971, followed shortly thereafter by Libya. In the following year, Iraq nationalized the concessions of Western companies. In 1973 Iran also nationalized its domestic oil industry.

> **The Seven Sisters controlled 85 percent of the world's oil reserves until the 1970s.**

The power of the Seven Sisters was dwindling, and OPEC—founded in 1960 and the cartel's counterpart on the supply side—was gaining in importance.

Today, OPEC countries supply about 40 percent of the world's crude oil, and according to their own data, member countries together account for about 75 percent of global crude oil reserves, while oil production in Western countries has declined over recent years.

> **Four of the Seven Sisters still exist today—ExxonMobil, Chevron, Royal Dutch Shell, and BP.**

To counter strong price fluctuations and a continuous drop in oil prices below 10 USD, the large oil companies used mergers and acquisitions. For example, Exxon (Standard Oil of New Jersey) and Mobil Oil (Standard Oil Company of New York) merged in 1999 to create

ExxonMobil, the world's largest oil company, whose annual revenue exceeds the economic power of many small countries.

From Standard Oil of California came Chevron, which took over US Gulf Oil in 1985 and in 2001 incorporated Texaco as well. The British Anglo-Persian Oil Company first became the Anglo-Iranian Oil Company and then British Petroleum. Following the acquisition of Amoco (the former Standard Oil of Indiana) and Atlantic Richfield, the company finally changed its name to BP in 2000. As a result, four of the original seven dominant companies were left: ExxonMobil, Chevron, Royal Dutch Shell, and BP.

Big Oil today is made up of BP, Chevron, ConocoPhillips, ExxonMobil, Royal Dutch Shell, and Total.

Further mergers, such as Total and Petrofina (1999), Total and Elf Aquitaine (2000), and Conoco and Phillips Petroleum (2002), have put the US firm ConocoPhillips and the French company Total into the same category as the other four. There are now six super-majors—BP, Chevron, ConocoPhillips, ExxonMobil, Royal Dutch Shell, and Total—all often referred to as "Big Oil" in the financial press. However, their influence today is significantly lower than that of the Seven Sisters 50 years ago. Together, Big Oil today controls less than 10 percent of global oil and gas production, and the group's share of global reserves is again significantly lower.

In contrast, the "new Seven Sisters" of the oil industry together control about a third of global oil and gas production and global reserves: These include Saudi Aramco (Saudi Arabia), Gazprom (Russia), China National Petroleum Corporation (China; CNPC), National Iranian Oil Company (Iran), Petróleos de Venezuela (Venezuela), Petrobras (Brazil), and Petronas (Malaysia).

The "new Seven Sisters" are Saudi Aramco, Gazprom, CNPC, National Iranian Oil, Petróleos de Venezuela, Petrobras, and Petronas.

Aramco, based in Dhahran, Saudi Arabia, is the most important of the group. As the world's largest oil company, it produces 12 million barrels of crude oil daily and has reserves of approximately 260 billion barrels of crude oil—almost a quarter of global reserves. With its Ghawar oil field, Saudi Aramco also operates the largest oil field in the world. After a dramatic drop in oil prices in 2015–2016, the kingdom of Saudi Arabia speculated about an IPO of Saudi Aramco to raise money. But plans have not yet been realized.

At the end of 2006, Russian Gazprom and Petro China, a subsidiary of CNPC, had left the market value of most Western energy companies far behind. CNPC, the China National Offshore Oil Corporation (CNOOC), and Sinopec are China's three largest oil companies.

The power of the former Russian state-owned company Gazprom—the world's largest producer of natural gas—was felt in Europe in late 2005 due to the gas dispute with Ukraine. (The enterprise also holds a monopoly on the export of gas from Russia.)

The state-owned National Iranian Oil Company (NIOC), based in Tehran, is part of the Iranian Ministry of Petroleum and is also active worldwide. Petróleos de Venezuela (PDVSA) was the instrument of power of former Venezuelan president Hugo Chávez. Established as part of the nationalization of the country's oil industry, PDVSA is today the largest oil company in Latin America. In the Campos Basin, the semipublic Petrobras (formally Petróleo Brasileiro) accounts for more than 80 percent of Brazil's oil production. The company is also a leader in offshore drilling and deep drilling. With the Tupi field, the Brazilians have probably discovered the third-largest oil field in the world. Petronas (full name Petroliam Nasional Berhad), a state-owned petroleum company known for its landmark Petronas Towers in Kuala Lumpur, is one of the largest international oil and gas companies, with more than 100 subsidiaries and representations in more than 30 countries.

Key Takeaways

* After the breakup of Rockefeller's Standard Oil empire, a consortium known as the "Seven Sisters" emerged. Included were Standard Oil of New Jersey, Standard Oil Company of New York, Standard Oil of California, Gulf Oil, Texaco, Royal Dutch Shell, and the Anglo-Persian Oil Company. This consortium controlled 85 percent of global crude oil reserves until the mid-1970s.

* The influence of the Seven Sisters diminished with the founding of OPEC and the rise of state oil companies outside the Western world. OPEC today controls about 40 percent of global oil and gas production.

* The legacy of the Seven Sisters lives on in a group of super-majors, six integrated oil and gas companies also referred to as "Big Oil": BP, Chevron, ConocoPhillips, ExxonMobil, Royal Dutch Shell, and Total. Compared to the original Seven Sisters, they control less than 10 percent of global oil and gas production.

* The "new Seven Sisters" are Saudi Aramco, Gazprom, CNPC, National Iranian Oil, Petróleos de Venezuela, Petrobras, and Petronas. Together these seven companies control about a third of global oil and gas production and reserves.

27

Wheat and the "Millennium Drought" in Australia

After seven lean years for Australia's agricultural sector, a Millennium Drought drives the price of wheat internationally from record to record. Thousands of Australian farmers expect a total failure of their harvest. Is this a preview of the effects of global climate change?

> *"This is more typical of a 1 in a 1000-year drought, or possibly even drier, than it is of a 1 in a 100-year event."*
> —**David Dreverman**, Head of the
> Murray-Darling Basin Authority

The Aboriginal term *uamby* means "where the waters meet," except that on the Uamby farm, 50 kilometers northwest of the Australian wine-making and sheep-breeding city of Mudgee, no more water was flowing. The year 2006 was one of the hottest since weather records began on this continent and also one with the least rainfall.

Though the extreme drought had already affected the farm severely, it was only the beginning of the worst summer months—which fall between December and March in Australia. Water reserves were running low, and the animals could no longer find food. The pastures were bare and parched, necessitating purchases of water and food. Of the original 4,800 sheep on the farm, only 2,800 were left; the remainder had to be sold for 5 USD per animal, though the owners had expected about 40 USD.

The World's Wheat

With an annual production of just under 600 million tons, various wheat varieties, together with corn and rice, are among the most widely cultivated cereals in the world. Wheat accounts for around one-fifth of the world's calorie needs. It's an important food for livestock and is also used to produce biofuels like ethanol. The average yield per hectare is just under 3 tons worldwide (1 hectare = 10,000 square meters, comparable to a soccer field). Large parts of the harvest are consumed by the producer countries themselves, so that only about 100 million tons of the total amount produced reach the world market—a factor that can affect price fluctuations in times of shortages.

More than 400,000 people were working in Australia's agriculture sector, one of the country's most important industries, and the situation was dire. At the beginning of 2007, due to the adverse circumstances, a farmer was taking his own life every four days. At the beginning of the next year, more than 70 percent of the agricultural land, about 320 million hectares, was affected by lack of rain and high temperatures.

The "granary" of Australia, the Murray-Darling Basin, produces 40 percent of the country's wheat.

The situation was especially tense in the Murray-Darling Basin. The river system spans thousands of kilometers, an area about the size of France and Spain combined, supplying some 15 percent of Australia's water. Officially, the rivers supplied around 50 percent less water in 2007 than the previous year, and 2006 itself had been a record low-water year. The basin is considered the granary of Australia, because this area alone grows 40 percent of the food on the continent. Meanwhile, small towns like Dimboola, about 330 kilometers from Melbourne, in the Australian wheat belt, were becoming ghost towns.

For the international market, Australia's role as the second-largest exporter of wheat was of particular importance. In "normal" times, Australia exports 25 million tons every year. But normal times had not existed in Australia for seven years, making the drought the country's longest. The year 2006 was the third-driest year since records began in 1900, and the Australian Bureau of Agricultural and Resource Economics (ABARE) was estimating the 2006–2007 winter harvest at just 26 million metric tons, 36 percent less than the previous year. Even so, 2007 proved to be hotter, and experts began talking about a Millennium Drought. Australian prime minister John Howard declared it "the worst drought in living memory." The direct cause was the phenomenon known as El Niño—a rise in Pacific Ocean temperature that affects weather patterns, and a phenomenon whose frequency and intensity has increased significantly through global climate change, according to environmental and weather experts.

El Niño Acts Up

El Niño ("the boy" in Spanish, referring to the Christ Child, since El Niño usually occurs around Christmastime) describes a weather phenomenon in which the sea surface temperature in the equatorial Pacific

continued

rises, wind systems over the Pacific change, and as a result, the cold Humboldt current west of South America weakens. A layer of warm water travels through the tropical East Pacific from Southeast Asia to South America, and water temperatures off Australia and Indonesia drop. The result is a change in global weather patterns: There are usually heavy rains on the South and North American West Coasts and drought, crop failures, and bush fires in Australia, India, and Southeast Asia.

In contrast, La Niña ("the girl") is an exceptionally cold current in the equatorial Pacific, whose effects are excessive rain in Indonesia and drought in Peru.

The Australian harvest was crucial because the *global* 2006–2007 wheat harvest, at 598 million metric tons, was also significantly lower than the previous year's 621 and 628 million tons. The 15 largest producing countries provided about 80 percent of that total. Australia, the second-largest exporter after the United States at the time, accounted for about 16 percent of global wheat exports.

The harvest came at a time of increasing demand, growing prosperity, and robust economic growth. For global wheat *consumption*, the forecast for this period was 611 million metric tons.

The collapse of Australian wheat production first hit Asia and the Middle East, since these countries traditionally imported grain from Australia. They were now looking for wheat in the United States and Canada. The Europeans were also affected by the heat. In Ukraine, the 2006 crop had shrunk by half.

In February 2008 the price for wheat more than tripled, compared to 2006, to almost 13 USD per bushel.

The price of wheat on the Chicago Board of Trade (CBOT) soon began an unprecedented rally. The typical trading band for wheat in the years before 2006 was between 2.50 USD and 4 USD. At the beginning of 2004, however, inventories fell to their lowest levels since 1980. Bad harvests in Europe and China meant that the Middle Kingdom had to import wheat for the fourth year in a row. The price of grains was picking up dynamically.

In October 2006, wheat broke through the 5 USD mark for the first time and remained there. Then, in June 2007, wheat prices rose to 6 USD, climbed to 7 USD in August, 8 USD at the beginning of September, 9 USD at the end of that month, and rose to 9.50 USD at the beginning of October.

Meanwhile, global inventories continued to fall and reached a 26-year low. In addition, in Canada—another major wheat exporter on the world market—grain reserves plunged 29 percent year-on-year at the end of July, while Egypt, Jordan, Japan, and Iraq placed buying orders for large quantities of wheat.

Figure 24. Wheat prices in US cents/bushel, 2005–2008, Chicago Board of Trade. Data: Bloomberg, 2019.

After this fast-paced rally, international wheat prices took a breather, but in hindsight that turned out to be just a short break. At the beginning of February 2008, wheat prices broke through the 10 USD barrier, and the price momentum continued. The closing price on February 27, 2008, was 12.80 USD, a dramatic tripling since early 2006!

The devastating drought had caused losses of around 50 percent in the recent Australian harvest. The situation began to relax slightly with the 2007–2008 harvest of 609 million tons, as the rapid increase in wheat prices had proved an incentive for many farmers to plant previously fallow land. A harvest of 688 million tons worldwide was estimated for 2008–2009. By then the unprecedented Australian drought finally had come to an end. However, weather experts painted a bleak picture for the country's agriculture in the future.

Key Takeaways

- The year 2006 was the third driest in Australia since weather records started in 1900, but 2007 topped it. That year turned out to be the hottest year in history.

- After several lean years, the Millennium Drought caused devastating damages to Australian agriculture. The national wheat harvest dropped by 50 percent, and global grain markets panicked, since Australia was the biggest global exporter of wheat after the United States.

- In October 2006, wheat topped 5 USD for the first time. In summer 2007, the rally in wheat prices intensified. In February 2008, wheat prices broke the psychological barrier of 10 USD and closed the month at 12.80 USD. Prices had tripled since early 2006.

- The Millennium Drought in Australia was caused by El Niño, a weather phenomenon whose strength and frequency could be directly linked to global climate change, according to environmental and weather experts.

28

Natural Gas: Aftermath in Canada

The new CEO of the Bank of Montreal, Bill Downe, must report a record loss for the second quarter of 2007 due to failed commodity price speculation. Half a year after Amaranth's bankruptcy, another natural gas trading scandal shakes market participants' confidence.

> *"How all of a sudden does a USD 450 million loss just materialize like this? Was it a lack of control from a risk perspective or was somebody hiding trades in a desk drawer?"*
> —**Leigh Parkinson**, Risk Advisory

It was the middle of April when three of the directors of Optionable, a New York commodity broker, unloaded a share package worth nearly 30 million USD. Just days later, the auditor Deloitte and Touche released a report to its principal, the Bank of Montreal (BMO), stating that there was a 350 to 450 million CAD loss in its natural gas portfolio. This came as a nasty surprise for CEO Bill Downe, who had been in his position for only a month and who was about to announce BMO's quarterly figures.

A Canadian Institution

Founded in 1817, the Bank of Montreal (BMO) is the fourth-largest bank in Canada in terms of deposits and has played a major role in the development of the country, having financed the construction of the first transcontinental railroad in the 1880s. Today BMO's business activities are divided into private and commercial clients (retail banking), investment banking (BMO capital markets), and wealth management. Tony Comper served as CEO from 1990 to 2007, and during his leadership, in 2000, a small trading scandal occurred in futures trading of natural gas, causing damage of around 30 million CAD. Seven years later, Bill Downe took over.

The responsible trader at BMO was David Lee, who dealt in natural gas options both on the New York Mercantile Exchange (NYMEX) and over the counter. Lee had joined BMO in his mid-20s, coming from the Bank of New York, where he had been involved in building the commodity derivatives business from scratch. Beginning as an analyst, he soon switched to trading and specialized in natural gas options.

At BMO, Lee handled a large portion of his trades via Optionable. For a broker like Optionable with fewer than 20 employees, these trades represent almost 30 percent of his total revenue. It was no wonder that Lee and Kevin Cassidy, the CEO of Optionable, were close friends.

BMO's commodity trading achieved a huge profit in 2006.

Trading in natural gas delivered an attractive additional income for BMO. Its commodity trading was 15 to 20 times larger than that of the Canadian market leader, the Royal Bank of Canada (RBC). BMO's energy-trading business had grown to 25 traders. The bank had offices in Houston, New York, and Canadian energy metropolis Calgary, where in March 2006, at BMO's annual general meeting, Tony Comper had announced excellent results in the investment banking segment, driven primarily by trading profits in oil and gas.

The commodity business was booming. Due to the damage caused by Hurricane Katrina in 2005, the price of natural gas was rising. In 2004 and the first half of 2005, the price hovered between 6 and 7 USD, but after the hurricane season, corporate clients increasingly were interested in price-hedging transactions. In December 2005, the price of US natural gas went over 15 USD/MMBtu.

This trend did not go on forever, though. Within weeks benchmark gas prices in New York had lost around two-thirds of their value. A mild winter ensured a sufficient supply of the commodity, which this time was unaffected by hurricanes. Customer interest cooled down significantly, but energy trading at BMO continued to grow.

The BMO team around David Lee was betting on a rebound in prices.

BMO's star trader David Lee got it massively wrong with natural gas options.

Market participants could see that someone was building massive options positions on the NYMEX and over the counter, but prices continued to fall and volatility declined. The value of call options imploded.

The trading positions in Lee's team were getting out of balance, but he was able to disguise his losses with the help of Optionable. Later the law firm Schatz Nobel Izard would accuse Optionable of having helped the BMO trader falsify his book and, among other things, of confirming incorrect trading prices. When Deloitte and Touche examined the upcoming quarterly figures, the loss could no longer be concealed. The auditors estimated the deficit came to 350 to 450 million CAD. BMO canceled collaboration with Optionable immediately, and Optionable stock lost almost 90 percent of its value.

Figure 25. Natural gas prices in USD/MMBtu, 2003–2007, New York Mercantile Exchange. Data: Bloomberg, 2019.

At the end of April 2007, just days before the announcement of its quarterly figures, BMO announced a profit warning and pointed to the bank's deferred trading positions in the commodity market, namely positions in natural gas, that would weigh heavily on quarterly profits. Companies such as Goldman Sachs and Citadel, a major Chicago hedge fund manager, showed interest in taking over the portfolio. However, BMO's managers were convinced that they could handle the situation themselves. It turned out, though, that publicizing the trading positions before they could be reduced was the wrong strategy. The losses continued to increase.

When the quarterly figures came out in May, BMO had upped the losses on its commodity trading book to 680 million USD, the equivalent of about 12 percent of its total annual profit. Gritting his teeth, Downe reported the biggest trade loss of any Canadian bank in history, blaming market illiquidity and lower volatility. His rationale was not wrong, but market participants were skeptical, and analysts asked some unpleasant questions, about both the bank's business strategy and the quality of its risk management. Bob Moore, executive managing director for commodity products, and David Lee had to leave the company. Lee was fined 500,000 USD and was banned from working in the banking industry. The total cost of the BMO trade scandal added up to around 850 million USD.

Key Takeaways

- Half a year after Amaranth Advisors' bankruptcy, another natural gas trading scandal shook the commodity markets in 2007.

- David Lee was a celebrated star trader at BMO, and he and his team bet on a rebound of natural gas prices, after prices had declined from a record high of 15 USD due to damages from a record hurricane season.

- But prices declined further. Natural gas even traded temporarily below 4 USD again. For a while, Lee could disguise his loss of 350 to 450 million USD with the help of his broker Optionable. But auditors uncovered the problem.

- After earning record profits the year before, Lee's energy trading imploded. Losses from the trading scandal added up to more than 800 million USD.

29

Platinum:
All Lights Out in South Africa

Due to ongoing supply bottlenecks of electricity from Africa's largest energy provider, Eskom, South Africa's major mining companies restrict their production, and the price of platinum explodes.

> *"South Africa needs at least 40 new coal mines*
> *to prevent shortages over the long term."*
> **—Brian Dames**, Eskom

> *"Restoring energy security for the country*
> *is an absolute imperative."*
> **—Cyril Ramaphosa**,
> president of South Africa in 2019

Two years before the World Cup kickoff in June 2010 in South Africa, the country faced its worst electricity supply bottleneck in decades. In spring 2008 the government declared an energy emergency. The national utility company Eskom—the largest electricity provider in Africa—shut down power for several hours every day for weeks, since its capacity lagged far below demand. For 20 years the country's economy had been growing at a rapid pace. Electricity demand had risen 50 percent since the end of apartheid in 1994, but the South African government and Eskom had failed to provide additional capacity. The electricity company had repeatedly stressed that the nation's power plants would have to be overhauled and new power plants built, but government agencies ignored these warnings.

Because there was not enough power available, electricity was rationed at various intervals and in different zones, resulting in two- to three-hour power outages every day. Particularly affected were Johannesburg and the Gauteng region, the center of gold and platinum production. Around half of the mining companies' energy demand was needed just to maintain infrastructure. Without electricity, the water could no longer be pumped out

Eskom turned off the power for the mining companies.

of the mines, and getting sufficient oxygen several kilometers deep became critical. The impact on actual production was even more dramatic. The Miners' Union said that the companies sent tens of thousands of workers home or for training. At the end of January, the situation worsened. The energy company operated the world's largest coal-fired power plant, the Kendal power plant, and Eskom's coal reserves were being soaked by rainfall. At this point international precious metal prices began to react.

Precious Platinum and Palladium

The group of platinum metals (PGMs) includes platinum, palladium, rhodium, iridium, osmium, and ruthenium, but the economically important metals in this group are platinum and palladium, whose trading is overseen by the London Platinum and Palladium Market (LPPM). South Africa and Russia together account for around 90 percent of the world's platinum metals production. Smaller producer countries are Canada, the United States, and Zimbabwe. The major companies are Anglo American Platinum (Amplats), Impala Platinum (Implats), Lonmin in South Africa, and Norilsk Nickel in Russia. In recent years, Sibanye has also grown into a new player through take-overs and acquisitions.

Platinum is mainly used for catalysts (50 percent) and jewelry (25 percent); while for palladium, in addition to those applications, dentistry and electronics are important. Price-determining factors for both metals are Russian and South African production, Russian inventories, and global growth rates.

South Africa had been the center of global gold production since the end of the 19th century, though it had fallen back over the past 30 years to eighth place. However, South Africa still has a dominant position in producing platinum. Around 80 percent of the world's production comes from that country, with the overwhelming majority being produced in the Bushveld complex. The prices for platinum are correspondingly sensitive to any negative news from South Africa.

Prices for platinum had been rising steadily since mid-2005, but the momentum increased significantly in late 2007 and early 2008. For the first time in seven years, the multinational firm Johnson Matthey, the world market leader in auto catalysts and thus the largest customer of platinum, expected falling shipments for the entire year.

Figure 26. Platinum prices in USD/troy ounce, 2004–2009.
Data: Bloomberg, 2019.

At the end of January 2008, the news that the three largest gold producers in South Africa and the largest platinum producer were reducing
production in all mines caused prices to jump. Amplats, with a 40 percent
market share, expected production losses of 9,000 ounces per day. The
number-two firm, Impala Platinum, claimed to lose about 3,500 ounces
per day. Overall, South Africa's platinum miners feared a 2008 production
loss of 0.5 million ounces.

By March 2008 the price of platinum rose to more than 2,200 USD/oz.

In addition to gold, the price of platinum in particular rose overnight
by almost 100 USD to more than 1,700 USD. At the beginning of March
2008, the price of a troy ounce of platinum closed at more than 2,250
USD, a temporary price maximum.

Electricity supplier Eskom slowly began to regain control of the
situation, but industry production was still running at only 90 percent

capacity, and the company predicted that supply problems would continue until at least 2020.

And the years of mismanagement and corruption continued. In February 2019 the situation escalated again, as Cyril Ramaphosa, the president of South Africa following Jacob Zuma, declared Eskom to be "too big and too important to fail" during the Indaba mining conference in Cape Town. Besides its aging coal-fired plants, the company suffers from a debt level of more than 30 billion USD. A breakup, a government rescue plan, as well as a 15% increase in its tariffs to its industrial customers are in the cards for 2019. At the same time, an ounce of platinum costs 800 USD—a new price rally is about to unfold!

Key Takeaways

- In 2008, South Africa faced its worst electricity supply bottleneck in decades, and the government declared an energy emergency. Eskom, the national utility company and the largest electricity provider in Africa, shut down power for several hours every day.

- Although South Africa's golden days of gold mining were over, it remained the dominant force in platinum group metals, with about 80 percent of the world's production.

- At the end of January 2008, the three largest gold producers and the largest platinum producers all reduced their mine production as a result of continuing power outages.

- That development spurred prices for platinum, which had been rising steadily since mid-2005 and had already reached 1,000 USD. By March 2008, the price of platinum climbed above 2,200 USD per troy ounce, its highest price ever!

30

Rice:
The Oracle

2008

The Thai "Rice Oracle," Vichai Sriprasert, predicts in 2007 that rice will increase in price from 300 USD to 1,000 USD, and he becomes a figure of ridicule and mockery. However, a dangerous chain reaction affecting the rice harvest is about to start in Asia and, with Cyclone Nargis, culminates in a catastrophe.

"National hoarding really doesn't help the market."
—Robert Zeigler,
International Rice Research Institute

A t 65, Vichai Sriprasert was one of Thailand's largest rice exporters, nicknamed the "Rice Oracle." Years of experience with the interrelationship between supply, demand, and price development had earned Vichai a lot of money as well as the honorary chairmanship of the Thai Association of Rice Traders. As the world's largest exporter of rice, Thailand was a determining factor in international trade.

Disbelief and ridicule were the initial reactions to Vichai's prediction, in 2007, that rice prices were likely to exceed 1,000 USD per ton in the following year. At the time Thai export rice was priced at around 300 USD per ton. After a rapid increase in the price of oil and dramatically higher prices for wheat and corn, however, the laughter disappeared. In spring 2008, the price of rice actually broke Vichai's targeted 1,000 USD mark. And it would continue to rise. For Vichai, the situation was comparable to the 1970s, when in the shadow of the oil crisis, rice prices rose to around 2,700 USD per metric ton.

Rice Realities

According to figures from the Food and Agriculture Organization (FAO), rice—along with corn and wheat—is one of the most widely cultivated cereals in the world, with an annual production of around 650 million metric tons. The largest producer countries are China, India, Indonesia, Bangladesh, Vietnam, and Thailand. Due to its predominantly wet cultivation, between 3,000 and 5,000 liters of flowing water are needed per kilogram of rice. On the one hand, this has a positive effect in terms of lower pest and weed infestation; on the other hand, this can lead to serious crop failures in periods of dry weather.

Despite the importance of rice, futures trading is insignificant, with less liquidity than the wheat or corn market. The most important trading place for rice is the Chicago Board of Trade (CBOT) in the United States. Traded contracts are quoted in US cents per American centner or hundredweight (1 cwt equals 100 lb equals 45.359 kg), with one contract covering 2,000 hundredweights.

What had happened? Driven by the rising price of crude oil, the prices of many agricultural goods rose sharply in 2007, a condition called "agflation." The food price index, calculated by the FAO, had risen by 57 percent within just one year, from March 2007 to March 2008. Wheat and soybean prices also doubled, and the price of corn had increased by 66 percent since autumn 2007.

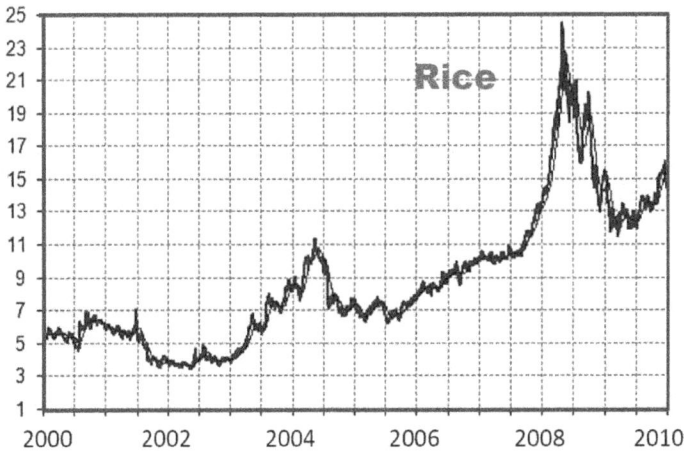

Figure 27. Rice prices in US cents/cwt, 2000–2010, Chicago Board of Trade. Data: Bloomberg, 2019.

However, the price of rice was still well above that of other agricultural goods and was developing its own momentum in spring 2008. From June 2007 to April 2008, rice prices rose by around 75 percent—even more in Asia. Prices increased from 400 USD per metric ton to more than 1,000 USD.

The price spike had widespread consequences. Rice is a staple food for around three billion people, and in many countries nearly half of household income is spent on nutrition. The rise in prices threatened political stability in several countries and caused serious unrest around the world. In Haiti several people were killed in protests, and uprisings were reported in Egypt, Burkina Faso, Cameroon, Indonesia, Côte d'Ivoire, Mauritania, Mozambique, and Senegal. How did all this happen?

> The globally traded rice volume of 30
> million tons was very low compared to the
> total production of 650 million tons.

The rice market is generally subject to structural deficits. The average amount of rice traded on the world markets per year—around 30 million metric tons—is very low compared to global production of around 650 million tons. This makes global prices extremely vulnerable to short-term fluctuations in supply and demand. Urbanization, demographics, and the demand for alternative energies and weather conditions all are influential factors and also apply to other agricultural goods to some extent.

For example, rapid urbanization in Asia has destroyed more and more agricultural acreage, and increasing prosperity on that continent has also led to more meat consumption, increasing the amount of grain needed to feed livestock. The consumption of meat in China alone increased by about 150 percent in the past 30 years. Furthermore, the rice fields of Asia have had to absorb an annual birth rate of about 80 million babies in the region. Indirectly, the high price of oil and a related increase in demand for biofuels are also driving up the price of rice, as many farmers switch to the more profitable cultivation of corn, wheat, and oilseeds.

Some countries recorded significant losses in their rice harvest due to weather in 2007–2008. Thunderstorms and floods destroyed more than 20 million hectares of fields within one year, twice the total acreage of Thailand. Bangladesh, generally a major exporter of rice, suffered significant crop losses in 2007 from floods and Tropical Storm Sidr, which destroyed almost the entire crop. The rice harvest in Vietnam was also hampered by severe pest infestation and disease. As a result, the price of rice continued to rise, and the situation gradually worsened.

With panic buying and export restrictions, the dominoes were falling: In Asia, supplies continued to be stretched. The rice-exporting countries of Vietnam and India issued restrictions on the export of rice, while India slowed exports to stabilize prices at home. Other exporting countries, such as China, Egypt, and Cambodia, joined in with quotas and taxes. China was so worried about supplying its own population that it waived exports until further notice, while in Thailand, farmers, traders, and rice mills began to hoard their rice.

In Asia, hoarding and export restrictions worsened the already tight supply.

Everywhere in the region there was panic buying. Even in the United States, Wal-Mart rationed its sales to customers. The world's largest importer, the Philippines, announced massive purchases to forestall further supply shortages. Importing countries like Bangladesh, Indonesia, and Iran were also affected. And then, on the night of May 3, a catastrophe occurred.

Cyclone Nargis hit the coast of Myanmar, devastating the rice supply region in the middle of the harvest season and leaving between 50,000 and 100,000 people dead. The price of rice shot up again, and the risk of famine and revolts caused by hunger rose. As the price of rice quadrupled, many regions were threatened by unrest. In addition to the tight supply and the unfavorable weather, export restrictions and hoarding had created an artificial shortage, dramatically exacerbating the situation. Even Vichai did not foresee how bad the situation would become.

In May 2008, however, the supply situation eased. Pakistan, one of the largest rice producers, loosened its export restrictions, and the crop in India was more than 2 million metric tons larger than expected. However, the structural problems of the rice market would remain. Given a comparatively small international market, repeated supply bottlenecks in Asia are to be expected in the future.

Key Takeaways

- In the beginning of 2007, Vichai Sriprasert, the "Rice Oracle" of Thailand, predicted a massive increase in the price of rice, a ridiculous thought at that time.

- Later in 2007, however, prices of many agricultural goods rose sharply, driven by increasing crude oil prices ("agflation"). The situation in the rice market was especially critical.

- From June 2007 to April 2008, rice prices in Asia increased from 400 USD to more than 1,000. Hoarding and export restrictions worsened an already tight supply.

- When Cyclone Nargis hit Myanmar in May 2008, it devastated that country's rice harvest and left as many as 100,000 people dead.

- The price of rice quadrupled, and many regions were threatened by unrest, causing difficulties that even the Rice Oracle did not foresee.

31

Wheat:
Working in Memphis

The price of wheat speeds from record to record. Trader Evan Dooley bets on the wrong direction, juggling 1 billion USD and dropping the ball. This results in a loss of 140 million USD for his employer, MF Global, in February 2008.

> *"I simply do not know where the money is."*
> —**Jon Corzine**, CEO of MF Global

L ess than a month after Jérôme Kerviel's catastrophic bet on European equity indices, which resulted in losses of nearly 5 billion USD to French investment bank Société Générale, another trader caused difficulties for his employer.

This time it was through speculation on wheat futures. At the end of February 2008, MF Global, one of the world's largest futures and options brokers, had to admit that one of its traders in Memphis, Tennessee, had speculated on wheat futures with corporate accounts. Within hours, a loss of about 140 million USD occurred.

Spun out of Man Financial Group in 2007, MF Global was a commodity brokerage house that offered clearing and execution services. It had ambitions to become a financial services firm on the order of a Goldman Sachs or JPMorgan, and its CEO was Jon Corzine, former chairman of Goldman Sachs and onetime governor of New Jersey. Although it was a niche player on Wall Street, MF Global was a force on the Chicago Mercantile Exchange (CME), with 3 million futures and options positions open with a face value of more than 100 billion USD. Its customers made up almost 30 percent of the trading volume on the CME.

Trading Wheat

After corn, wheat is the second-biggest agricultural crop in the world, and it is traded worldwide on commodity futures exchanges. On the Chicago Board of Trade (CBOT), wheat is traded under the symbol W and the current contract month (e.g., W Z0 for wheat December 2020). One contract refers to 5,000 bushels of wheat, and each bushel is equivalent to 27.2 kilograms.

Priced at 7.50 USD per bushel in November 2007, US wheat was already trading above 8 USD by the beginning of 2008. In part this was due to a tightening supply, but the increase was also increasingly driven by speculative capital, along with a weak US currency. The price broke through 9 and 10 USD per bushel within days, and at the end of February the situation had really gotten out of hand. On February 27, wheat contracts close to delivery experienced price movements of as much as 25 percent within a day. Although trading opened positive, by noon the price had fallen to 10.80 USD.

Trader Evan Dooley speculated on falling prices of 2 million tons of wheat.

In the afternoon, however, the price jumped again, to 13.50 USD per bushel. The news that Kazakhstan, one of the largest exporters of wheat, wanted to introduce export taxes to reduce sales was boosting the US wheat price. It was the strongest intraday price movement in wheat ever observed.

However, there was also another explanation for the price swings: Evan Dooley, who had been a trader at MF Global since November 2005, had quickly entered significant positions in wheat futures on his own account in the morning hours of February 27. With these unauthorized actions, the 40-year-old trader exceeded his limits by far.

Betting on a falling wheat price, Dooley is said to have traded around 15,000 futures—2 million metric tons of wheat. The value of the position varied between 800 million and 1 billion USD. However, as the wheat price continued to rise sharply, the company was forced to close the position with losses, that is, to buy further futures contracts. This led to a further price jump to a level that the market would not reach again, despite continuing strength, for several years.

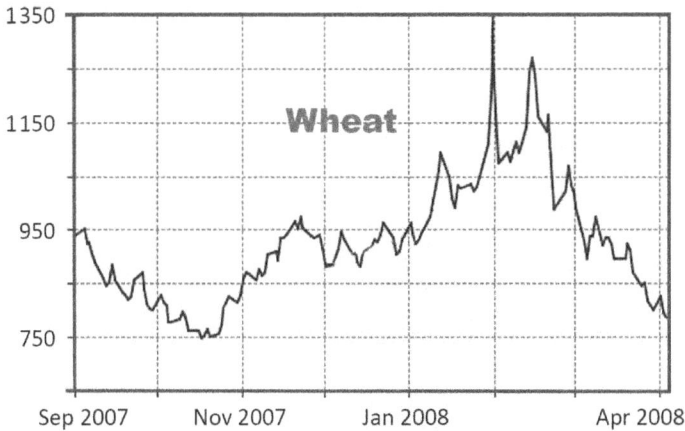

Figure 28. Wheat prices in US cents/bushel, 2007–2008, Chicago Board of Trade. Data: Bloomberg, 2019.

MF Global shares lost more than 25 percent in value on that day. The losses came to approximately 140 million USD and represented four times the previous quarter. Concerned about the extent of the loss, MF Global promised to revise its internal policies and risk management. Dooley was fired immediately, and MF Global was fined 10 million USD for lack of supervision of its traders. Dooley himself was sentenced to five years in federal prison and had to make restitution of 140 million USD.

On a side note, MF Global collapsed in 2011 when the company reported a 192 million USD quarterly loss. Client funds disappeared in the aftermath, which became a huge scandal. However, the failure of MF Global, with more than 40 billion USD in assets—the eighth-biggest bankruptcy in US history—was modest compared with the chaotic 2008 failure of Lehman Brothers, which had a 691 billion USD balance sheet. Regulators were eager to show that not all Wall Street firms were too big to fail. They happily let MF Global go under.

Key Takeaways

- Less than a month after Jérôme Kerviel's catastrophic bet on European equity indices in 2008, another trader caused trouble for his employer: Evan Dooley of MF Global speculated on falling wheat prices and built up a short position of almost 1 billion USD.

- Wheat prices kept climbing higher and higher, however, from 7.50 USD per bushel in late 2007 to more than 10 USD per bushel in January 2008.

- On February 27, 2008, the price of wheat traded in Chicago fluctuated in the course of the day by 25 percent—falling back to 10.80 USD per bushel, then jumping again to 13.50 USD in the afternoon. MF Global accumulated a loss of about 140 million USD within hours.

32

Crude Oil:
Contango in Texas

The price of West Texas Intermediate (WTI) crude oil collapses, unsettling commodity traders around the world. A 10,000-person community in Oklahoma becomes the center of world attention. The concept of "super-contango" is born, and investment banks enter the tanker business.

> *"Super-Contango is a state in which a forward price of a commodity is higher than the spot price to a greater extent than can be explained by the interest and storage costs that explain the usual state of contango."*
> —Moneyterms.co.uk

Cushing is a small town in Oklahoma with fewer than 10,000 residents: There's a Wal-Mart, some fast-food restaurants, and a few gas stations. Only massive tanks, pipes, and refineries hint that the town is somehow special. In the south of the city is a complex for the strategic oil reserves of the United States, with a capacity of 35 million barrels—one of the largest in the country.

Suddenly, at the beginning of 2009, Cushing—the only delivery location for West Texas Intermediate (WTI), the US benchmark for crude oil—became the focus of the world's attention. In the oil market, big-time inventory building had begun. And it began on a large scale.

Trading in Crude

Because of the many different types and qualities of crude oil, market participants have agreed to trade in a few local varieties for reference: At the New York Mercantile Exchange (NYMEX), this is US West Texas Intermediate (WTI) oil, at the Intercontinental Exchange (ICE) in London it's North Sea Brent, and in Singapore the Asian reference is Tapis. Additionally, there is an OPEC basket price, which calculates the average price of seven different types of crude: Sahara Blend (Algeria), Minas (Indonesia), Bonny Light (Nigeria), Arab Light (Saudi Arabia), Dubai (United Arab Emirates), Tia Juana Light (Venezuela), and Isthmus (Mexico). On commodity futures markets, WTI and Brent are the primary references for the price of oil, which is traded in 1,000 barrels per contract under the abbreviations CL (WTI) and CO (Brent) as well as the corresponding contract months (e.g., Z9 for December 2019).

In the wake of the financial market crisis and the deteriorating economic outlook, the price of crude oil had come under massive pressure in the second half of 2008. That summer, crude oil had briefly traded at more than 145 USD for a short time. But then, the price dropped to less than 45 USD. The withdrawal of investment capital ("deleveraging") also contributed significantly to the price decline. This became obvious through an analysis of the short-term crude oil contracts in which financial investors are typically invested, and which were now much more affected than long-term contracts.

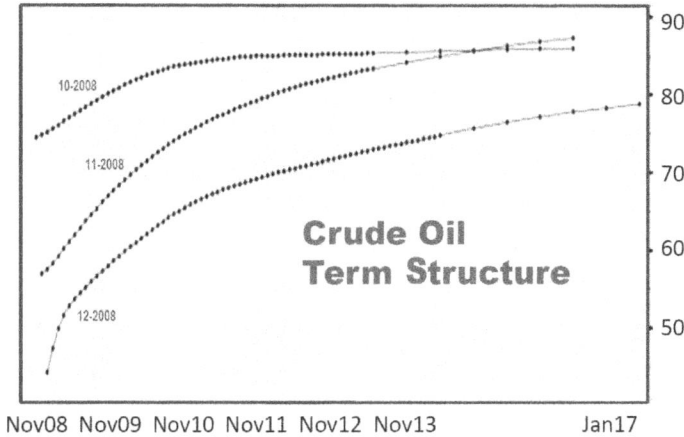

Figure 29. Crude Oil (WTI) Term Structure in USD/barrel, 2008. Data: Bloomberg, 2019.

The forward term structure, which tracks the price of future crude oil deliveries over a period of several years, was still nearly flat in summer 2008, but from there, the contango structure of crude oil (WTI) increased. Contango refers to the situation in which spot prices are below the level of futures prices. This could be due to warehousing costs, including insurance and interest, for example, although those can be superseded by the effects of supply and demand.

Between October and December 2008, the contango became extreme. The price decline at the short end of WTI contracts led to a record price difference (the spread)—in excess of 20 USD—between contracts for WTI January 2009 and WTI December 2009. Commodity traders introduced the term "super-contango" to describe what was happening, and commodity analysts called the price distortion of crude oil "absurd." WTI decoupled completely from other crude oil reference prices such as Brent and, as a barometer for international crude oil markets, was "as useful as a chocolate oven glove," noted a commodity analyst of Barclays, the British investment bank. What led to this situation? And, more importantly, what were the implications?

> Super-contango! Front-end WTI traded as
> low as 35 USD, while later crude contracts
> with later dates stayed above 50 USD.

The world's attention turned to Cushing, the world's "pipeline cross-roads" and the only source of WTI crude oil. Contango favors stockpiling, because instead of a low current price, oil can be sold for more at a later date. The only obstacle is that the owner of the crude needs to have appropriate storage facilities. At Cushing, due to the increasing contango, the storage level of oil was steadily increasing.

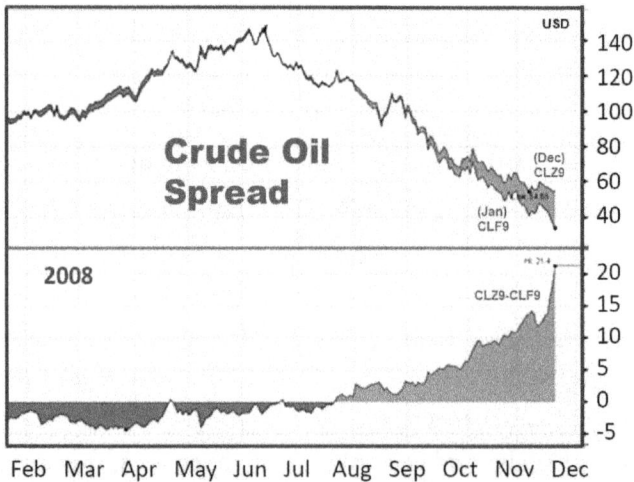

Figure 30. Price spread of crude oil January (CLF9) and December 2009 (CLZ9) in USD/barrel. Data: Bloomberg, 2019.

In January, oil inventories counted more than 33 million barrels (1 barrel equals 159 liters), and the remaining capacity literally was disappearing like ice in sunshine. The super-contango led to "super-storage," because every holder of crude oil futures without the appropriate capacity had to sell crude oil, if needed, regardless of price. At its low, US crude oil was trading below 35 USD.

It's hard to know whether the super-contango was merely an expression of the short-term oversupply of the crude oil market due to the economic slowdown, or whether this was the effect of disinvestment of index and hedge fund capital in the forward contracts. In any case, the steepness of the crude oil forward curve continued to increase.

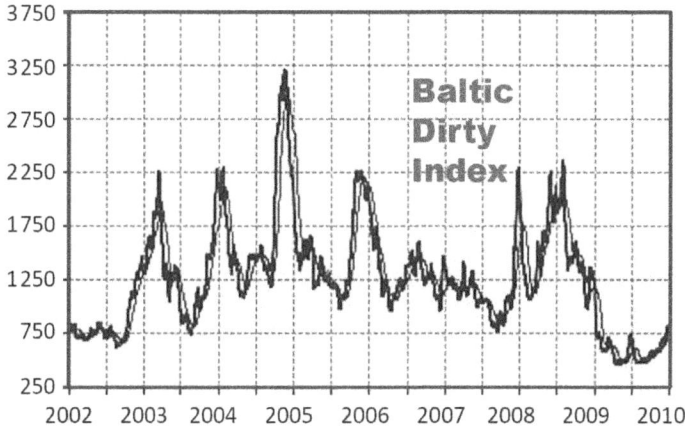

Figure 31. Baltic Dirty Tanker Index, 2002–2010. Data: Bloomberg, 2019.

An additional factor, apart from the price differences, distinguished this situation from past events: The economic slowdown and the effects of the credit crunch had put international freight rates under extreme pressure. At the beginning of 2009, freight rates for oil tankers were around 85 percent below their highs in summer 2008.

> ## The crude oil super-contango, combined with low freight rates, provided a lucrative business for investment banks.

For a short while early in 2009, the price difference between a current crude oil contract and a December 2009 contract exceeded 30 percent. The combination of super-contango and the low crude oil tanker freight rates opened up a new field not only for crude oil traders but also for investment banks, since it was possible to store crude oil in oil tankers on the high seas.

With sufficient inventories, it made no sense to sell oil at prices below 40 USD, if you could sell above 55 USD risk-free through a futures contract. January crude oil prices were trading 20 USD below December contracts, while the cost of storage aboard on a supertanker in January 2009 averaged around 90 US cents a barrel. Assuming that transportation, insurance, and financing were secured, there was an opportunity for immense profit for oil companies and traders.

Tanker Talk

The Baltic Exchange is a global marketplace for shipbrokers, shipowners, and charterers. The various indices of the stock exchange offer an important overview of freight rates differentiated according to cargo types, ship sizes, and shipping routes. The Baltic Clean Tanker Index tracks tankers carrying clean cargo, such as oil *products* (petrol, diesel, fuel oil, or kerosene); the Baltic Dirty Tanker Index is for tankers that carry cargo such as crude oil. In 2009, freight rates for bulk carriers—summarized in the Baltic Dry Index—had fallen by 94 percent since the previous summer, due to the economic slowdown and the credit crunch during the international financial crisis. In comparison, the freight rates for tankers lost a little less. Freight rates for crude oil fell by around 85 percent.

Tanker lease periods between three and nine months were particularly sought after.

In February 2009, Frontline, the world's largest owner of supertankers, reported that 25 tankers had been chartered, and there were still open inquiries about 10 more ships. Any tanker that held less than 2 million barrels of oil was not statistically recorded, but industry experts estimated that there were as many as 80 million barrels on the water at the time, more than twice as much oil as was in official storage in Cushing. The profitable business had also taken on a new dimension. The new customers were no longer BP or Exxon, but Merrill Lynch, Morgan Stanley, Goldman Sachs, Citibank, Barclays, and Deutsche Bank.

Ship brokers around the globe were surprised by the extent of storage inquiries. After all, 35 supertankers accounted for roughly 10 percent of crude oil tanker capacity worldwide. Due to additional demand, tanker freight rates recovered slightly from their lows. However, the floating inventories prevented a significant spike in oil prices during the year, despite any improvement in underlying economic data. After a nearly 75 percent drop in crude oil prices in just one year, the supply surplus of floating stock unsettled the market. For 2008, the International Energy Agency (IEA) reported a decline in oil demand for the first time since 1983.

Key Takeaways

- Cushing, a small town in Oklahoma, is the pipeline capital of the world—the only delivery point for WTI, the most important benchmark for crude oil.

- In the summer of 2008, crude oil was trading above 145 USD. But then the price collapsed to less than 45 USD, and WTI switched from backwardation into a deep contango. A super-contango was born.

- In combination with low freight rates due to the economic crisis, the oil super-contango provided a lucrative business for investment banks, which could physically buy oil, store it in supertankers, and sell it on futures exchanges, locking in a secure profit.

- The super-contango led to a massive supply glut in crude oil for a number of years.

33

Sugar: Waiting for the Monsoon

A severe drought threatens India's sugar harvest, and the world's largest consumer becomes a net importer on the world market. Brazil, the largest exporter of sugar, has its own problems. As a result, international sugar prices rise to a 28-year high.

> *"The peacocks are not dancing.*
> *It will not rain."*
> —P. K. Dubey in *Monsoon Wedding* (2001)

June 2009 was the driest summer month in India for more than 80 years, and the dry season was nowhere near ending. In the first week of August, rainfall was only one-third of its normal level. In the main agricultural areas in the north of the country, the weather phenomenon called El Niño had practically stopped the monsoon, whose season on the subcontinent usually lasts from the beginning of June to the end of September.

One consequence of El Niño in India is significant crop failures, but India's frequent experience of drought and famine has historically led to large storage facilities. According to the US Department of Agriculture, about 20 million metric tons of rice and about 30 million tons of wheat were stored in 2009. For sugar, however, the situation was quite different.

Crop failures were so severe, especially in the state of Uttar Pradesh, that India—the second-largest sugar producer in the world—changed from being a net exporter of the crop to becoming a net *importer*. After producing more than 26 million metric tons of sugar the year before, the country was initially expected to consume 22 million tons of sugar in 2009. However, in August, the Indian Ministry of Agriculture revised the harvest estimates downward, first to 17 million tons and later to 15 million tons. It was not until 2011 that the Indian authorities expected a harvest of around 25 million metric tons of sugar.

Sweet!

Almost three-quarters of the sugar produced in more than 100 countries comes from sugarcane, grown primarily in tropical and subtropical regions. Sugar beets come mainly from the European Union and Russia. Brazil, the largest sugar producer and exporter, is responsible for about 16 percent of the world's sugar, followed by India (14 percent), China (6 percent), and the United States (5 percent). In Brazil, more than half of the sugar harvest is processed into fuel (ethanol).

Sugar is traded on multiple futures exchanges in different classifications. The most liquid trading is in Sugar No. 11 (ticker SB) on the New York Board of Trade (NYBOT), where futures contracts are traded in US cents per pound and comprise approximately 50 metric tons of sugar (112,000 pounds). Together with wheat, corn, and soybeans, sugar is the most liquid traded agricultural commodity.

In 2008, the global trading volume of sugar was about 45 million tons, which equates to almost one-third of the quantity produced worldwide. Two-thirds of total sugar production is consumed directly in producer countries and is excluded from global trade. If other trade barriers, such as quotas and trade agreements, are taken into account, only about 25 percent of the world's sugar is available to the global market, and about 40 percent of that comes from Brazil, which has quadrupled its sugar production since the early 1990s.

**With severe weather in India and Brazil,
the price of sugar shot up.**

Like India, Brazil also had to cope with severe weather conditions in 2009. The problem there was not drought, however, but too much water.

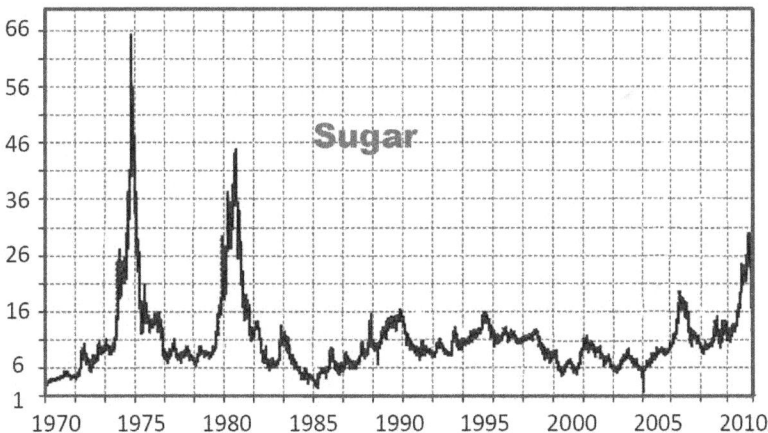

Figure 32. Sugar prices in US cents/lb, 1970–2010. Data: Bloomberg, 2019.

Over the past 40 years, the price of sugar has been very volatile. Starting with prices as low as 1 US cent per pound in 1967, the price exploded in the mid-1970s to more than 60 US cents. Then, in 2004, the price of sugar slipped below 6 US cents—levels that had not been seen for more than 20 years.

In 2010, however, there was a sugar rush! Massive imports from India and weather-related delivery delays in Brazil pushed the raw sugar price to a 28-year high. Futures contracts closed at 29.90 US cents per pound on January 29, 2010, a premium of more than 150 percent compared to the previous year. The situation calmed down only after the March contracts expired on February 26, 2010. At that point positive data from Brazil signaled that the worst scarcity was over.

Key Takeaways

- The three most important sugar producers worldwide are Brazil, India, and China, and the latter two mostly produce the crop for their own use.

- The summer of 2009 was the driest summer in India for more than 80 years. El Niño caused significant crop failures, India became a net importer of sugar on the world market, and Brazil had weather-related problems as well. The price of sugar spiked around the globe.

- Sugar prices rose to just under 30 US cents per pound by the end of January 2010—more than 150 percent over the previous year. Compared to prices in 2004, when sugar traded below 6 US cents, it represented a staggering increase of 500 percent and the highest price in almost 30 years.

34

Chocolate Finger

Due to declining harvests in Côte d'Ivoire (the Ivory Coast)—the largest cocoa exporter on the world market—prices are rising on the international commodity futures markets. In the summer of 2010, cocoa trader Anthony Ward, "Chocolate Finger," wagers more than 1 billion USD on cocoa futures.

> *"Of course they are people. They're Oompa Loompas."*
> —Willy Wonka in the movie
> *Charlie and the Chocolate Factory*

Cocoa, native to Central and South America, was considered by the Maya and the Aztecs to be a gift from the gods and therefore sacred. The seeds of the cacao tree also served as a means of payment. In the treasuries of Aztec king Moctezuma II, the Spanish conquistadors discovered, in addition to gold, more than 1,200 tons of cocoa—tax revenues and a huge currency reserve.

Today cocoa is an important cash crop, an export commodity for many developing countries, and the raw material for the production of chocolate. (In Germany, one of the countries with the highest per capita consumption of chocolate worldwide, every person eats an average of around 9 kilos per year.) Production costs for chocolate depend on the cocoa content, cocoa quality, and processing time, so that for a normal chocolate bar, the price of cocoa accounts only for about 10 percent of the cost of production.

Cocoa is traded in New York on the New York Board of Trade (NYBOT) and in London on the London International Financial Futures Exchange (LIFFE) in contracts of 10 tons each in USD and GBP, respectively.

The 10 largest cocoa producers account for more than 90 percent of the world's crop. Côte d'Ivoire dominates global production with a market share of more than a third of world production.

In July 2010, market rumors in London suggested that the Armajaro hedge fund had placed a 1 billion USD bet in the cocoa market. Fund manager Anthony Ward was said to have bought around 240,000 tons of cocoa in an attempt to corner the market. This would have accounted for about 7 percent of global cocoa production and the majority of the available quantities. While some traders saw this as a bet that cocoa prices would continue to rise due to a declining supply, others argued that Ward was creating an artificial shortage and manipulating the market through his massive purchases just before the start of the annual cocoa harvest in October.

Where's the Cocoa?

Cocoa's main growing areas have shifted in recent years from Central America to Africa. The 10 largest producer countries account for more than 90 percent of the global cocoa harvest. Of these, Côte d'Ivoire is the largest supplier of cocoa in the world, with a market share of more than 33 percent. Indonesia, Ghana, Nigeria, Brazil, and Cameroon follow far behind. By 2010, however, cocoa production in Côte d'Ivoire had fallen by more than 15 percent over the previous five years, largely due to poor crop maintenance and pest infestation. Cocoa production in 2008–2009 was the smallest harvest in the previous five years, at just 1.2 million metric tons, a trend that market participants expected for the 2009–2010 crop as well.

At age 50, Anthony Ward was considered a genius in trading cocoa. His attempt to corner the market for cocoa was spectacular but not an isolated event. In 2002, Ward had purchased more than 200,000 tons of cocoa—the equivalent of 5 percent of the world's cocoa market—through futures contracts. That was not the biggest cocoa transaction, however. The cocoa trading desk at Phibro, Salomon Smith Barney's commodity trading business, had taken a position of 300,000 tons of cocoa in 1997. The head of the cocoa trading desk at that time? Anthony Ward.

Anthony Ward had been a cocoa trader and industry expert since 1979. In the first months of 2010, the price rose more than 20 percent because of his trades.

Anthony Ward gained his first trading experiences in 1979 with tea, rice, cocoa, and rubber. In 1998 he co-founded Armajaro with Richard Gower, initially focusing on cocoa, then adding coffee and, later, other agricultural goods. Today Armajaro manages 1.5 billion USD and, with a local presence in Côte d'Ivoire, Indonesia, and Ecuador, is one of the largest cocoa suppliers to the world market. After Ward's trades in July 2010, the British press dubbed Ward "Willy Wonka," after the character in *Charlie and the Chocolate Factory*, and "Chocolate Finger," in homage to a James Bond villain.

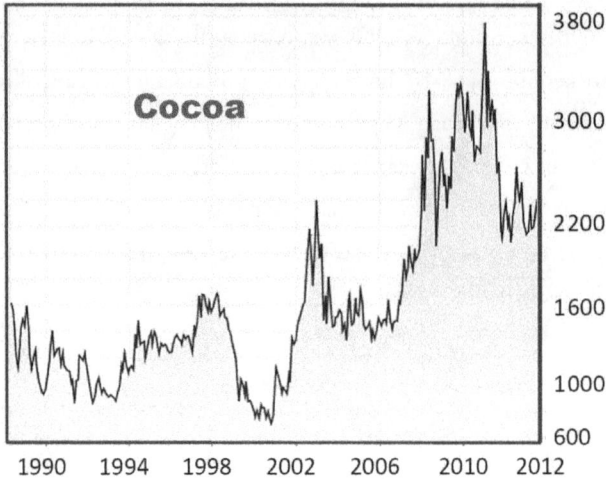

Figure 33. Cocoa prices in USD/ton, 1990–2012. Data: Bloomberg, 2019.

In 2009 and 2010, increasing demand, declines in production, and price speculation by hedge funds caused cocoa prices to rise more than 150 percent within two and a half years and to reach their highest level since 1977. A ton of cocoa in mid-July cost more than 3,600 USD. Because of Armajaro's purchases, the short-term price of cocoa rose: A July contract carried a 300 USD premium compared to a December 2010 contract. Customers had to pay a premium of around 15 percent compared to a later delivery (backwardation).

In a letter to the NYSE and LIFFE, 16 companies and trading houses complained about market manipulation of the cocoa market. However, LIFFE declared that "indications for a market manipulation are not recognized."

Key Takeaways

- The cocoa market is relatively small and highly concentrated: Côte d'Ivoire dominates global cocoa production with a market share of more than a third of world production. The 10 largest cocoa-producing countries account for more than 90 percent of the world's crop.

- During the summer of 2010, rumors spread that hedge fund Armajaro had placed a bet of 1 billion USD in the cocoa market. Fund manager Anthony Ward, nicknamed "Willy Wonka" and "Chocolate Finger," is said to have bought around 240,000 tons of cocoa in an attempt to corner the market.

- Compared to price levels in early 2009, cocoa prices in London and New York rose by more than 150 percent and reached their highest level since 1977. A ton of cocoa cost more than 3,600 USD in July 2010—an increase of more than 500 percent compared to 2002. It was a successful bet for Chocolate Finger.

35

Copper:
King of the Congo

2010

The copper belt of the Congo is rich in natural resources, but countless despots have looted the land. Now Eurasian Natural Resources Corporation (ENRC) is reaching out to Africa, and oligarchs from Kazakhstan aren't shy about dealing with shady businessmen or the corrupt regime of President Joseph Kabila.

"The West exploited Africa and now it wants to save it.
We have been living with this hypocrisy for too long.
Africa can only be saved by Africans."
—**Joseph Kabila,** President of the
Democratic Republic of the Congo

"We bought an asset from the
Democratic Republic of Congo that was for sale."
—**Sir Richard Sykes,** ENRC

On Friday, August 20, 2010, investors in the city of London listened closely as Eurasian Natural Resources Corporation (ENRC), a 12 billion USD, London-listed Kazakh mining company, took over the majority stake in Camrose Resources, which held the Kolwezi mining licenses recently expropriated by the government of the Congo. The previous owner of the extremely lucrative licenses? The Canadian mining company First Quantum Minerals. This was explosive news!

All of a sudden, after decades of colonialism, dictatorship, and warfare, the Democratic Republic of the Congo (DRC) was once again the focus of media attention and the international mining industry. The Congo, one of the poorest countries in the world, nevertheless has an immense wealth of natural resources. The African copper belt stretches from the Congolese mining province of Katanga to northern Zambia. Here lies around 10 percent of the world's copper reserves. And in 2010, copper was scarcer and more expensive than ever before: Based on its 52-week low, the price of the metal had increased that year alone by 50 percent. For the first time, copper traded above 9,000 USD per metric ton on the London Metal Exchange (LME).

An Introduction to the Congo

The Democratic Republic of the Congo, formerly Zaire, is the third-largest country in Africa, after Sudan and Algeria. Neighboring countries—the (formerly French) Republic of the Congo, the Central African Republic, Sudan, Uganda, Rwanda, Burundi, Zambia, Tanzania, and Angola—are all much smaller. With its wealth of natural resources, such as cobalt, diamonds, copper, gold, and other rare minerals, the Congo is a prime example of the "resource curse" thesis: The 70 million inhabitants of the Democratic Republic of the Congo are among the world's poorest. Only Zimbabwe has a lower per capita GDP.

The Congo, whose capital is Kinshasa, gained independence from Belgium in 1960 under President Kasavubu and the popular Prime Minister Patrice Lumumba. A period of instability and military intervention followed, beginning in 1965, under the long dictatorship of Mobutu Sese Seko, during which Mobutu and the elite of the country (now called Zaire) systematically looted the wealth of the nation.

The system collapsed in 1997, when Mobutu was ousted by Laurent-Désiré Kabila. In January 2001, L.-D. Kabila was murdered by one of his bodyguards under unclear circumstances, and the presidency passed to his son, Joseph Kabila. The latter stayed in power until the end of 2018. In January 2019, opposition leader Felix Tshisekedi was declared the fifth president of Congo-Kinshasa since its independence of Belgian colonial supremacy.

Despite the official end of the second Congo war in July 2003 (the first took place in 1997–1998), conflicts still persisted in the country up until today. In the course of this "African World War," which involved eight African states and 25 armed groups, more than 5 million people died. It was the bloodiest armed conflict since World War II.

The Kamoto Mine near the town of Kolwezi is in the heart of the Congo's mining district, where more than 3 million tons of copper and more than 300,000 tons of cobalt are believed to be in the ground. The current market value of copper reserves alone exceeds 30 billion USD. When the mine was still in operation, the machines of state-owned mining company Gécamines, once the largest company in Africa, moved about 10,000 tons of rock each day. In September 1990, however, the central part of the mine collapsed, burying many miners. The operation came to a standstill. Under the Mobutu dictatorship, reinvestments were neglected, and the largest mines fell into decay. In the late 1990s, Gécamines sold most of its projects to international mining corporations.

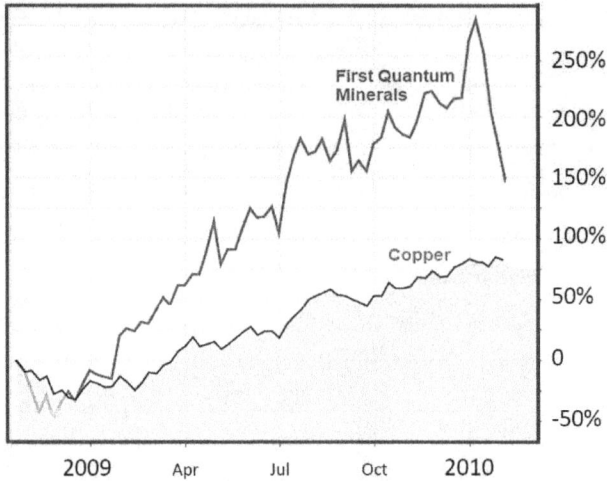

Figure 34. Copper and share price of First Quantum Minerals, 2009–2010. Data: Bloomberg, 2019.

Beginning in 2007, the Congolese government undertook a review of more than 60 foreign mining agreements in order to increase state involvement and ownership in the mining sector. Since then, the revision of mining licenses has created multiple sources of conflict.

The government was aiming for at least 35 percent government ownership in future mining projects. In addition, newer regulations called for a signing bonus of 1 percent of the project value, a 2.5 percent license fee on the gross income, and a stipulation that the mine would go into production within two years.

The value of the mineral reserves of the African copper belt between the DRC and Zambia exceeded the GDP of half the African continent.

In August 2009, after a 2½-year review by the government, Canadian First Quantum Minerals' Kolwezi license was terminated. The government accused First Quantum of breaching the 2002 mining regulations, though First Quantum denied it. One of the contentious issues was the increase of the Gécamines' share by 12.5 percent—for zero costs involved.

The situation for the Canadian company was precarious, since it had already invested more than 700 million USD in expanding Kolwezi. Moreover, after First Quantum couldn't come to an agreement with the Kabila government, the Congolese Supreme Court also revoked the company's licenses for the Frontier and Lonshi mines in favor of the state mining company Sodimico—another bitter blow to First Quantum.

Sly Foxes

The wealth of natural resources in the Katanga province of the Congo smoldered into a power struggle among the three craftiest businessmen on the continent: George Forrest, Billy Rautenbach, and Dan Gertler. Sixty-seven-year-old Forrest, head of the Forrest Group, had been born in the Congo and was the old man of the Congolese mining industry. In early 2004, a few months after the end of the war in the Congo, Forrest and Kinross Gold entered into a joint-venture agreement with the government over the Kamoto Copper Company (later Katanga Mining).

Rautenbach, founder of Wheels of Africa, the largest transport company in southern Africa, was a friend of Zimbabwean president Robert Mugabe. He went after the jewel, Katanga Mining, through the British company Camec. However, after a short takeover battle, the Congolese government announced a review of those mining licenses, and Rautenbach took the hint. He pulled back in September 2007.

continued

Rautenbach had previously been the manager of Gécamines but was replaced by Forrest, which accounted for the hostility between the two men.

Meanwhile, Gertler was laughing on the sidelines. Just 30 years old, he closed a joint-venture contract with the government of the Congo in 2004 for the development of KOV (Kamoto-Oliveira Virgule, later the company Nikanor). KOV was the only mine in Katanga with more resources than Kamoto Copper Company. More than 6.7 million metric tons of copper and 650,000 tons of cobalt—twice as much as in Kamoto—were estimated to be in the ground. According to market prices in 2018, the value of these resources alone exceeds half the GDP of Africa.

During the takeover battle for Katanga, Gertler bought shares in that mine through Nikanor. Camec finally lost its bid at the beginning of 2008, and Nikanor and Katanga Mining merged. In addition to his financial resources, Gertler had excellent connections: He is the grandson of the founder of Israel's diamond exchange, a friend of then-Israeli prime minister Ariel Sharon, and the same age as Congo president Joseph Kabila, whom he considered a close friend.

In January 2010 the newly established Highwinds Properties, owned by Dan Gertler, was awarded the Kolwezi license in a shady deal. A few months later came the bombshell. On August 20, 2010, ENRC confirmed that it had secured the licenses to Kolwezi through its 50.5 percent acquisition of Camrose Resources for 175 million USD. The company said it intended to cooperate with Cerida Global, another Dan Gertler–controlled company. With the acquisition of Camrose, ENRC was also committed to a 400 million USD loan for Highwinds and a loan guarantee of another 155 million USD for Cerida's debts.

The Kazakh company ENRC aggressively expanded its business in Africa and was not shy about dealing with African despots like Joseph Kabila.

Camrose also offered a majority stake in its subsidiary Africo to ENRC, whose copper and cobalt projects were located near its Camec properties. This was of high strategic importance for the Kazakh company, since ENRC had acquired the Central African Mining and Exploration Company (Camec) for 955 million USD in 2009. This is where Dan Gertler came into play, as Camec was 35 percent owned by the Israeli investor, who quickly unified the three Kazakh oligarchs—Alexander Mashkevitch, Patokh Chodiev, and Alijan Ibragimov—who owned 40 percent of ENRC.

The deals between Camec and Camrose were important milestones for ENRC's aggressive expansion policy in Africa, along with a 12 percent stake in Northam Platinum in South Africa that ENRC acquired in May 2010. Regardless of pending possible expropriations and a skeptical attitude by many institutional investors, only time would show whether ENRC would have a more favorable outcome in Congo than its Canadian rival, First Quantum.

Sometimes time flies. In November 2013, ENRC delisted its shares from the London stock exchange. The following April, an official investigation into bribery and sanction-busting began in England, and the founding partners decided to take the company private again. In February 2014, news spread that the company needed to sell all its international assets—including the copper mines in the Democratic Republic of the Congo—to repay debts. President Kabila, however, stayed in power until the end of 2018.

In January 2019, the opposition leader Felix Tshisekedi was declared the fifth president of Congo-Kinshasa. Leader of the opposition, Martin

Fayulu, complained that Kamila, despite officially stepping down from office, would with his associates most likely continue controlling the levers of powers. Presidential elections had been due for more than two years, but elections had been postponed several times despite forceful protests. Since the end of Belgian colonial supremacy in 1960, the country had never seen a peaceful transfer of power.

Key Takeaways

- The African copper belt that runs between the Congo and Zambia holds an incredible wealth of natural resources. In 2010 it became the focus of upheaval when President Kabila revoked the mining license of Canadian firm First Quantum Minerals.

- Copper was now big business, as copper prices traded at record highs of more than 9,000 USD per ton on the London Metal Exchange (LME).

- The Kazakh (but London-listed) resource company Eurasian Natural Resources Corporation (ENRC) began to massively expand its footprint in Africa. The firm's leaders were willing to deal with shady businessmen as well as with President Kabila's corrupt regime.

- In a murky transaction involving Dan Gertler's Highwinds Properties, the expropriated assets of First Quantum were sold to ENRC. International investors were shocked, and the company went private a couple of years later.

36

Crude Oil:
Deep Water Horizon
and the Spill

2010

Time is pressing in the Gulf of Mexico. After a blowout at the Deepwater Horizon oil rig, a catastrophe unfolds—the biggest spill of all time. About 780 million liters of crude oil flow into the sea. Within weeks BP loses half its stock-market value.

> *"This well did not want to be drilled . . . it just*
> *seemed like we were messing with Mother Nature."*
> —**Daniel Barron**, survivor of the
> Deepwater Horizon disaster

> *"I would like my life back."*
> —**Tony Hayward**, CEO of BP

Deepwater Horizon was one of the world's most advanced deepwater rigs. Installed in 2001, it was 121 meters long, 78 meters wide, and 23 meters high and cost 350 million USD. In April 2010, the giant lay about 40 miles off the coast of Louisiana in the Gulf of Mexico. Since February, the platform had been busy in the Mississippi Canyon Block 252, drilling in the Macondo reservoir about 4,000 meters below sea level.

April 20, 2010, promised to be a successful day, because the drill hole identified as API Well No. 60-817-44169 was about to be completed. The well would be sealed and

Twenty years after the *Exxon Valdez* oil spill, an even bigger environmental catastrophe was looming on the horizon.

prepared for production by a production platform. Every day counted because platform operators like Transocean charged oil companies on a daily basis. And in this case, BP was already concerned because Deepwater Horizon had been behind schedule for 43 days. The delays had already cost the big oil company more than 20 million USD.

The *Exxon Valdez*—A Past Catastrophe

Shortly after midnight on March 24, 1989, the most severe environmental disaster in the history of the United States occurred. The 300-meter-long oil tanker *Exxon Valdez* was on its way from the oil-loading station of the Trans-Alaska Pipeline, in the port city of Valdez, Alaska, when it collided with Bligh Reef in Prince William Sound. The accident caused a spill of almost 40,000 tons of crude oil. Around 2,000 km of coastline were contaminated, and hundreds of thousands of fish, seabirds, and marine animals died. Captain Joseph

Hazelwood was drunk in his room at the time of the accident, and third officer Gregory Cousins had the bridge.

Despite an extensive cleanup, the ecosystem remains severely disturbed three decades later.

That morning, four BP managers arrived by helicopter to monitor the completion of the drilling. Only a few hours before, experts from the oil services company Halliburton had cemented the drill hole closed, but employees of Schlumberger, who were about to test the cement seal, were sent back to shore by the BP managers before they had accomplished their task.

Deepwater Horizon drilled for black gold in the Gulf of Mexico on behalf of BP.

To accelerate completion of the work, BP urged rapid replacement of the drilling mud in the well with seawater to prepare for early production. This decision precipitated an argument between BP and the Transocean managers, who considered that step premature. Unlike seawater, drilling mud holds back rising gas and oil. However, the managers of BP prevailed, and the work began.

The decision would prove disastrous. The hole had a leak, and drilling mud and gas bubbles began to spill out. The cement plug also appeared to be leaking. Work continued into the night, until suddenly a sharp hiss of methane was heard and a fountain of mud shot out of the derrick, signaling a blowout.

As the methane ignited, a huge column of flame rose into the sky. Suddenly the entire derrick was on fire, and four workers on the drilling deck were dead.

The alarm sensors designed to warn of fire and a concentration of toxic or exploding gases had been turned off to keep workers from being disturbed by false alarms in the middle of the night. Now, below deck, it was chaos. Workers, some of them barely awake and dressed in little more than a life jacket, were jumping off the platform into the water, trying to save themselves. But with the Deepwater Horizon in flames, the oil on the water's surface had caught fire as well. Chaos also reigned in the rig's two lifeboats.

Around 11 pm, the *Damon B. Bankston*, an 80-meter-long supply ship, rescued the survivors. Eleven people had died in the explosion. Two days later, the oil platform sank in the Gulf of Mexico.

The demise of the platform marked the beginning of the biggest environmental disaster in the history of the United States, an event that would provide the plot for a Hollywood blockbuster movie, starring Mark Wahlberg, in 2016.

The Macondo drilling ended in disaster. In the largest oil spill in the United States, nearly 780 million liters of crude oil ran out, and the market value of BP fell by half.

When fire broke out on the deck of the Deepwater Horizon, engineer Christopher Pleasant pressed the emergency button for the blowout preventer (BOP), a series of shut-off valves mounted directly above the well bore to interrupt the flow of oil into it. Like huge pliers, the massive shear jaw of the BOP was supposed to cap and close the well in case of disaster. The automatic emergency system was activated, but nothing happened.

A commission of inquiry later found that the Deepwater Horizon blowout preventer was poorly maintained, the hydraulic system was leaking, and the safety instructions had not been properly maintained. In addition, the ring valve of the device had been damaged weeks before. Not only was the blowout preventer in poor condition, as early as September 2009, BP had reported almost 400 defects on the rig to Transocean. However, maintenance had been delayed, and more than 26 systems were in poor condition. There were even problems with the ballast system.

After the platform sank, an oil slick formed. Approximately 1.5 km by 8 km at first, it expanded to almost 10,000 square kilometers within a few days. Between 5 and 10 million liters of crude oil were flowing out every day, and Louisiana, Florida, Mississippi, and Alabama all declared a state of emergency. According to the US Department of the Interior's Flow Rate Technical Group (FRTG), the amount of oil that flowed out every 8 to 10 days matched the total amount of oil from the *Exxon Valdez* disaster. BP estimated that there were around 7 billion liters of crude oil in the source. Thus, it would take another two to four years until the entire amount of oil had oozed into the sea.

Shortly after the platform sank, BP initiated two independently made side-to-side relief wells (called the "bottom-kill method"), but the drilling would have taken about three months. Meanwhile, the capture of the oil with the aid of large steel domes was failing.

The depth of the seabed—around 1,500 meters—complicated the work. At the end of May 2010, several attempts were made to plug the leak with mud and cement (the "top- kill method"), but they,

It took five months to seal the oil leak.

too, were unsuccessful. In the middle of July, BP succeeded in significantly reducing the oil flow with a new sealing attachment—a temporary closure was successful. As a result, on August 6, the leak was finally sealed permanently using a modified variant of the top-kill method ("static-kill")—pumping in liquid cement through side relief holes. On September 19, five months after the Deepwater Horizon sank, BP declared the well "officially dead."

It was estimated that nearly 5 million barrels of oil, around 780 million liters, had run out, and BP's stock-market value fell by half in the course of the disaster. The company announced that it would divest 10 billion USD worth of assets to defer the cost of the spill.

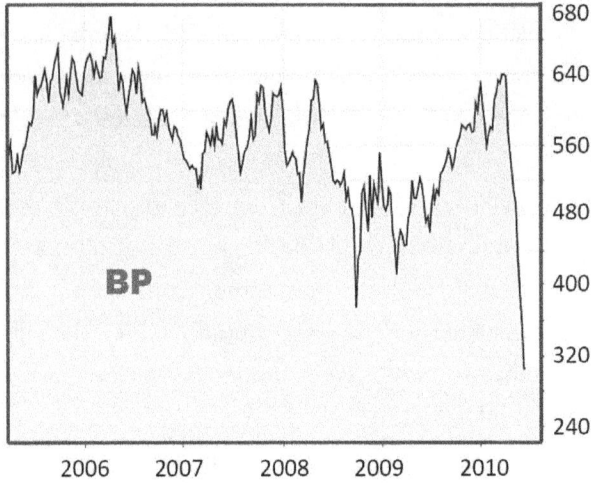

Figure 35. BP, share price fluctuation during first half of 2010. Data: Bloomberg, 2019.

At that point only about 3 billion USD in costs had accumulated. But BP also set up a trust fund of more than 20 billion USD for the future consequences of the catastrophe. Still unanswered is the question of who bears the responsibility for the disaster. Undoubtedly, BP took high risks, applied non-industry-compliant practices to save costs, and, as the principal, bears the financial responsibility. Transocean's role as operator of the oil platform also needs to be clarified, especially since the platform was in relatively poor condition. For Halliburton, the questions revolve around the doubtful completion of the cement seal of the well, and initial claims have also been made to BP's partner companies Mitsui and Anadarko.

The disaster heightened public awareness of the risks associated with deepwater drilling, both in the Gulf of Mexico and in planned projects off Brazil and Africa. As a direct result of the catastrophe, the US government passed a deep-sea moratorium, temporarily banning all new deep-sea drillings. Although this was later repealed, no new licenses have been awarded. As a further consequence, President Barack Obama fired the head of the Minerals Management Service, Elizabeth Birnbaum. The agency, now renamed the Bureau of Ocean Energy Management, Regulation and Enforcement, had grossly and negligently violated its oversight responsibilities.

It is impossible to estimate the economic consequences of the disaster, let alone the environmental consequences, which include not only the direct effects of the oil pollution but also the burning of oil and the use of toxic chemicals like Corexit, which have been used to combat the oil spill. BP said in 2018 that it would take a new charge over the Deepwater Horizon spill after again raising estimates for outstanding claims, lifting total costs to around 65 billion USD. The story of the disaster in the Gulf of Mexico will play out for decades in the future.

Key Takeaways

- At the Deepwater Horizon oil rig in the Gulf of Mexico, the Macondo drilling, at about 4,000 meters below sea level, ended in disaster. Nearly 780 million liters of crude oil ran out, and the market value of BP, the oil and gas company in charge, fell by half within weeks.

- The oil spill caused the biggest environmental catastrophe in the history of the United States, far more devastating than the oil spill of the *Exxon Valdez* 20 years earlier.

- As a consequence, US authorities temporarily froze all deepwater drilling licenses. BP is estimating a price tag of more than 65 billion USD.

37

Cotton:
White Gold

2011

The weather phenomenon known as La Niña causes drastic crop failures in Pakistan, China, and India due to flooding and bad weather conditions. Panic buying and hoarding drive the price of cotton to a level that has not been reached since the end of the American Civil War 150 years ago.

"It's not something you're going to see again in your lifetime."
—**Sharon Johnson**, senior cotton analyst

"I think there's still hope for prices to go higher."
—**Yu Lianmin**, Chinese cotton farmer

In ancient Babylon, cotton was known as "white gold," and the fabric has remained popular throughout history, woven by hand for hundreds of years. At the end of the 18th century, however, spinning and weaving mills began to produce fabrics and clothing at a much lower cost than could be done by hand. By the 19th century, the cotton business was booming, due to recent inventions such as the steam engine, the cotton gin, the spinning jenny, and mechanical looms.

The textile industry of the United Kingdom required ever larger quantities of the raw material, which was produced in its colonies or elsewhere abroad, especially in the southern United States, where cotton had expanded tremendously in the early 1800s. The crop thrived everywhere that was moist and warm, and labor was cheap in the American South. For about 250 years enslaved Africans had toiled on southern plantations, and cotton production grew from just 10,000 bales a year to more than 4 million until slavery was abolished after the end of the American Civil War in 1865. During that war, the price of cotton rose to dizzying heights that would only be reached again in spring 2011, almost 150 years later.

> The last time cotton reached almost 2 USD per pound was after the American Civil War.

Since 1995, cotton had traded mostly between 0.40 and 0.80 USD, but at the end of September 2010, for the first time in 15 years, the price of cotton broke the 1 USD/lb level. A few months earlier, in May, the German magazine *Der Spiegel* had bemoaned "the end of cheap jeans," as it noted the price explosion in cotton. But that was only the beginning. By November, cotton prices had increased another 40 percent. A sharp correction followed, but by the end of December cotton was up to 1.40 USD. And, beginning in January 2011, the market was unstoppable. The price spiked to more than 2.15 USD in March 2011—four times the level of early 2000 and a 480 percent increase over the November 2008 price.

It was the highest price ever paid for cotton since the introduction of cotton trading on the New York Cotton Exchange in 1870.

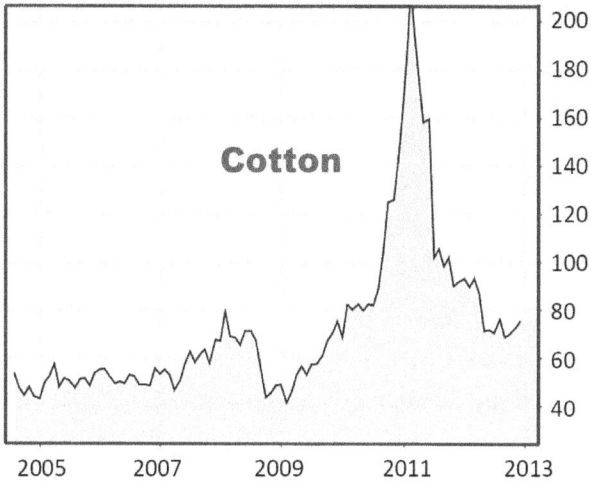

Figure 36. Cotton prices in US cents/lb, 2005–2013. Data: Bloomberg, 2019.

The price had actually been rising for several years. At the end of 2009, the global textile industry had forecast robust growth of around 3 percent for the following year. However, flooding and bad weather conditions in several important producer countries such as China, India, Pakistan, and Australia led to significant crop losses. Because of the falling inventory, high premiums were paid for material that was available in the short term.

> Once again, severe weather conditions
> influenced agriculture prices.

In Pakistan, the world's fourth-largest cotton-producing country, floods hit more than 14 million people in 2010, according to UN estimates. The exceptionally heavy monsoon season was considered the strongest in more than 80 years, and rain destroyed more than 280,000 hectares of cotton. According to the Pakistan Cotton Ginners Association, the flood destroyed 2 million bales of cotton. The All Pakistan Textile Mills Association also reported a worrying shortage of cotton. Only 30 percent of the mills had raw material in stock for the next 90 days, and Pakistan would soon stop exporting cotton.

A few weeks later, India, the second-largest cotton producer in the world, followed suit. The Indian Ministry of Textiles stopped exports, since without the ban the Indian textile industry would not have been guaranteed an adequate supply of cotton. Indian exports dropped to 0.5 million metric tons, having exceeded 1.5 million tons in the 2007–2008 season.

There were several reasons for the shortage beyond the dynamic growth of the domestic Indian textile industry. The world's largest cotton producer and importer, China, was also enduring a shrinking cotton harvest for the second year in a row, due to low temperatures and too much rain. China Cotton Association statistics in December 2010 showed monthly imports doubling year over year.

Cotton Basics

Most cotton species and varieties are cultivated as annual plants and have high requirements for heat and water. In the Northern Hemisphere, sowing takes place from the beginning of February to the beginning of June, depending on the location.

China, India, the United States, Pakistan, Brazil, and Uzbekistan together account for around 85 percent of the world's cotton production, with China and India producing more than half of the global market volume. In the 2009–2010 harvest, the amount of cotton grown worldwide reached 25 million metric tons.

Cotton is used mainly in textiles, accounting for about one-third of the world's textile fibers. These can be categorized into natural fibers—such as vegetable fibers (e.g., cotton or linen) and animal fibers (e.g., wool, hair, and silk)—or artificial (synthetic) fibers. Synthetic fibers actually dominate the industry, accounting for almost 60 percent. They can be divided into cellulosic fibers (e.g., viscose) and those derived from petroleum. The most important synthetic fibers are polyester, polyamide, and polyacrylic fibers.

Cotton is traded on the commodity futures exchanges in the United States under the symbol CT and the respective contract month in a contract size of 50,000 lb per contract.

In late 2010 and early 2011, flooding and Cyclone Yasi caused severe damage in Australia, which ranked eighth among the top 10 cotton producers worldwide. The Australian Cotton Shippers Association, which had predicted a bumper harvest of more than 4 million bales, reduced its forecast by more than 10 percent.

Blocks on cotton exports worsened the situation, and panic buying and hoarding were the result.

Cotton processors in the region reacted in panic. Willing to pay any price for raw material, they pushed prices ever higher. Cotton farmers who still had inventory continued to aggravate the situation. The China National Cotton Information Center estimated that around 2 million tons of available material never reached the market in China. For example, in Huji, in Shandong province, about 220 kilometers from Beijing, growers held back more than 50 percent of their harvest at the end of January, expecting prices to continue to rise. Because of the short shelf life of cotton, that strategy could only be maintained until April or May.

In any case, the price boom in cotton was short lived. The International Cotton Advisory Committee in Washington estimated that the acreage for the 2011–2012 season would increase to 36 million hectares, the most in 17 years. It was a natural response to record prices. In the short term, however, most processors had no choice but to mix cheaper synthetic fibers with the more expensive cotton.

Key Takeaways

- If you thought that the exciting times of trading cotton took place more than 100 years ago, events in 2010 proved you wrong.

- The first impacts of global climate change were evident in a series of extreme weather events. Flooding and bad weather conditions caused by La Niña accounted for significant crop losses in several important cotton-producing countries, such as China, India, Pakistan, and Australia.

- Cotton processors in the region reacted in panic, driving prices higher. Cotton farmers who still had stocks held back their supply in expectation of even higher profits.

- As a consequence, cotton prices shot through the roof. Cotton, which once traded at 40 US cents per pound in 2009, doubled in value within a year to 80 US cents and skyrocketed to 2 USD in 2011. This was an increase of 500 percent in two years!

- Because of short supplies, export restrictions, panic buying, and hoarding, the price of cotton rose to a level not reached since the end of the American Civil War 150 years ago.

38

Glencore:
A Giant Steps Into the Light

In May 2011, the world's largest commodity trading company—a conspicuous and discreet partnership with an enigmatic history—holds an IPO. The former owners, Marc Rich and Pincus Green, have been followed by US justice authorities for more than 20 years. Without mandatory transparency or public accountability in the past, they were able to close deals with dictators and rogue states around the world.

"Glencore is Marc Rich's legacy."
—**Daniel Ammann**, author of *The King of Oil*

"My business is my life."
—**Marc Rich**

It was the week before the Easter holidays in 2011, on a warm, sunny day in the banking metropolis of Frankfurt am Main, Germany. For the first time that year, temperatures climbed above 72 degrees Fahrenheit, and the city was full of people enjoying the sun's warm rays. It was also the first week of "investor education" concerning the biggest IPO of the year, for Glencore.

Equity sector specialists were explaining corporate strategy and the business model of the world's largest commodity trading house and the reasons why institutional investors should participate in its initial public equity offering. In a meeting room in one of the bank towers, high above the city center, 11 people nibbled on light snacks. The analyst was late, however, thanks to too many meetings and telephone conferences. And much of the information about corporate returns remained unclear. It seemed that Glencore was not being completely transparent. How exactly did the commodity giant—whose value was estimated at between 60 and 80 billion USD by the banks in the consortium and whose management team was known only to industry insiders—earn its money? Until the IPO, the Switzerland-based company had cherished one thing above all: secrecy.

Glencore (the name was derived from Global Energy Commodity Resources) was one of the world's leading commodity players. Its business activities included the production, processing, and trading of aluminum, copper, zinc, nickel, lead, iron ore, coal, and crude oil as well as agricultural products. In terms of sales, the company was the largest in Switzerland and the largest individual shareholder, with 33 percent, of the multinational mining company Xstrata. Before the IPO, Glencore was completely owned by its management and employees, but until 1993 it had had a turbulent history determined by only one man: Marc Rich, nicknamed "The King of Oil."

Marc Rich was the world's most successful commodity trader. Together with Pincus Green, he broke the Seven Sisters cartel, the dominant oil companies until the 1970s.

Within commodity markets, Marc Rich was a legend. No commodity trader before or after him has ever been so successful. As a son of

German-speaking Jews, Rich began his career in 1954 with Philipp Brothers, then the world's largest commodity trader. Strong economic growth in Europe, the United States, and Asia made the 1960s a boom decade for commodity trading. But in 1973, when the company earned a record profit in which Marc Rich and Pincus Green played a decisive role, a dispute about future payments arose.

Rich and Green left Philipp Brothers and convinced Jacques Hachuel, Alexander Hackel, and John Trafford to follow them. Together they founded Marc Rich + Co AG in Zug, Switzerland, on April 3, 1974.

Rich and Green revolutionized commodity trading, breaking the multinational Seven Sisters oil companies cartel and becoming major players in international petroleum trading. In the early 1980s Rich was the world's largest independent oil trader. Marc Rich + Co generated more profit than UBS, the biggest bank in Switzerland, and Rich's private wealth was estimated to total more than a billion USD.

Initially, the company focused on the physical trading of iron, nonferrous metals, and minerals. Crude oil and coal marked an expansion into energy. With the acquisition of an established Dutch grain distribution company in 1982, Rich + Co also entered the agricultural sector. Through further acquisitions in mining, smelting, refineries, and processing, the company continued to grow in the 1980s and 1990s.

Who Was Marc Rich?

Marc Rich, born Marcell David Reich on December 18, 1934, in Antwerp, Belgium, was the son of German-speaking Jews. Fleeing war and persecution, the family immigrated to the United States and changed the family name to Rich. As a young man, Rich studied at New York University but left after two semesters to join Philipp Brothers in 1954,

continued

then the largest commodity trading company in the United States. He started his career under Ludwig Jesselson, and between 1964 and 1974 he worked as a manager of the Philipp Brothers offices in Spain. In 1974 Rich left the company and with Pincus Green and others founded Marc Rich + Co AG.

Within the next two decades, the new commodity trading company would become the most successful in the industry. But because of business ties to Iran—despite American political and economic sanctions and the US abolition of diplomatic relations in April 1980—Rich and Green became the focus of the US Justice Department. Accused of organized crime and tax fraud, Rich avoided prosecution by fleeing to Switzerland, where for 20 years he and Green proceeded with business as usual, while they were pursued by US justice.

After a management buyout in 1993, Rich separated from the firm, and the group was renamed Glencore. At the time, *Forbes* magazine estimated his private assets at more than 1.5 billion USD.

Rich never went to trial, and on his last day of office, January 20, 2001, President Bill Clinton granted full and unconditional pardons to Rich and Green in a still-controversial act.

In June 2013, Rich died of a stroke at a hospital in Lucerne, Switzerland, at the age of 78.

As it hunted for the next source of profits, the company was not picky. The list of its business partners read like a "Who's Who" of international rogue states and dictatorships. The company traded commodities with Iran during the hostage crisis and with Fidel Castro's Cuba, as well as with Slobodan Milosevic's Yugoslavia, North Korea, Muammar Gaddafi's Libya, the Soviet Union under Brezhnev, South Africa's apartheid regime, and Nigeria and Angola in the late 1970s.

In the 1990s, though, the tables turned. Pincus Green and Alexander Hackel resigned, and the press relentlessly excoriated the company's business behavior. Finally, after heavy trading losses, Rich lost the support of other senior managers.

In November 1993, the 39 most important employees of Marc Rich + Co met at the Parkhotel in Zug to discuss the future of the company without Rich. Led by Willy Strothotte, they agreed on a management buyout, and by the following November, Rich had gradually sold his shares of the firm to management and senior employees, about 200 people in all. The value of the company—an industry leader in trading crude oil, metals, and minerals —was estimated to be between 1 and 1.5 billion USD. The new owners renamed the company Glencore, eliminating all traces of the Marc Rich name after 20 years.

Strothotte took over as chairman of the board of directors of Glencore but also moved into a top position at Schweizerischer Südelektra, which was renamed Xstrata in 1999 and was 33 percent owned by Glencore. The two companies maintained a close relationship. While Xstrata concentrated on commodity production, Glencore focused on marketing and trading raw materials. Xstrata, listed in London, offered transparency for investors. However, Glencore's business continued to play out behind the scenes.

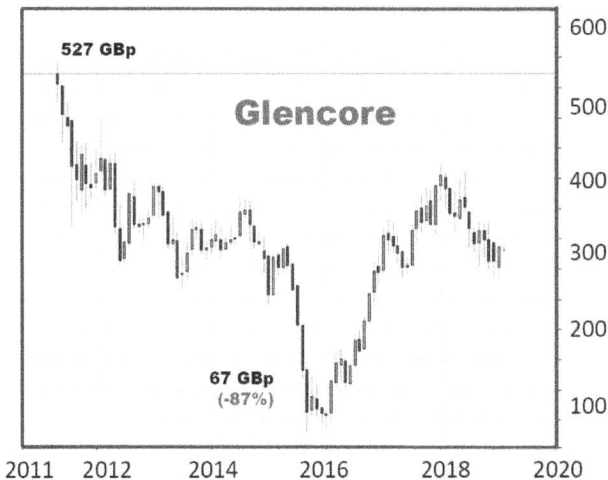

Figure 37. Glencore (GBP). Equity price performance since IPO on May 19, 2011. Data: Bloomberg, 2019.

As Glencore reached the limits of growth within its corporate structure, it badly needed fresh capital, a situation exacerbated by the fact that some of the management team had to be reimbursed within the next couple of years. The initial public offering, which raised 12 billion USD, satisfied that hunger for cash. On May 19, 2011, shares of Glencore were listed for the first time in London at 5.27 GBP. In February 2012, the company announced a merger with Xstrata that would be concluded almost a year later under CEO Ivan Glasenberg. The CEO of Glencore since 2002, Glasenberg had been with the company since 1984 and, with an estimated 5 billion USD net wealth, he became one of the top 10 richest people in Switzerland.

It turned out that Glencore's management had cashed out at the peak of the cycle: The share price of the initial IPO has never been reached again. Instead, during a commodity sell-off, shares plunged to 67 GBP on September 28, 2015, a loss of 87 percent since the IPO. In January 2019, however, Glencore's share price had recovered to 3 GBP, which shows that its business model as a listed company was working.

Key Takeaways

- The commodity trading company Glencore had a turbulent history that, until 1993, was determined by one man—Marc Rich, nicknamed "The King of Oil." Rich had founded Glencore's predecessor company, Marc Rich + Co AG, in Zug, Switzerland, in 1974.

- With private wealth of more than 1 billion USD, Rich became the most famous commodity trader by breaking the Seven Sisters cartel, and by becoming the world's largest independent oil trader. His list of business partners read like a "Who's Who" of international rogue states and dictatorships.

- Glencore and other commodity trading companies generally maintain an aura of secrecy, since they prefer to strike their deals in private. However, to overcome financing constraints, Glencore, which was completely owned by its management and employees after 1993, raised 12 billion USD in its initial public offering in May 2011. It merged with mining giant Xstrata one year later and became a leader in both mining and commodity trading.

- In May 2011, shares of Glencore were listed for the first time in London at 5.27 GBP. In hindsight, that was the top of the cycle; during the following bear market in commodities, the shares plunged to 0.67 GBP in September 2015. Today, shares of Glencore have recovered to 3 GBP.

39

Rare Earth Mania:
Neodymium, Dysprosium,
and Lanthanum

China squeezes the supply of rare earths, and high-tech industries in the United States, Japan, and Europe ring the alarm bell. But the Chinese monopoly can't be broken quickly. And the resulting sharp rise in rare earth prices lures investors from around the globe.

"The Middle East has oil. China has rare earths."
—Deng Xiaoping, 1992

In 2013, geologist Don Bubar bought 4,000 hectares of land in the wilderness of Canada for less than half a million USD, hoping that in a few years the area would be worth billions. Bubar and his company, Avalon Resources, planned to develop a mine for rare earths and to start production by 2015. Gold fever had seized the mining industry. Almost 300 companies worldwide were exploring for rare earths and other exotic metals like lithium, indium, or gallium. Investors were happy to spend their money on these projects, because the supply of rare earths is limited, demand was high, and prices were soaring, reflected in press headlines almost every day.

Rare earths have become indispensable for modern high-tech applications—in computers, mobile phones, or flat screens, for example, and the growth of regenerative energy can't be achieved without rare earths in electric/hybrid cars or in wind power plants. But these metals have been at the center of a trade conflict between the main producer, China, and the industrialized countries, a situation that has been worsening over the past few years.

What Are Rare Earths?

Rare earths consist of 17 metals: scandium, yttrium, and the lanthanides group of lanthanum, cerium, dysprosium, europium, erbium, gadolinium, holmium, lutetium, neodymium, praseodymium, promethium, samarium, terbium, thulium, and ytterbium. In most deposits, light rare earths (cerium, lanthanum, neodymium, and praseodymium) are found in large quantities, while the occurrence of heavy rare earths (yttrium, terbium, and dysprosium among others) is considerably lower.

One of the most extensively used metals is neodymium, which is indispensable for the production of permanent magnets, that is, magnets that do not discharge. Neodymium is used in mobile phones and computers, wind turbines, and electric/hybrid cars. Each megawatt of power from a wind generator requires between 600 and 1,000 kg of permanent magnets made of iron-boron-neodymium alloys. Moreover, in every wind turbine, there are several hundred kilos of neodymium and dysprosium.

Lanthanum is also used in many high-tech applications. For example, about one kg of neodymium is needed for the hybrid engine of a Toyota Prius, but the batteries contain about 15 kg of lanthanum. The German Federal Institute for Geosciences and Natural Resources expects the demand for rare earths to rise to 200,000 metric tons a year. At current prices, this means a market size of 2 billion USD. Compared to other metal markets, such as that for copper, with an annual production volume of almost 20 million metric tons and a market value of almost 140 billion USD, rare earths are a tiny but profitable segment.

China has dictated world market prices of rare earths, since its production accounts for about 97 percent of the global volume of 120,000 tons per year. China also has almost 40 percent of the world's reserves, while other significant reserves are located in Russia, the United States, Australia, and India.

Similar to OPEC's actions during the oil crises of the 1970s, China has been manipulating exports for years, and the United States, Japan, and Europe have all complained about export restrictions and high export duties. In 2005, exports were around 65,000 metric tons per year, but the volume has shrunk dramatically since then. As a result, prices for rare earths rose sharply from 2005 to 2008, and there was another price push in the third quarter of 2009. For the first half of 2011, the Chinese government announced exports of just 14,500 metric tons, and prices rose again. A kilogram of neodymium in May 2011 cost almost 300 USD, compared to just 40 USD 12 months earlier.

China also used its dominance in rare earth production as a political weapon. When Japan detained a Chinese ship captain, China banned rare earth exports to Japan in September 2010.

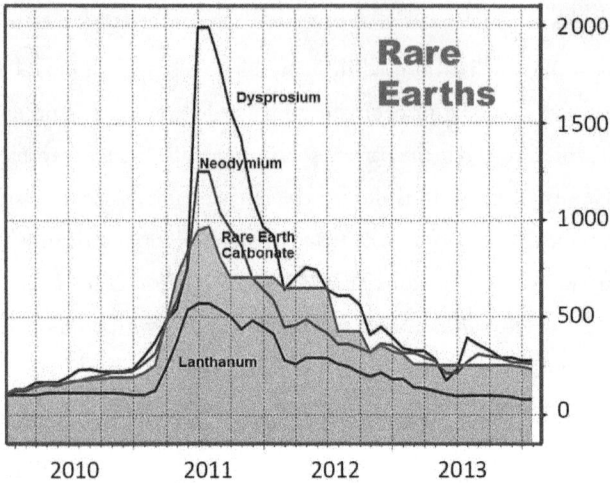

Figure 38. Rare earth carbonate, neodymium, dysprosium, and lanthanum, 2010–2013. Chinese onshore prices in RMB, indexed 30.12.2009=100. Data: Bloomberg, 2019.

Over the past 20 years, industrialized nations have maneuvered themselves into this economic dependency. In the mid-1960s, the United States began producing rare earths in the Mountain Pass Mine, in the Mojave Desert of California. Until the late 1990s, this mine alone covered the world's demand for these metals. Within the industry, this time period is known as the "Mountain Pass era."

However, due to environmental constraints and low prices for rare earth metals, the mine closed in 2002. Since the beginning of the 1990s, the Chinese—able to produce the rare earths more cheaply and without worrying about environmental requirements—have begun to flood the world market.

The main Chinese production comes from Mongolia, where only a few kilometers away from the city of Baotou, with its multimillion population, is Bayan Obo, one of the world's largest open-air mines.

It is estimated that up to 35 million metric tons of rare earths—more

Bayan Obo in China is the world's
largest mine for rare earth minerals.

than half of total Chinese production—come from Bayan Obo. Another large segment of the Chinese supply derives from the southern provinces, where there are numerous small illegal projects in addition to official government mines. Production has its price, however. Processing rare earths generates large amounts of poisonous residues, which leads to heavy pollution by thorium, uranium, heavy metals, acids, and fluorides. Thus, untreated sewage has turned the nearby 12-kilometer-long drinking-water reservoir at Baotou into a waste dump enriched with chemicals and radioactive thorium.

Such heavy environmental damages are ironic, since these rare earths are indispensable to the clean energy industry, especially wind turbines and electric/hybrid cars. There's no short-term, easy way out of the West's self-inflicted scarcity. Development of an independent production capacity without environmental problems

> **Skyrocketing prices of rare earths have attracted many adventurers.**

is a very capital-intensive undertaking. Exploration and exploitation of rare earth deposits is somewhat less problematic; despite their name, rare earths are not really scarce. Even the rarest metal in the group is around 200 times more common than gold.

Skyrocketing prices in 2011 attracted investors and adventurers around the globe, as small mining companies began to search for rare earths and other exotic metals, and investors looked for attractive rare earth deposits to invest in. However, the majority of new rare earth deposits will never be developed or even have the slightest chance to go into production.

The two most promising companies were Molycorp and Lynas. Molycorp, which had an IPO in 2010, planned to reactivate the Mountain Pass Mine, while Lynas aimed to start production at the Mount Weld Mine in Australia in 2011. All other projects were looking at a planning horizon of at least five years. Meanwhile, the absence of a processing infrastructure was an even greater obstacle than the need for capital-intensive funding.

In 2015, Molycorp filed for bankruptcy after facing challenging competition and declining rare earth prices. The company was then reorganized as Neo Performance Materials. Lynas successfully got into production and made a first shipment of concentrate in November 2012. Today it operates a mining and concentration plant at Mount Weld and a refining facility in Kuantan, Malaysia. In September 2018, however, the processing facilities in Malaysia came under government review because of environmental concerns, and shares of Lynas began to tumble.

China will continue to be the dominant source of rare earths, which perfectly fits into the strategic plan issued by Chinese premier Li Keqiang and his cabinet in May 2015: Made in China 2025.

Key Takeaways

- The group of 17 rare earth metals, with exotic names like neodymium, dysprosium, or lanthanum, have become indispensable for modern high-tech applications like wind turbines and e-mobility.

- In 2011, China squeezed the supply of rare earths, using its dominance in rare earth production as a political weapon. Because its production accounts for more than 90 percent of global supply, China has been able to dictate world market prices.

- High-tech industries in the United States, Japan, and Europe sounded the alarm, but it was impossible to break the Chinese monopoly on the supply of rare earths in the short term. As a consequence, rare earth prices increased sharply, an average of 10 times between 2009 and 2011. Prices of neodymium and dysprosium, which are in the highest demand, increased even more drastically. This price spike attracted global investors who were eager to invest in rare earth deposits.

40

The End?
Crude Oil Down the Drain

2016

A perfect storm is brewing for the oil market. There is an economic slow-down and too much storage because of contango. The world seems to be floating in oil, whose price falls to 26 USD in February 2016. But the night is always darkest before dawn, and crude oil and other commodities find their multiyear lows.

> *"Everybody be cool. You—be cool."*
> —**Seth Gecko** in *From Dusk till Dawn*

> *"The crude oil supply glut is gone."*
> —**Nick Cunningham**, www.oilprice.com

The Armageddon of the global financial crisis had been stopped by the massive bailouts and unconventional monetary policy of central banks around the world. As for oil, WTI crashed from almost 150 USD/barrel in June 2008 and traded temporarily below 33 USD during spring 2009. By the end of that year, crude prices had recovered to 80 USD, and between 2011 and 2014 the reference point for crude oil was 100 USD.

But in hindsight, the summer of 2014 proved to be just the quiet before a massive storm: WTI fell from almost 110 USD to less than 26 USD—a drop of 76 percent, even lower than it had been during the financial crisis. (Actually it was the lowest level for crude prices since 2003.)

Crude oil was not the only victim. The year 2016 began as an ugly one for all commodities as the Chinese domestic stock market plunged, and many other equity indices around the world followed in a case of Asian contagion. Demand in China was of fundamental importance for commodities because of demographics, growth, and the country's immense raw material purchases. The US dollar retreated massively from highs of 100 on the Dollar Index, and raw material prices dropped further.

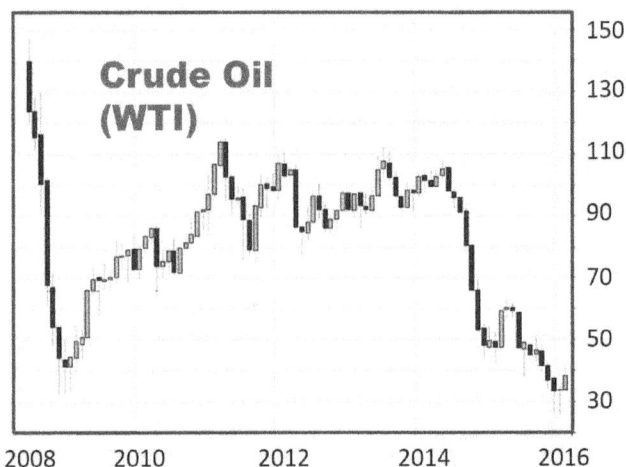

Figure 39. Crude oil (WTI): recovery and bear market, 2008–2016. Data: Bloomberg, 2019.

The massive price drop during the financial crisis had caused the term structure for crude oil to flip into contango, in which spot prices are below those of future delivery dates. It made more sense to store oil than to sell it, but the glut in supply overtaxed existing holding facilities, eventually leading to the use of supertankers as floating storage.

By the end of summer 2015, crude inventories were still rising and prices had started to crash. In early 2016, storage levels had barely declined from their 80-year highs of 490 million barrels in the United States alone, leading to pessimism about the future.

The International Energy Agency (IEA) noted that crude oil markets could "drown in over-supply" because of rising storage levels around the world. The agency said that the world had added 1 billion barrels of oil in storage in 2015, and storage levels were still rising. Even in the fourth quarter, normally when stocks are drawn down, inventories continued to climb.

Crude oil crashed because of a massive global supply glut. Oil prices fell to less than 26 USD.

There were dire warnings that the world could soon run out of storage space for oil, which would depress prices even further. Oil tumbled to its lowest level in more than 12 years, as the crude stockpiled at the delivery point for New York futures reached a record.

On February 11, 2016, when the S&P 500 index posted a 12 percent loss on the year, the Baltic Dry Index—which measures the shipping activity of dry bulk cargos around the world—fell to an all-time low of 290. The activity in commodity markets came to a halt, and the Bloomberg Commodity Index posted a 30 percent loss on the year. However, February 11 marked the lows for many assets, and the markets began to improve in the weeks and months that followed.

OPEC and Russia agreed to a joint production cut to fight the supply glut. Finally prices started to recover.

Capitulation Price Levels

In early February 2016, the S&P Goldman Sachs Commodity Index and Bloomberg Commodity Index, two important commodity market references, posted double-digit losses. Investors were devastated since 2015 had already been a bloodbath for commodities. Crude oil traded as low as 26 USD/barrel, copper below 2 USD/lb, and even gold traded as low as 1,050 USD/oz. Cryptocurrencies weren't given much attention from investors at that time. Bitcoins, for example, had a bad year in 2015, trading below 200 BTC/USD, and started to recover in 2016.

Gold was the first among the group of more than 20 commodities to indicate a turnaround, as prices started to climb, and exceeded its 200-day moving average rather quickly, a strong technical indicator for bullish markets.

In the face of the massive supply glut, OPEC and Russia agreed to a joint cut in production. It was OPEC's first agreed cut since 2008, when oil prices collapsed late in the year after hitting record levels during the summer. And it had the potential to restore some longer-term stability to the global oil market. The wild card was renewed production in the United States, pushed by shale oil and fracking on the back of rising prices. Some feared that this could simply end up prolonging the glut and pushing prices back down.

But there was also evidence that the massive inventories of raw materials were declining, and demand was finally picking up. And demographic trends continued to support the rationale that more people in the world would require more commodities in the years ahead. Both classic economic theory and common sense dictate that as demand rises, inventories fall and prices rise.

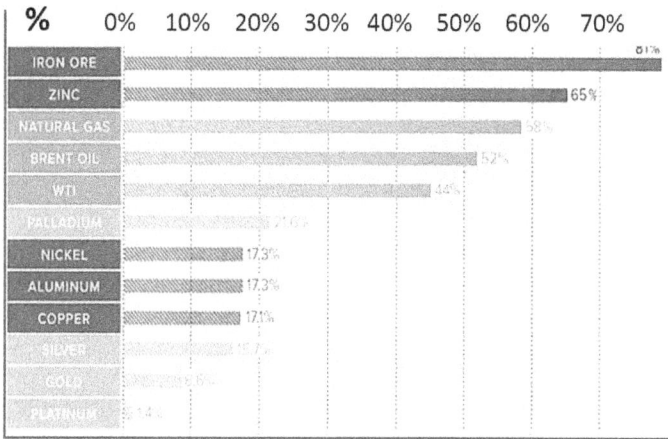

Figure 40. Commodity performance in 2016. Data: Bloomberg, 2019.

Meanwhile commodity prices were rising, with gold leading the way. The precious yellow metal traded to more than 1,380 USD in the wake of Britain's Brexit vote, and silver shot up above 21 USD. Crude oil rose from just above 26 USD per barrel in February to more than 50 USD at the beginning of October. The price of sugar increased from 10 US cents per pound in August 2015 to more than 24 US cents on September 29, 2016. The prices of iron ore, zinc, tin, nickel, and lead all posted double-digit gains in 2016. In perhaps the most optimistic signal for commodity markets, the Baltic Dry Index rose from 290 in February to 915 in early October, an increase of more than 215 percent.

> **Crude oil prices doubled from their lows in 2009, and commodities started to shine again.**

It appeared that prices for raw materials had reached a significant bottom. Commodities as an asset class posted impressive gains, rising by more than 20 percent from its lows in 2016 to the end of the year. WTI more than doubled in that period to above 55 USD/barrel.

Production cuts that had been in place since the start of 2017 helped halve the excess of global oil stocks, although, according to OPEC, those remained above the five-year average, at 140 million barrels. It was not until May 2018 that OPEC said the global oil supply surplus had nearly been eliminated.

Key Takeaways

- "Super-contango" had caused a massive supply glut in crude oil, during which storage facilities for WTI in Cushing, Oklahoma, reached maximum capacity: The world seemed to be floating in oil, and WTI crashed from almost 110 USD to less than 26 USD in February 2016—a drop of 76 percent and the lowest level for crude oil prices since 2003.

- During 2016, the Chinese domestic stock market plunged, and many other equity indices around the world followed, leading commodity markets lower as well. However, in spring 2016, commodity markets found a bottom, and commodities as an asset class posted impressive gains over the full year, rising by more than 20 percent. The price of WTI more than doubled in that period to more than 55 USD/barrel.

- Nevertheless, it would take until May 2018 until OPEC confirmed that the global oil supply surplus had nearly been eliminated.

41

Electrification: The Evolution of Battery Metals

Elon Musk and Tesla are setting the pace for a mega trend: electrification! Demand from automobile manufacturers, utilities, and consumers pushes lithium-based battery usage to new heights. For commodity markets, it is not only lithium and cobalt but also traditional metals like copper and nickel that are suddenly in high demand again. Electrification might prove to be the "new China" for commodity markets in the long term.

> *"Tesla is here to stay and keep fighting*
> *for the electric car revolution."*
> —Elon Musk

The year 2016 issued a wake-up call for the automotive and oil industries. OPEC, the mighty oil cartel, massively revised its growth expectations for electric vehicles (EVs) upward by 500 percent. Instead of the 46 million EVs by 2040 it had envisioned in 2015, OPEC was now looking at a forecast of 266 million EVs.

If those projections turn out to be correct, by 2040 demand for oil could fall by 8 million barrels a day. That is about what the United States currently produces in a day, or roughly 8 percent of global consumption. (The world consumes almost 100 million barrels of crude oil every day, of which 75 percent is related to the transportation sector.)

Elon Musk and Tesla

Elon Musk, founder and CEO of SpaceX, Tesla, and Neuralink, was born in Pretoria, South Africa, in 1971. As of February 2018, Musk had a net worth in excess of 20 billion USD and was listed by *Forbes* as the 53rd-richest person in the world. In December 2016, he was ranked 21st on the *Forbes* list of "The World's Most Powerful People." Musk also founded PayPal, which was bought by eBay for 1.5 billion USD in October 2002.

Tesla, based in Palo Alto, California, specializes in electric vehicles (EVs), lithium-ion battery energy storage, and solar-panel manufacturing through its subsidiary company SolarCity. Tesla operates multiple production and assembly plants near Reno, Nevada, while its main vehicle-manufacturing facility is in Fremont, California. The Gigafactory in Reno primarily produces batteries and battery packs for Tesla vehicles and energy storage products. According to *Bloomberg*, over the past 12 months Tesla has been burning money at a clip of about 8,000 USD a minute (roughly 500,000 USD an hour).

In 2017 Tesla produced and sold 100,000 cars. It might be the beginning of a revolution, but so far EVs are hardly making a dent. German automakers BMW, Mercedes, and Audi together sold 6.6 million cars, and for these traditional car companies, the electric catchup has just started. In Germany, new car registrations of EVs reached 55,000, half of which were plug-in hybrids. This represented 1.6 percent of the new car market, based on 3.4 million new cars in Germany. Compared to 43.8 million total cars in use in that country, it was basically a grain of sand in the desert.

EVs made up 1.6 percent of new car registrations in car-crazy Germany in 2017. However, Bloomberg New Energy Finance estimates that by 2040, EVs will make up to 40 percent of global new car registrations—tremendous growth!

Currently China makes up half of the global EV market, according to the International Energy Agency's *Global EV Outlook 2018*. In 2017, China sold 579,000 EVs, a 72 percent increase compared to 2016. Meanwhile, the global stock of electric passenger cars exceeded 3 million last year.

But compared to the bigger picture, that's merely a drop of water in the ocean, since according to BMI Research, the global car fleet can be estimated at around 1.2 billion cars. And global sales of passenger cars are forecast to exceed 81 million vehicles in 2018. Along with China, the United States is among the largest automobile markets worldwide, in terms of both production and sales.

Therefore, it is all about the future as automakers start to expand their business into the electric mobility sector. Bloomberg New Energy Finance (BNEF) estimates that by 2040, global EV penetration of new car registration could reach 35 to 40 percent.

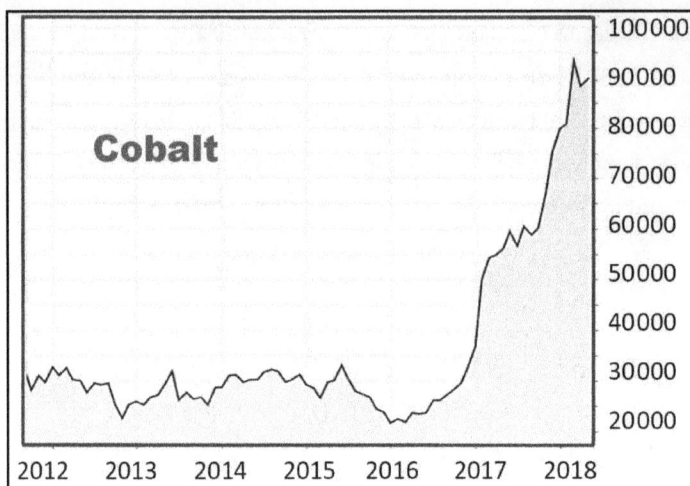

Figure 41. Cobalt prices, 2012–2018. Data: Bloomberg, 2019.

For commodity markets, this might signal the beginning of an avalanche, as electric cars demand additional raw materials. For example, studies done by the investment bank UBS and BNEF suggest that by 2040 there will be a significant surplus demand for graphite, nickel, aluminum, copper, lithium, cobalt, and manganese. Other commodities, like crude oil, steel, as well as platinum and palladium, would be negatively affected.

> For commodity markets, the mega trend
> of electrification could turn out to be an
> enormous new source of demand.

Prices for cobalt and lithium, which are both essential for different types of batteries, are experiencing a bull market. Lithium-based batteries first had commercial applications a couple of years ago. Now we have them in almost all mobile devices: laptops, smartphones, electric tools, and cars. Gigafactories have been ramped up in the United States and China, and battery prices are falling because of economics of scale and scope. That, in turn, triggers new applications.

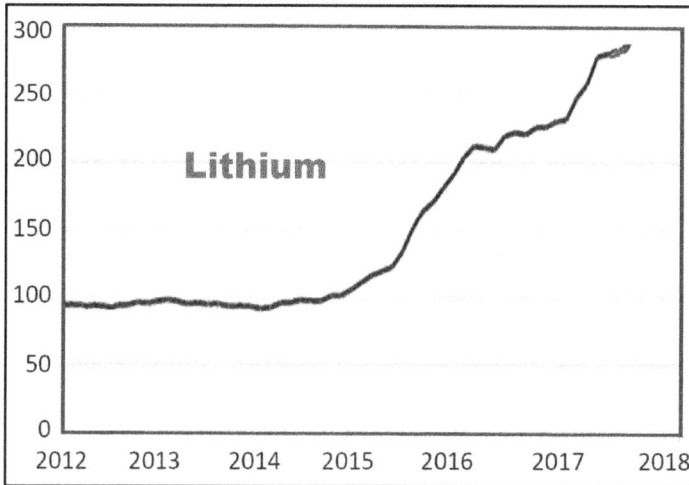

Figure 42. Benchmark Lithium Index, 2012–2018. Data: Benchmark Mineral Intelligence, 2019.

Tesla might lose its leadership in electric cars, but Elon Musk kicked off a revolution in electrification and energy usage—a revolution that works to the good of humanity and, as a side benefit, will be good for commodity markets as well.

The electrification of the automobile industry is a gigantic step, but only the tip of an iceberg. The ability to store energy is the missing link in growing alternative (wind, solar, and water) energy production. By 2025, power banks and power walls—instruments for decentralized energy storage at home, for example—might exceed sales for lithium-based batteries for the car industry. And this market is much bigger and promises much higher growth!

Key Takeaways

- There is a bull market for battery metals like lithium and cobalt, as battery-producing facilities shoot up like mushrooms. Prices for cobalt quadrupled from 25,000 to 100,000 USD per ton in 2017.

- Elon Musk and Tesla are at the forefront of a mega trend in electrification. Although sales of electric vehicles today are minuscule, industry estimates peg them at 40 percent of global new car registrations by 2040. We might be witnessing the beginning of a revolution.

- E-mobility is the first step, but energy storage is the missing link to alternative energy production by wind, sun, and water.

- Together, e-mobility and energy storage might prove to be the "new China" for commodity markets in the long term, since demand is climbing not only for lithium and cobalt, but also for traditional metals like copper and nickel.

42

Crypto Craze: Bitcoins and the Emergence of Cryptocurrencies

2018

Bitcoins, the first modern cryptocurrency, emerged in 2009, described in a white paper the previous year by the pseudonymous Satoshi Nakamoto. The value of bitcoins explodes in 2017 from below 1,000 to above 20,000 USD, attracting worldwide attention. This stellar price rise, followed by a crash of almost 80 percent in 2018, makes bitcoins the biggest financial bubble in history, dwarfing even the Dutch tulip mania of the 17th century. Today, in 2021, bitcoins are about to take a run-up to 100,000 USD. Despite the boom and bust, the future looks bright, as underlying blockchain technology reveals its potential and starts to revolutionize daily life.

> *"[Bitcoin/Blockchain] is the next major IT revolution that is about to happen."*
> —Steve "Woz" Wozniak, co-founder of Apple

> *"With all of the calls of 'bubble,' it's worth remembering that we're in the early stages of global adoption as well as the early stages of development of the technology."*
> —Ari Paul, *Forbes*

The punch came fast. Before boarding a flight to leave the country on April 1, 2018, Robert Farkas, co-founder of Centra Tech, was arrested by local criminal authorities in the United States. Half a year earlier, in September 2017, celebrity boxer Floyd Mayweather had posted happy pictures of himself living la dolce vita, spending money in expensive shops in Beverly Hills with his cryptocurrency-based Centra card.

Farkas and his Centra Tech co-founder Sohrab "Sam" Sharma had claimed to offer a debit card, backed by Visa and Mastercard, that would allow people to convert cryptocurrency to US dollars to spend on everyday goods. The Securities and Exchange Commission alleged that Centra had no relationship with either card company. Sharma and Farkas had created fake biographies of fictional executives and paid celebrities to tout the upcoming initial coin offering (ICO)—an unregulated process by which a company can issue a new digital coin in exchange for real money—and the promise of quick riches on social media. Sharma and Farkas had swindled about 32 million USD from investors.

Centra Tech is just one example of multiple scams and frauds in the crypto and ICO market in 2018, but it was dwarfed by other ICO scams like Modern Tech, which had made off with more than 660 million USD.

It is still pioneer days in the technology sector, where ICOs are more popular and better known than companies' traditional initial public offerings (IPOs). ICOs have quickly become a more important source of project funding than endless discussions with venture capital companies. There's a dark side, however. The opportunities of a fast-developing market always attract fraud and black sheep. That is part of the game.

The bitcoin was born in 2009. Today, more than 10,000 alternative coins exist.

December 2018 is still the Wild West in an industry that just entered its teenage years. Bitcoins (BTC), described in a white paper in November 2008 and first released as open-source software in January 2009 by the pseudonymous Satoshi Nakamoto, are generally considered the first decentralized cryptocurrency. It was originally created as an alternative, decentralized payment method. Since then, more than 10,000 alternative coin variants have been created. Like Napster 10 years earlier, the system works without a central bank, as a peer-to-peer network in which transactions take place directly between users, without an intermediary. Blockchain is the technology behind cryptocurrencies, and it is fast becoming a platform for a vast number of innovations in peer-to-peer transactions.

A blockchain is a cryptographically protected distributed ledger. It's what protects you or anyone else from making a copy of that bitcoin you just bought. In fact, anything that you can make a mental list of, you can manage with blockchains—everything from tracking land and real estate ownership to the way we distribute medicine and how we grant certificates and diplomas. Some of these ideas are brilliant, while others are ridiculous.

Digital Assets, Cryptocurrencies, and Tokens

A digital asset is anything that exists in a binary format and comes with the right to use it, while the term "cryptocurrency" refers to coins that fulfill the characteristics of standard paper-based money (fiat money). The characteristics are its function as a store of value, a unit of account, and fungibility. Examples include bitcoin, ethereum's ether, and ripple's XRP. Note that ethereum and ripple refer to the underlying blockchain and not to their cryptocurrencies. Crypto tokens are similar to cryptocurrencies in that they are built on blockchains.

Cryptocurrencies are the most common form of tokens, but crypto tokens are broader representations of a blockchain's value. That value is manifested across a diverse range—from cryptocurrencies to loyalty

continued

points and even to assets built on the blockchain.

Ethereum, for example, is the underlying blockchain for several tokens that use its platform to develop services and products. The difference between cryptocurrencies and crypto tokens becomes important within the context of investment. For example, cryptocurrency valuation is derived from a coin's success in adhering to the characteristics of money. On the other hand, crypto token valuations depend on a different set of factors, such as protocol adoption and robustness.

Originally, cryptocurrencies were designed to offer a decentralized alternative to traditional fiat currencies. Even at peak valuation in April 2021, bitcoins—plus the sum of all other cryptocurrencies a decade after their invention—represented just a fraction of physical money in US dollars, euros, pound sterling, or yen in terms of value. In volume, bitcoins are still by far the biggest cryptocurrency, followed by ether, ripple, and dash. In 2021, the 500 biggest coins had a combined market capitalization of 2 trillion USD, of which bitcoins made up 50 percent. Physical US dollar notes in circulation are valued at 1.5 trillion USD, and that is only a minor fraction of the total US dollar supply. Next in line is physical gold, whose circulating value is estimated at 8 trillion USD, before taking the whole currency market into consideration. All fiat currencies together add up to a value of 83 trillion USD, which includes all physical money in circulation and electronic, that is, virtual money.

Another important factor is the concentration of holdings. About 40 percent of bitcoins are held by perhaps 1,000 users. The top 100 bitcoin addresses control 17.3 percent of all the issued currency, according to Alex Sunnarborg, co-founder of the crypto hedge fund Tetras Capital. That's important, since the cryptocurrency was designed to reach a maximum of 21 million bitcoins. Bitcoins are added by "mining," a process by which transactions are verified and added to the public ledger. Currently, one bitcoin is added approximately every 10 minutes. With ether, the top 100 addresses control 40 percent of the supply, and with smaller currencies top coin holders control more than 90 percent because many of them are members of the teams running these projects.

Bitcoins were first explained to the public as a form of digital money, and that is how its successors and competitors like litecoin and ether have been framed as well. Each of these currencies resembles traditional money in certain ways: They

> **Bitcoins are more than digital money.**

are abstractions of economic value and can be traded. But none of them offers the most basic role of a currency as a relatively stable medium of exchange. There is too much friction involved. Each transaction takes too long, uses too much energy, and involves too many risks.

The biggest problems with bitcoins have emerged because the mechanics of buying and holding them are so inscrutable that nearly everyone pays third parties to handle them. Those wallet-service middlemen become points of failure for the whole system. They get hacked, their systems go down, and they are ordered by governments and regulators to report transactions that users thought would be anonymous.

The Mt. Gox Heist

Launched in 2010 by Jed McCaleb, who later founded ripple, Mt. Gox, by 2013, had become the largest bitcoin exchange in the world. Based in Shibuya, an area in Tokyo, Japan, at that point Mt. Gox was handling more than 70 percent of all bitcoin transactions worldwide. In June 2011, when Mt. Gox was acquired by Mark Karpelès, the company was hacked the first time, and 2,000 bitcoins were stolen.

continued

As a consequence, a number of security measures were initiated, including arranging for a substantial number of bitcoins to be taken offline and held in cold storage. As a result of an investigation by the US Department of Homeland Security regarding the company's license, the US government seized more than 5 million USD from Mt. Gox, and the company had to announce a temporary suspension of US dollar withdrawals. But that was not the biggest problem. As it turned out, the company had been the victim of an ongoing hack for more than two years.

In February 2014, Mt. Gox suspended trading, closed its website and exchange service, filed for bankruptcy protection in Japan and the United States, and began liquidation proceedings soon after. The crypto exchange announced that approximately 850,000 bitcoins belonging to customers and the company were missing (valued today at 4.2 billion USD). Although 200,000 bitcoins were eventually recovered, the remaining 650,000 have never been found.

CEO Mark Karpelès was arrested in August 2015 in Japan and charged with fraud and embezzlement and manipulating the Mt. Gox computer system to increase the balance in an account. US authorities followed the trail of money, and in July 2017 Alexander Vinnik was arrested in Greece and charged with playing a key role in the laundering of bitcoins stolen from Mt. Gox. Vinnik is alleged to be associated with BTC-e, an established bitcoin exchange, which was raided by the FBI as part of the investigation. The BTC-e site has been shut down, and the domain has been seized by the FBI. But no money has been found so far.

What is a fair price for a bitcoin? Is it 1 or 100,000 USD? Some financial analysts today emphasize that bitcoins have no intrinsic value at all, and some economists refer to the Fisher equation, which pins the current value of a bitcoin to 20 to 25 USD in regard to the total available number of bitcoins, transaction speed, and trading volume. But it's important to note that for this equation it is not the status quo but the future potential of the technology and application that is relevant for a bitcoin's value. And it is hard to see limits to the application of blockchain technology.

In May 2010 Laszlo Hanyecz bought two pizzas in Jacksonville, Florida, for 10,000 BTC. It was the first real-world bitcoin transaction.

Bitcoins became a hot topic in 2017 in the financial mainstream because of tremendous price fluctuations. Let's take a step back: Prices initially were measured in US cents and single-digit US dollars in the land of Dungeons and Dragons or World of Warcraft. But on May 22, 2010, Laszlo Hanyecz made the first real-world bitcoin transaction by buying two pizzas in Jacksonville, Florida, for 10,000 BTC, valuing one bitcoin at 0.003 USD. One year later, in spring 2011, bitcoins were traded at parity with US dollars. And six years after that, on December 17, 2017, bitcoins surpassed 20,000 USD for the first time.

Bitcoins traded at 0.03 USD in May 2010 and above 20,000 USD in December 2017.

That same month, in December 2017, the Chicago Mercantile Exchange (CME) introduced and listed futures contracts on bitcoins in the commodity segment, allowing a hot speculative bubble to unfold. Bitcoins became commoditized and open to new investors and the mainstream, beyond the niche of electronic wallets. Until then, bitcoin and other cryptocurrency trading had been limited to specialized exchanges like Bitfinex, Kraken, or OKCoin, where you had to exchange US dollars or euros into bitcoins with your electronic wallet, though bitcoins were exchangeable into any other cryptocurrency. From its high in December, bitcoins crashed to below 6,000 USD within two weeks.

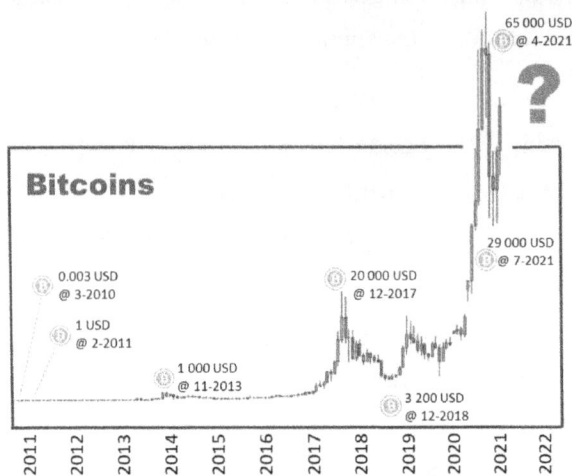

Figure 43. Price of bitcoins surpassed 1,000, 5,000, 10,000, and finally 20,000 USD in 2017. Data: Bloomberg, 2021.

In December 2018, bitcoins tumbled below 3,500 USD to a 13-month low before stabilizing. The slide fueled a sell-off among rival tokens ether, litecoin, and XRP. After months of stability at around 6,000 to 6,500 USD, bitcoins and other cryptocurrencies had lost more than 700 billion USD in market capitalization since their peak in December 2017.

Regulatory concerns played a role, as the US Securities and Exchange Commission announced penalties against two companies that hadn't registered their initial coin offerings as securities. Also, the US Justice Department was in the process of investigating whether the previous year's rally was fueled by market manipulation.

As Robert Shiller noted in his book *Irrational Exuberance*, it is impossible to spot a bubble and time its burst if you are part of it. That is possible only in hindsight. But after the stellar rise from less than 1 USD before 2011 and the crash by almost 80 percent from its December 2017 peak, the verdict is official: The bitcoin craze is the biggest financial bubble in history! It even dwarfs the tulip mania of the 17th century, which had previously exceeded every historic financial market bubble, including the Mississippi or South Sea Bubble, the run-up in equity prices before the busts of the Great Depression and Black Friday, or—more recently— the dot-com bubble and the rally before the world financial crisis hit in 2008.

It may comfort investors that an 80 percent crash is not a unique event in the crypto space. In the past five years, the value of bitcoins was cut in half three times, and crashed by more than 25 percent 16 times, only to rise to new highs until 2018. Think back . . . how many years did it take to recover your losses from the dot-com bubble? Measured by the NASDAQ Composite, on average that took about 15 years! In the past, recoveries in the crypto universe have been much faster.

> The year 2013 was a rough ride for bitcoins.
> And the Mt. Gox heist almost became an
> extinction event for the cryptocurrency.

In percentage terms, the bitcoin crashes of 2013 were almost as bloody as 2018. Prices ran up from a couple of US dollars to more than 1,200 USD, before plummeting. In April 2013, bitcoin prices fell from 230 to 67 USD overnight, a massive 70 percent drop in 12 hours. It took seven months to recover. After April, bitcoin prices hovered around 100 to 120 USD until later in the year, when prices suddenly skyrocketed to 1,200 USD in late November. However, in December the price tumbled back to less than half of that.

Adding to the long road of recovery after the collapse in December 2013 was the Mt. Gox scandal. Bitcoins steadily increased in price through January and February, when they suddenly dropped by nearly 50 percent from 880 to below 500 USD because of the Mt. Gox heist.

Percent decline

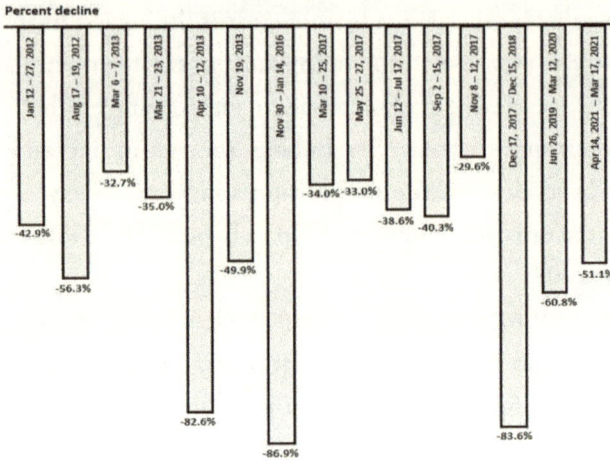

Figure 44. Historic bitcoin price corrections, 2013–2021. Data: Coindesk.com.

One of the results of the erratic price swings of 2013–2014 is the emergence of an active cryptocurrency trading scene with its own slang, a special language established by crypto enthusiasts. The term "HODL" is probably the best known. During a massive price crash in 2013, someone called "GameKyuubi," apparently drunk, posted "I AM HODLING" in a Bitcoin Talk forum. What the user in the post wanted to convey was the fact that despite the sharp drop in price, he was choosing to hold on to his bitcoins. The post went viral, and #HODL has been interpreted as "Hold On for Dear Life," which corresponds to "Buy & Hold," an investment strategy every long-term investor can relate to.

#HODL.
Hold On for
Dear Life.

Crypto slang today is very colorful, with a multitude of new terms and phrases whose meanings go way beyond their traditional definitions. There are words and abbreviations such as "mooning," "fudding," ADDY, JOMO, BTFD, and DYOR—the list goes on and on. HODL, however, is by far the most popular of these terms, and one that almost all cryptocurrency investors can identify with.

Anti-money-laundering measures and the Chinese ban on cryptocurrencies and ICOs weighed heavily on bitcoins in 2018.

How does one account for the extraordinary bitcoin rally and its bust? Originally, bitcoins were founded to redistribute value and move money away from banks and other financial institutions to people. Anyone could become a bank, a payment service, or a lender. But bitcoins and other cryptocurrencies also became a loophole for money laundering and capital flight. Because of the low level of legal regulation, the use of cryptocurrency spread into the shadow economy. The implementation of an automatic exchange of information in 2017 led to last-minute panic as a new global standard on the automatic exchange of information targeted tax evaders. The new system provides for the exchange of non-resident financial account information with the tax authorities in the account holders' country of residence. Data was exchanged for the first time in September 2017, but the majority of the 100-plus jurisdictions had implemented the system by January 1, 2018.

The Top 5 Crypto Billionaires

1. Chris Larsen (57), co-founder of ripple, owns 5.2 billion XRP, the token launched by ripple, whose current value is 8 billion USD.

2. Joseph Lubin (53), co-founder of ethereum, has an estimated wealth of 1–5 billion USD.

continued

3. Changpeng Zhao (41), founder and CEO of Binance, the world's largest cryptocurrency exchange, has an estimated wealth of 1–2 billion USD.

4. Cameron and Tyler Winklevoss (36) were early investors in bitcoins and the founders of Gemini in 2015. Their estimated wealth is 0.9–1.1 billion USD.

5. Matthew Mellon (45), an early investor in ripple's XRP, has an estimated wealth of 0.9–1 billion USD.

Source: *Business Insider*, 2018.

Capital flight has also worried the government of China. By buying bitcoins, the Chinese have been able to move funds abroad. In September 2017, renminbi-to-bitcoin trades made up more than 90 percent of all bitcoin transactions. The government outlawed fiat money from being used in cryptocurrency purchases and even imposed travel bans on Huobi and OKCoin executives, two of the nation's largest crypto exchanges. Chinese regulatory authorities also imposed a ban on ICOs and finally termed them illegal in China in September 2017. Huobi was forced to move its operations to Singapore, while OKCoin, renamed OKEx, was embraced by Malta. Many Chinese simply transferred their bitcoins to the now-offshore exchanges and carried on trading—until February 2018.

That February, the People's Bank of China (PBOC), which is the central regulatory authority, issued a statement that "it will block access to all domestic and foreign cryptocurrency exchanges and ICO websites," basically shutting down all cryptocurrency activities in the country. And the authorities were not bluffing: In April 2018, police stormed a large-scale bitcoin mining operation in the city of Tianjin and confiscated 600 computers in the raid

For bitcoins and blockchains, 2018 was like 1992 for the internet—early days. To reveal the cryptocurrency's full potential, another 10 years are needed.

The Chinese government has been successful in imposing stricter capital controls, banning bitcoin trading and ICOs, and shielding its people from bad influences by its Great Firewall. But China will not be able to turn back time for blockchain technology and its applications.

The blockchains and cryptocurrencies will achieve their full potential in a decade, said Steve Wozniak, co-founder of Apple, in 2018, and according to Jack Dorsey, CEO of Twitter, bitcoins will become the world's "single currency." Previously, from 2014 to 2017, Jamie Dimon, CEO of JPMorgan Chase, was regularly quoted about his views of bitcoins: "Bitcoin is a fraud," he said, as well as "Bitcoin will not survive," and "Bitcoin is going nowhere." In 2018, Jamie Dimon regretted that he had called bitcoin a fraud but still remained bearish. Meanwhile, earlier in that year, overwhelmed by client demand, JPMorgan Chase's top rival, Goldman Sachs, announced the setup of a cryptocurrency trading desk.

As for a distributed ledger technology like blockchain, its situation today is like that of the internet in 1992, with immense potential but a steep and messy learning curve. Every successful new technology undergoes an explosion of growth in which we try to use it for everything, until time reveals what the best applications and limitations are. Investing in dot-com stocks in the late 1990s was a roller-coaster ride, and many of the pioneers in that field ultimately failed. The real impact of the internet has taken decades to unfold, but the future of e-commerce and society has been changed forever.

In September 2021, bitcoins became legal tender in El Salvador. The boom and bust of 2017–18 was followed by a crypto winter, which lasted until the summer of 2019. From there, bitcoins took off and traded above 60,000 USD in the spring of 2021.

Blockchain technology has the potential to be just as impactful as the invention of the internet over time. Just as with the dot-com bubble, backing any single player in the crypto craze is like placing a bet on 27 red in a game of roulette. It is too early and the outcomes are too uncertain to identify potential winners. However, with the digital revolution we are experiencing right now, after the coronavirus pandemic, the economic landscape will be transformed in drastic ways. And, despite its sins of adolescence and the irrational exuberance of crypto trading's early years, crypto tokens and blockchain technology have already begun to revolutionize our world. The applications in real estate, property, banking and financial services, and health care, just to name a few, are limitless and can only be compared with the development of the internet or the rise of smartphone applications. It might be that we are witnessing the first glimpse of a tokenized and coin-based economy. The future looks bright.

Key Takeaways

- Bitcoins were introduced in 2009 as an alternative, decentralized payment method using blockchain technology. Today more than 10,000 alternative coins ("altcoins") exist.

- Over 10 years the price of bitcoins rose from 0.003 USD in 2010 to 1 USD in 2011, to more than 1,000 USD in 2017. It exceeded 20,000 USD in December 2017, but within weeks, bitcoins dropped by almost 80 percent to below 3,500 USD in December 2018.

- This tremendous boom and bust has made bitcoins the biggest financial bubble in history, greater even than the Dutch tulip mania of 1637.

- The boom and bust of 2017–2018 has been associated with the Chinese ban on cryptocurrencies and ICOs, as well as anti-money-laundering measures like the implementation of automatic exchange of financial information in more than 100 countries. The beginnings of new disruptive technologies often attract black sheep and fraud, and many of the ICOs did turn out to be scams.

- In 2021, bitcoins exceeded their boom and busts level of 2017–18, trading above 60,000 USD in the spring and targetting 100,000 USD.

- For bitcoins and blockchain applications, it is still early days. To reveal their true potential, another decade is needed. But from today's perspective, the applications seem limitless.

Outlook:
The Dawn of a New Cycle
and a New Era

We are at the dawn of the 2020s and the commodity and crypto markets are in the starting blocks for a new rally. At the beginning of 2016, commodity investors looked back on five painful bear market years. In 2015, the Bloomberg Commodity Index, which measures the performance of 22 commodities like crude oil, gold, copper, wheat, and corn, lost 25 percent of value. And it got worse: In January 2016, commodity markets traded down an additional 7 percent. The Bloomberg Commodity Index was trading at its lowest level since its inception in 1991. Since spring 2014, investors had lost almost half of their invested funds. Investors in gold and silver mining companies, in particular, were hit hardest. The Arca Gold BUGS Index and Philadelphia Gold and Silver Index, both representing the biggest gold and silver mines, traded down to levels last reached at the beginning of 2000, when a troy ounce of gold was 260 USD.

From summer 2011 to the beginning of 2016, investors saw 80 percent of their principal vanish into thin air, while gold in the same period traded down from above 1,900 USD to 1,050 USD (–45 percent). Mining in general suffered greatly. Market capitalization of companies included in the MSCI World Metals & Mining Index dropped by more than 80 percent since their peak valuation during the commodity super cycle in 2008. Shares of Glencore, the biggest mining and commodity trading company in the world, traded down to 67 GBP at the end of September 2015. From its highest prices in 2011, investors lost more than 80 percent of their capital. Compared to its closing price of 527 GBP for its initial public offering in May 2011, this represented a loss of shareholder value of almost 90 percent!

Market exaggerations drove credit default swaps for mining companies into the stratosphere. For example, Glencore's 2.5 percent yielding bond, maturing in 2019, dropped by 25 percent within three months to 75 US cents per dollar, offering a yield to maturity of more than 17 percent per year for investors. The same held true, for example, for bonds of Freeport-McMoRan, Teck Resources, First Quantum, or Lundin Mining, all large cap mining companies. Investors anticipated the bankruptcy of a whole industry.

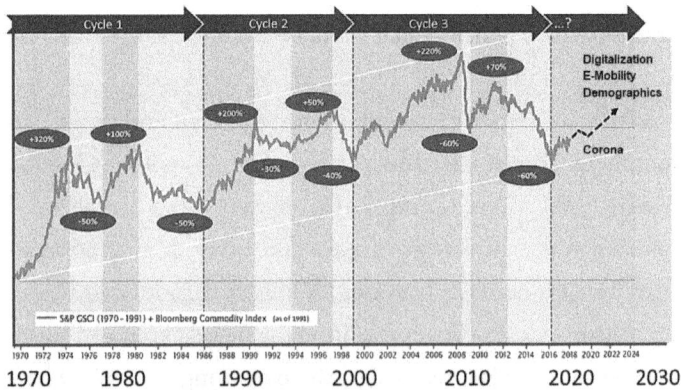

Figure 45. 50 years of commodity markets ups and downs. Did we see the beginning of a new bullish cycle in 2016? Data: Bloomberg, 2021.

In retrospect, we witnessed capitulation levels at the beginning of the year 2016. However, bold investors were able to make a killing in commodities during an early recovery. Compared to January 2016, gold mines tripled in value in just half of a year while gold gained 30 percent. Shares of Glencore approached 300 GBP, quadrupling in value compared to its lows just a couple of months before.

While commodity markets crumbled and value in mining evaporated, world equity and bond markets celebrated the time of their life. MSCI

World increased steadily after its drop by almost 60 percent during the financial crisis of 2008–2009. In the United States, the Dow Jones and S&P 500 were both trading at all-time highs in late 2016 and continued their path of success until January 2018. At the same time, yields of 10-year bonds in the United States fell below 1.5 percent, while in Europe, German 10-year bonds dropped into negative territory. Bond investors woke up every day believing their party would never stop.

Looking at the long-term relationship between equities and commodities by taking the ratio of S&P Goldman Sachs Commodity Index versus the S&P 500, one fact is striking: Relative valuation is extreme. Compared to equities, commodities have been stuck in the penalty box since the China-fueled commodity super cycle burst. Similar to the tech bubble 15 years ago, Alphabet (Google) today is valued equal to the aggregated market capitalization of all companies included in MSCI World Metals & Mining Index (more than 180 companies, including mining giants like BHP Group, Rio Tinto, Glencore, Vale, Barrick Gold, and Newmont Mining)! One has to ask: What is cheap, and what is expensive?

Figure 46. Relative valuation of commodities versus equities. Buy commodities!
Data: Bloomberg, 2021.

Therefore, it is no surprise that after a severe five-year bear market, a 15 percent rise in commodity markets in 2016 passed the majority of investors unnoticed. From their intra-year lows, commodity market indices like the Bloomberg Commodity Index (BCOM), S&P Goldman Sachs Commodity Index (S&P GSCI), and Rogers International Commodity Index (RICI) all gained more than 25 percent and surpassed equity-index performance. Furthermore, metals and mining as well as oil and gas led the equity-index sector performance in the United States and Europe, but fund manager surveys show that investors continued to be massively underweighted in resources equities.

Recent history aside, investors can refer to several commodity markets that are still in oversupply. But in terms of supply-demand imbalances following the boom of the commodity super cycle, the worst is behind us. Slashes of industry investments in mining, as well as in oil and gas, will have brutal results in 2020–2030, when natural depletion will combine with and outweigh reduced exploration and development expenditures. With fundamental market data for commodities just starting to improve, commodity prices reached a technical bottom. A shift of the 200-day moving average to the upside in April 2016 was a first positive sign for a bullish market environment in commodities in the future.

In conclusion, 2016 might prove to have been the dawn of a new cycle for commodity investors, a multiyear period of rising prices, which was only put on hold by the outbreak of the conronavirus and the pandemic in 2020. In the coming years, new trends like battery metals for electrification, e-mobility, and the megatrend of digitalization, which includes cryptocurrencies, will become an important and enormous driver for productivity, growth, and commodity markets. Electric vehicles might not need gasoline or diesel, but demand for gold, copper, nickel, cobalt, lithium, and rare earths increases drastically. If this scenario holds true, we witnessed the beginning of a new cycle which can only be compared to the awakening of the Chinese economy almost 20 years ago. It is also the beginning of a more mature stage in blockchain and bitcoins, as the exuberance of the early years is gone and opens the path to future applications.

Epilogue

Let us take a short time trip back to the year 2001. The average price for a barrel of crude oil was 26 USD. In the course of the year, the price of a ton of copper dropped from 1,800 to below 1,400 USD. Gold traded between 255 and 293 USD per troy ounce and made its first serious attempt in modern times to jump above 300 USD.

Prices for wheat and corn averaged 2.70 and 2.08 USD per bushel. The terror attacks of 9/11 on the World Trade Center and the Pentagon, which killed about 3,000 people, were the most traumatizing events in 2001. Although the head of Al-Qaeda, Osama bin Laden, was shot in an elite U.S military mission in 2011, the war against global terrorism still has not been won today, almost 20 years later. But at least a military victory against the Islamic State seems imminent. In the White House, Democrat Bill Clinton was replaced by Republican George W. Bush; 15 years later Republican Donald Trump took over the presidency from charismatic Democrat Barack Obama. Cynical observers note that 9/11 has been replaced by 11/9, the date Donald Trump's election was announced.

In 2001, commodities as a professionally recognized and investable asset class were still in their infancy. The Bloomberg Commodity Index, as a measure of commodity market performance, had been launched just a few years earlier, in 1998, as the Dow Jones AIG Commodity Index. Alternative investments in addition to traditional investments in equities and bonds have since become more fashionable, thanks to the investment strategies of endowment funds such as those at Yale and Harvard Universities. In 2005, Gary Gorton and K. Geert Rouwenhorst published "Facts and Fantasies about Commodity Futures," which also helped anchor commodities as an integral part of a global asset allocation.

At the end of 2001, China entered the World Trade Organization (WTO), an event that marked the beginning of rapid growth of the Chinese economy and caused massive turbulence for global commodity markets. Within a few years, China had evolved as a dominant factor in global commodity demand, and the commodity super cycle was born.

Crude oil reached 147 USD per barrel, copper traded above 10,000 USD per ton, gold surpassed 1,900 USD per troy ounce, and wheat and corn shot up to 9.50 and 8.40 USD per bushel. But depression followed euphoria in the form of years of sluggish growth in the aftermath of the global financial and economic crisis. The year 2008 was an annus horribilis for global capital markets, as equity and commodity markets dropped by more than 50 percent. A period of deleveraging and sluggish growth followed a nonsustainable recovery. Thereafter, commodity markets faced five years of a severe bear market.

Today, approaching 2022, we are witnessing the beginning of a new commodity bull market and a maturing of the market for cryptocurrencies. The exuberance of the commodity super cycle is gone, invested assets are rising again for the first time in years, and commodity market performance is up ahead of equities. The price of a barrel of oil turned negative during the coronavirus crisis of 2020 but has since recovered to 80 USD. Copper traded in excess of 10,000 USD per ton again. Gold rose above 2,100 USD per troy ounce. In the agricultural sector, wheat and corn prices averaged 7 and 5 USD per bushel. From a technical perspective, bottom building was completed in 2016, as commodities went above their 200-day moving average and created a bullish chart pattern in 2017. A global pandemic paused this bullish pattern only temporarily, as supply shortfalls caused by supply chain disruptions and a pickup in growth spurned commodity demand.

In hindsight, 2016 proved to be the turning point for commodities, as the crypto winter of 2018-19 cleared for a new market cycle.

The 42 chapters of this book show, on the one hand, that commodity market speculation was not invented in this decade. On the contrary, in the 1980s and 1990s commodities had only disappeared from investors' radar screens, while the 1970s also saw tremendous commodity price spikes. Many of the episodes described here—from the Dutch tulip mania in the 17th century to the fantastic rise and fall of bitcoins in the 21st century—show how dramatically temporary imbalances on the supply or demand side can affect individual commodity markets. The real economic consequences should not be underestimated, as unlike stocks, bonds, or currencies, commodities are real assets. Political unrest and failing governments because of high food prices in Africa, which led to the Arab Spring, or current instabilities in Venezuela and Brazil due to low oil prices, are only two examples.

Tulips and bitcoins are linked as the two biggest financial bubbles in history, despite nearly 400 years between them. Meanwhile markets and events have given rise to 40 fantastic stories from the commodity world. The wheel of time continues to turn, and due to the cyclical nature of commodity markets, extreme events are doomed to repeat themselves, albeit in a modified form. Each market is determined in its extreme phase by greed and fear; and the short memory of capital markets is proverbial anyway.

The episodes summarized in this book are meant to highlight the booms and busts of commodity and crypto markets. Besides extreme price fluctuations, this book aims to show an insider's perspective on speculation, gains, and losses that determine individual fates. The extent and velocity of price spikes are stunning, even for long-term investors. Linking commodity market events over several hundred years demonstrates the parallels among events in the past and prepares us for future developments including blockchain and bitcoins.

Acknowledgments

This book is based on my personal experience in commodity and crypto markets throughout my professional career, from 2003 to the present.

From my time at Deutsche Bank, I thank Klaus Martini for leadership, motivation, and for bringing the story of Bre-X to my attention. Jochen, I thank you not only for your foreword but also for sharing the same passion for commodity markets (and for Italian wine). Thomas, lucky coincidence to meet in Munich: you connected the dots of precious metals and cryptos.

Of all the people who supported me with ideas and endorsements, I would like to thank Sasha in particular for his input on crude oil and the implications of the 1970s crisis for Soviet Russia. Valery, I thank you for bringing up new aspects on blockchains and bitcoins.

I thank my beloved wife, Alina, for all your love and support. And I will always remember your wedding vow to read all my books, even the German ones.

I thank my mother and dedicate this book to her with love and eternal appreciation. Without you, all of this wouldn't have been possible.

I thank Cristina Chiarasini, my literary agent in Paris, for making *From Tulips to Bitcoins* an international entry, especially in China and Korea.

I thank Leylanis Gamboa for a wonderful Spanish translation, Nunez for your commodity expertise and your preface, and Profit Editorial in Barcelona for a surprise on Saint Jordi's Day.

In Germany, I thank Christian Jund, Georg Hodolitsch, and Desiree Goldstein of FBV—FinanzBuch Verlag.

In Russia and Ukraine, I thank Alex Orlovych, Alex Sleptssov, and Andrew Yankovets for translation and publishing.

Finally, I would like to thank the team at Greenleaf Book Group in Texas for their help and support in the USA. In particular, Daniel, for transporting good news to Lago Maggiore, Italy. Jen, for flexibility in project management and schedules. Lindsey, for getting it all right; Marianne, for polishing; and Chase, for layout brainstorming! And Joan, my editor in Santa Barbara, for her sunny mood and fresh ideas.

We make sure that yo

The world finance system is facing massive uncertainty and risk making it imperative that one has wide-ranging knowledge about alternative investment opportunities. Ensure your financial future by taking control.

Diversification is the means to survive the current and future market difficulties with a specific focus on value investing such as quality stocks, precious metals and resources in general.

We, the Swiss Resource Capital, assist you and deliver clear and concise information pertaining to the precious metals and the resource sector as well as selected mining companies.

Through our new developed multimedia channels like the exclusive Resource-TV, you have access anytime and anywhere in the world to comprehensive data and information.

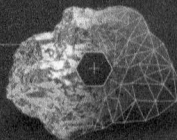

Glossary of Terms

Addy	Short version of "address," usually meaning your public key or the address of your crypto wallet. A bitcoin address is used to send and receive bitcoin transactions. The address is made up of a sequence of letters and numbers but can also be represented as a QR code.
Agflation	A period of rising food prices caused by increased demand for agricultural commodities, as was seen for both food and biofuels in 2007–2008. The word is a combination of the terms "agriculture" and "inflation."
Altcoin	Altcoins or coins are alternative cryptocurrencies launched after bitcoins. Today there are more than 4,000 altcoins, which differ from bitcoins in various ways. An example of an altcoin is litecoin.
Backwardation and Contango	In finance, the difference between a spot (or cash) price and future prices defines the term structure. Backwardation occurs when the price for future delivery is lower than the spot price (e.g., the price of crude oil delivered in 3 months is 60 USD/barrel and the spot price is 70 USD/barrel). Contango occurs when the price for future delivery is higher than the spot price (e.g., the price of gold delivered in 1 year is 1,400 USD/oz and the spot price is 1,300 USD/oz). Contango is common for financial futures and gold, whereas backwardation is often seen in commodity markets and implies a positive carry for investors.

Blockchain	A blockchain is a growing list of records, called blocks, that are linked using cryptography. Blockchain is a form of Distributed Ledger Technology (DLT), which is a consensus of replicated, shared, and synchronized digital data geographically spread across multiple sites, countries, or institutions. There is no central administrator or centralized data storage.
Bull and Bear Market	In finance, the terms bull and bear market describe the general direction of a market. The use of "bull" and "bear" derives from the way the animals attack their opponents. A bull thrusts its horns up into the air, while a bear swipes its paws downward. These actions are metaphors for the movement of a market. If the trend is up, it's a bull market. If the trend is down, it's a bear market. A bear market usually is defined when prices drop to 20 percent or more below their recent top, while a smaller price decline is considered to be a correction.
BTC	Bitcoin (BTC, or ₿). A cryptocurrency, a form of electronic money, 1 bitcoin is divided into 1,000 millibitcoins and 100,000,000 satoshis. A bitcoin is currently worth about 4,000 USD.
BTFD	An abbreviation for "Buy The Fucking Dip," a stock market term to buy stocks or other assets during a price correction.
Cornering a Market	In finance, cornering a market consists of obtaining sufficient control of an asset—for example, a stock, currency, or commodity—in an attempt to manipulate the market price. Control usually means to have a dominant share in ownership.

(Market) Crash	A crash in stocks, commodities, or cryptocurrencies is a sudden dramatic decline of prices across a significant cross-section of the market, resulting in a significant loss of paper wealth. Crashes are driven by panic as much as by underlying economic factors. They often follow speculative stock market bubbles.
Cryptocurrency	A cryptocurrency is a digital asset designed to work as a medium of exchange that uses a high level of cryptography to secure financial transactions, control the creation of additional units, and verify the transfer of assets. Cryptocurrencies are an alternative and digital currency, which use decentralized control as opposed to the centralized digital currency and central banking systems of fiat currencies. The most popular cryptocurrency is bitcoin. The most common categorization of cryptocurrencies are alternative cryptocurrency coins (altcoins) and tokens (which are not meant to be a medium of exchange).
DYOR	An abbreviation for "Do Your Own Research." It is used often in internet forums and blogs as a reminder for readers to do their own research on a subject, rather than take everything they read at face value.

Fiat Currency	A "regular" or "normal" currency today, such as the US dollar, euro, or pound sterling. Fiat money is a currency without intrinsic value that has been established as money, often by government regulation, and is backed by the government. (The term *fiat* comes from the Latin for "let it be done.") This approach differs from money whose value is underpinned by some physical good such as gold or silver (the "gold standard") or economic value like some cryptocurrencies.
FOMO / JOMO	An abbreviation for "Fear of Missing Out." It is defined as a fear of regret, which may lead to a compulsive concern that one might miss an opportunity for social interaction, a novel experience, a profitable investment, or other satisfying events. FOMO perpetuates the fear of having made the wrong decision. JOMO, on the other hand, describes the "Joy of Missing Out," the antithesis of FOMO.
FUD	This describes the spreading of "Fear, Uncertainty, and Doubt," typically through the media. It's a disinformation strategy broadly used in politics, public relations, sales, marketing, and investing. Generally, FUD is a strategy to influence perception by disseminating negative or false information and a manifestation of the appeal to fear.
Gold and Silver	Gold (symbol AU, from the Latin *aurum*) and silver (symbol AG, from the Latin *argentum*) are precious metals that have been used for thousands of years as a measure of value. Since the sixth century BCE, gold and silver have been minted as coins. In the past, a gold or silver standard was often implemented as a base of monetary policy. Officially, the world gold standard was abandoned for a fiat currency system after 1971 (the "Nixon Shock").

Gold Standard	The gold standard is a monetary system where a country's currency or paper money has a value directly linked to gold. (Variations include the silver standard or bimetallic standard.) Most nations abandoned the gold standard as the basis of their monetary systems at some point, although many hold substantial gold reserves. After World War II, a system similar to a gold standard was established by the Bretton Woods Agreements. Under this system, many countries fixed their exchange rates relative to the US dollar, and central banks could exchange dollar holdings into gold at the official exchange rate of 35 USD per ounce. All currencies pegged to the US dollar thereby had a fixed value in terms of gold. In August 1971, President Nixon ended the convertibility of US dollars into gold, which marked the beginning of the fiat currency system of floating exchange rates.
HODL	An abbreviation for "Hold On for Dear Life." HODL was originally a typo, originated in a December 2013 post on the Bitcoin Forum during a price crash. It became very popular within the cryptocurrency community as encouragement for holding the cryptocurrency rather than selling it (buy and hold).
ICO	An Initial Coin Offering (ICO) is a type of funding using cryptocurrencies. In an ICO, a quantity of cryptocurrency is sold in the form of tokens to investors in exchange for legal tender or other cryptocurrencies such as bitcoins or ether. ICOs can be a source of capital for startup companies and can usually avoid regulatory compliance and intermediaries such as venture capitalists, banks, and stock exchanges.

Long and Short	In trading, an investor can take two types of positions: long and short. An investor can either buy an asset (going long), or sell it (going short). In a long (buy) position, the investor is hoping for the price to rise. In a short position, the investor hopes for and benefits from a drop in the price of the asset. Entering a short position is a bit more complicated than purchasing the asset.
Mooning	In the cryptocurrency world, mooning refers to an instant surge in pricing in a positive way. If someone says, "the bitcoin is mooning," it means the price of a bitcoin has surged instantly for a certain time.
Pump and Dump	This is a form of securities fraud that involves artificially inflating the price of an owned stock through false and misleading positive statements, in order to sell the cheaply purchased stock at a higher price. Once the operators of the scheme dump—that is, sell—their overvalued shares, the price falls and investors lose their money. False or misleading information can be spread by spam email, social media, internet forums, or blogs. The scheme is most common with small cap cryptocurrencies and very small exchange listed corporations, that is, microcaps.

Rare Earth Metals or Rare Earth Elements	A set of 17 elements, specifically 15 lanthanides as well as scandium and yttrium. These are: cerium, dysprosium, erbium, europium, gadolinium, holmium, lanthanum, lutetium, neodymium, praseodymium, promethium, samarium, scandium, terbium, thulium, ytterbium, and yttrium. A common distinction differentiates between light rare earth elements and heavy rare earth elements. Rare earth elements are used in many high-tech applications, like electric motors of hybrid vehicles, wind turbines, hard disc drives, portable electronics, microphones, and speakers.
Sats	Short for "satoshi," the smallest fraction of a bitcoin. There are 100,000,000 satoshis in a bitcoin. The term derives from the pseudonym of bitcoin inventor Satoshi Nakamoto. Currently, 10,000 sats are equivalent to 65 US cents.
Strong and Weak Hands	In finance, strong hands refer to well-financed investors or speculators, typically long-term holders who are unlikely to exit their position based on small market movements. Weak hands refer to the opposite.
Rogue Trader	A trader who makes unauthorized trades, often in the gray area between civil and criminal transgression. A rogue trader may be a legitimate employee of a company yet enter into transactions on behalf of his or her employer without permission.
Tokens	(Crypto) tokens are a digital representation of a particular asset or utility and a category of cryptocurrencies. Tokens can represent basically any asset that is fungible and tradeable, such as property or real estate, commodities, loyalty points, or even other cryptocurrencies.

USD	The US dollar (USD, or $) is the official currency of the United States of America and its territories. Dollar is also the name of more than 20 currencies, including those of Canada, Australia, and New Zealand. One US dollar is generally divided into 100 US cents.
Wallet	If you want to store bitcoins or any other cryptocurrency, you will need to have a digital wallet. A cryptocurrency wallet is a software program that stores private and public keys and interacts with various blockchains to enable users to send and receive digital currency and monitor their balance. There are various forms of wallets: online, offline, hardware, and paper, all with varying levels of security.
Whale	The term "whale" is frequently used to describe a very big player or a very big investor in the market. The ocean is a metaphor for the market, since one can then extend it to include big fish and small fish, sharks, waves as the market moves, and so forth.

List of Abbreviations

BMO	Bank of Montreal
BTC	Bitcoin
CAD	Canadian Dollar
CBOT	Chicago Board of Trade
CHF	Confoederatio Helvetica Franc, or for short, Swiss Franc
CME	Chicago Mercantile Exchange
ct.	Carat
DOE	Department of Energy
EUR	The euro is the official currency of 19 of 28 member states of the European Union (EU).
EVs	Electric Vehicle(s)
FAO	Food and Agricultural Organization
GBP	Pound Sterling (Great Britain Pound)
ICE	Intercontinental Exchange
IEA	International Energy Agency
kg	Kilogram
lb	Pound

LIFFE	London International Financial Futures Exchange
LME	London Metal Exchange
LNG	Liquefied Natural Gas
LTCM	Long-Term Capital Management
NOK	Norwegian Krona
NYMEX	New York Mercantile Exchange
MMBtu	Million British Thermal Units
OECD	Organisation for Economic Co-operation and Development
OPEC	Organization of the Petroleum Exporting Countries
oz	Troy Ounce
RBC	Royal Bank of Canada
USD	US Dollar
USDA	US Department of Agriculture
WTI	West Texas Intermediate (crude oil)

List of Figures

References

1. **Tulip Mania: The Biggest Bubble in History (1637)**

   Dash, M. *Tulpenwahn. Die verrückteste Spekulation der Geschichte.* München: Claasen Verlag, 1999.

   Friedmann, J. "Tulpen-Wahn in Holland—Wie die große Gartenhure Investoren verrückt machte." www.spiegel.de, 1 August 2009.

   von Petersdorff, W. "Eine Blumenzwiebel für 87.000 Euro." www.faz.net, 18 March 2008.

2. **The Dojima Rice Market and the "God of Markets" (1750)**

   Mattheis, P. "Der Reishändler." SZ-Serie: *Die großen Spekulanten* 39. www.sueddeutsche.de, 28 October 2008.

   Needham, J. "Samurai trader!" www.financialsense.com, 20 January 2008.

3. **The California Gold Rush (1849)**

   Bojanowski, A. "Neuer Goldrausch in Kalifornien—'Es ist wie 1849.'" www.sueddeutsche.de, 17 June 2008.

   "Going to California—49ers and the Gold Rush." http://americanhistory.about.com, 2008.

   "Gold Rush." The California State Library, www.library.ca.gov/goldrush, 2007.

4. **Wheat: Old Hutch Makes a Killing (1866)**

   "B. P. Hutchinson dead—once leading grain speculator in this country." *The New York Times*, 17 March 1899.

   Ferris, W. G. *The Grain Traders. The Story of the Chicago Board of Trade.* East Lansing: Michigan State University Press, 1988.

   Geisst, Charles. *Wheels of fortune—The history of speculation to respectability.* Hoboken, NJ: John Wiley & Sons, 2002.

   "The great speculator fails—Mr. Hutchinson leaves Chicago and his trades closed out." *The New York Times*, 30 April 1891.

   Teweles, R. J., and Jones, F. J. *The Futures Game—Who Wins? Who Loses? And Why?* New York: McGraw-Hill, 1987.

5. **Rockefeller and Standard Oil (1870)**

   King, B. W. "John D. Rockefeller und das Zeitalter des Öls." http://finanzen.coart.de/BrsenKnowHow/Geschichtliches, 18 August 2006.

Kunz, M. "Reichster und meistgehasster Mann der Welt." www.focus.de, 23 May 2008.

6.   Wheat: The Great Chicago Fire (1872)

Ferris, W. G. *The Grain Traders: The Story of the Chicago Board of Trade.* East Lansing: Michigan State University Press, 1988.

Geisst, C. *Wheels of fortune—The history of speculation to respectability.* Hoboken, NJ: John Wiley & Sons, 2002.

"The wheat corner—sudden collapse of the grain gamblers' schemes in Chicago loss of the clique over USD 1,000,000." *The New York Times,* 23 August 1872.

7.   Crude Oil: Ari Onassis's Midas Touch (1956)

"Aristoteles Onassis—Reicher Mann ganz arm." www.stern.de, 13 January 2006.

"Kalkuliertes Risiko." *Der Spiegel* 29(1978), www.spiegel.de.

Seebach, W. "König Saud und Aristoteles Onassis." *Die Zeit,* www.zeit.de, 17 June 1954.

8.   Soybeans: Hide and Seek in New Jersey (1963)

Food and Agriculture Organization of the United Nations (FAO), www.fao.org, December 2008.

"The man who fooled everybody." www.time.com, 4 June 1963.

Miller, N. C. *The Great Salad Oil Swindle.* Baltimore: Penguin Books, 1965.

"Wall Street: spreading the losses." www.time.com, 6 December 1963.

9.   Wheat: The Russian Bear Is Hungry (1972)

"Another Soviet grain sting." www.time.com, 28 November 1977.

The Food and Agriculture Organization of the United Nations (FAO), www.fao. org, December 2008.

Mattheis, P. "Der Turtle-Chef." SZ-Serie: *Die großen Spekulanten* (33), www. sueddeutsche.de, 29 January 2008.

Peters, M., Langley, S., and Westcott, P. "Agricultural commodity price spikes in the 1970s and 1990s." United States Department of Agriculture (USDA), March 2009, www.ers.usda.gov.

10.   The End of the Gold Standard (1973)

Schulte, T. "Silber—das bessere Gold." Kopp Verlag, 2010.

"Die Silber-Panik" (1893). http://zeitenwende.ch.

"US-Bundesstaaten wollen einen Gold- und Silberstandard." www.bullion-investor.net, 7 March 2010.

11. 1970s—Oil Crisis! (1973 & 1979)

"Die Ölkrise 1973." http://zeitenwende.ch, 2009.

Organization of the Petroleum Exporting Countries (OPEC), www.opec.org, 2008.

US Department of Energy, www.eia.doe.gov, 2008.

12. Diamonds: The Crash of the World's Hardest Currency (1979)

Grill, B. "Herr der Diamanten." www.zeit.de, 2 October 2003.

"Im Griff des Syndikats." *Der Spiegel* 44 (1989), www.spiegel.de.

Kühner, C. "A diamond's best friend—Antwerpen, Weltzentrum des Diamantenhandels." *NZZ Folio,* December 1993.

Schulz, B. "Nicholas Oppenheimer—Der Diamantenkönig." www.faz.net, 22 October 2006.

13. "Silver Thursday" and the Downfall of the Hunt Brothers (1980)

Boehringer, S. "Aufstieg mit Öl, Absturz mit Silber." SZ-Serie: *Die großen Spekulanten* 17, www.sueddeutsche.de, 14 May 2008.

"Die Gebrüder Hunt verzocken sich am Silbermarkt." www.faz.net, 26 February 2004.

14. Crude Oil: No Blood for Oil? (1990)

"Fünf Jahre Irak-Krieg—Chronik eines umstrittenen Feldzugs." www.spiegel.de, 17 March 2008.

"Der Golfkrieg 1991." www.faz.net, 24 February 2001.

Pollack, K. "Der gefährlichste Mann der Welt." *Der Spiegel* 6 (2003), www.spiegel.de.

Pollack, K. *The Threatening Storm—The Case for Invading Iraq.* New York: Random House, 2002.

Thumann, M. "Trotz Blut kein Öl." www.zeit.de, 16 June 2009.

15. The Doom of German Metallgesellschaft (1993)

Knipp, T. *Der Machtkampf. Der Fall Metallgesellschaft und die Deutsche Bank.* Düsseldorf: Econ Verlag, 1998.

Landler, M. "Spotlight: Heinz Schimmelbusch's comeback." www.nytimes.com, 10 August 2007.

"Metallgesellschaft reports talks with ex-chief fail." *New York Times*, 5 April 1996.

"Missmanagement bei Metallgesellschaft." www.manager-magazin.de, 28 August 2001.

16. Silver: Three Wise Kings (1994)

Chasan, E. "Apex Silver Mines files for bankruptcy protection." www.reuters.com, 14 January 2009.

Fuerbringer, J. "Buffett likes silver; Soros, a silver mine." www.nytimes.com, 26 March 1998.

Morgenson, G. "Gates putting some money in silver miner." www.nytimes.com, 29 September 1999.

The Silver Institute, www.silverinstitute.org.

Weitzman, H. "Morales pledges to nationalize mining industry in Bolivia." www.ft.com, 9 May 2006.

17. Copper: "Mr. Five Percent" Moves the Market (1996)

Bastian, N. "Kupferfinger sucht einen neuen Job." www.handelsblatt.com, 12 December 2005.

www.kupferinstitut.de.

Neidhart, C. "Hamanaka—der Vorstadt-Spießer." SZ-Serie: *Die großen Spekulanten* 2. www.sueddeutsche.de, 29 January 2008.

18. Gold: Welcome to the Jungle (1997)

Behar, R. "Jungle Fever." *Fortune*, 9 June 1997.

BHP Billiton, Minerals Companion, 2006

"Goldenes Grab." *Der Spiegel* 16 (1997), www.spiegel.de.

Goold, D., and Willis, A. *The Bre-X Fraud.* Toronto: McClelland & Stewart, 1997.

19. Palladium: More Expensive Than Gold (2001)

Frank, R. "Eine Seltenheit: Palladium-Münzen." www.moneytrend.at, January 2001.

United Nations Conference on Trade and Development (UNCTAD), Market Information in the Commodities Area (InfoComm), www.unctad.org/infocomm.

Wolf, C. "Palladium—Rasante Rekordjagd." www.focus.de, 18 January 2001.

20. Copper: Liu Qibing Disappears Without a Trace (2005)

"Bad bets in the copper market." www.economist.com, 18 November 2005.

Busch, A. "China treibt den Kupferpreis von allen Seiten in die Höhe." www.handelsblatt.com, 12 December 2005.

Hoffbauer, A. "Die diskreten Kontrakte des Herrn Liu." www.handelsblatt.com, 12 December 2005.

Mortished, C. "City gripped by mystery of the phantom copper dealer." *The Times*, 15 November 2005.

Powell, B. "Buy! Sell! Run!" www.time.com, 20 November 2005.

21. Zinc: Flotsam and Jetsam (2005)

BHP Billiton, Minerals Companion, 2006.

International Lead and Zinc Study Group, www.ilzsg.org, 2009.

London Metal Exchange, www.lme.co.uk, 2009.

"A user guide to commodities." Deutsche Bank, September 2008.

"Zinc in New Orleans flooded warehouses." Reed Business Information, 2009.

"Zinc price soars after New Orleans supply freeze." www.telegraph.co.uk, 7 September 2005.

"Zinc under supply tightness." *Metalworld*, September 2005.

22. Natural Gas: Brian Hunter and the Downfall of Amaranth (2006)

"Amaranth trading led to MotherRock loss." Bloomberg, 25 June 2007.

Energy Information Administration, www.eia.doe.gov, 2009.

"Hedge-Fonds hat angeblich fünf Milliarden Dollar verwettet." www.handelsblatt.com, 19 September 2006.

"Hedge-Fonds MotherRock schließt." www.handelsblatt.com, 7 August 2006.

"In sieben Tagen 4,5 Milliarden Dollar Verlust." www.manager-magazin.de, 19 September 2006.

"Milliardenverlust von Hedge-Fonds läßt Märkte kalt." www.fazfinance.net, 20 September 2006.

US Department of Energy, www.energy.gov, 2009.

Copeland, R. "Ten years after blowup, Amaranth investors waiting to get money back." *Wall Street Journal*, www.wsj.com/articles/ten-years-after-blowup-amaranth-investors-still-waiting-for-money-back-1451524482, 1 January 2016.

23. Orange Juice: Collateral Damage (2006)

"Orange juice falls." *The New York Times*, 22 January 2004.

"Orange juice rises." *The New York Times*, 14 August 2004.

www.flcitrusmutual.com.

www.nws.noaa.gov.

US Department of Agriculture (USDA). Situation and Outlook for Orange Juice. www.fas.usda.gov, February 2006.

24. John Fredriksen: The Sea Wolf (2006)

Bomsdorf, B. "John Fredriksen—Milliardär und Tankerkönig." www.welt.de/wirtschaft/article1799093/John-Fredriksen-Milliardaer-und-Tankerkoenig.html, 14 March 2008.

"Kathrine und Cecilie Astrup Fredriksen Schnappen sich diese schönen Milliardärs-Töchter TUI?" www.bild.de/politik/wirtschaft/kaufen-diese-schoenen-milliardaers-toechter-tui-11713918.bild.html, 2 July 2010.

"Lachsfieber: Brisante Recherchen über einen Nahrungsmittelgiganten." www.ardmediathek.de.

OECD-FAO: Agricultural Outlook 2011–2012. www.fao.org.

25. Lakshmi Mittal: Feel the Steel (2006)

Feel the Steel is the logo of Pittsburgh Steelers (www.steelers.com).

"Arcelor und Mittal. Stahl-Giganten einigen sich auf Fusion." www.spiegel.de/wirtschaft/arcelor-und-mittal-stahl-giganten-einigen-sich-auf-fusion-a-423475.html, 25 June 2006.

"Der größte Stahlproduzent der Welt entsteht." http://www.faz.net/aktuell/wirtschaft/rohstoffe-der-groesste-stahlproduzent-der-welt-entsteht-1192255.html, 25 October 2004.

James, J. "Steel's new spring." *Time* magazine, www.time.com, 31 October 2004.

Kanter, J., Timmons, H., and Giridharadas, A. "Arcelor agrees to Mittal takeover." www.nytimes.com/2006/06/25/business/worldbusiness/25iht-steel.html, 25 June 2006.

Kroder, T. "Lakshmi Mittal: Der Stahlbaron aus Indien." www.ftd.de, 25 October 2004.

www.arcelormittal.com.

"Lakshmi Mittal 'Stahl-Maharadscha' mit Familiensinn." www.stern. de/wirtschaft/news/lakshmi-mittal--stahl-maharadscha--mit-familiensinn-3498140.html, 27 January 2006.

"Mittal/Arcelor Fusion perfekt." http://www.manager-magazin.de/unternehmen/artikel/a-428605.html, 26 July 2006.

Zitzelsberger, G. "Fusion der Stahlgiganten. Ein moderner Maharadscha." www.sueddeutsche.de/wirtschaft/fusion-der-stahlgiganten-ein-moderner-maharadscha-1.819924, 5 December 2008.

26. Crude Oil: The Return of the "Seven Sisters" (2007)

Hoyos, C. "The evolution of the Seven Sisters." www.ft.com/content/2103f4da-cd8e-11db-839d-000b5df10621, 11 March 2007.

Hoyos, C. "The new Seven Sisters: oil and gas giants dwarf western rivals." www.ft.com/content/471ae1b8-d001-11db-94cb-000b5df10621, 12 March 2007.

"Petro-China—Das teuerste Unternehmen der Welt." www.faz.net, 5 November 2007.

"The Seven Sisters still rule." www.time.com, 9 September 1978.

Vardy, N. "The new Seven Sisters: today's most powerful energy companies." https://seekingalpha.com/article/30922-the-new-seven-sisters-todays-most-powerful-energy-companies, 28 March 2007.

27. Wheat and the "Millennium Drought" in Australia (2007)

"Dried up, washed out, fed up." *The Economist*, 4 October 2007.

"Dramatische Dürre." www.spiegel.de, 20 April 2007.

"Dürre in Australien." www.faz.net, 10 November 2006.

"Dürre in Australien." www.stern.de, 2 January 2007.

"Dürre treibt Bauern in den Selbstmord." www.stern.de, 24 October 2006.

"Extremwetter—Jahrtausend-Dürre in Australien." www.spiegel.de, 7 November 2006.

International Grains Council (IGC), www.igc.org.uk, 2009.

"Der Weizenpreis läuft von Rekord zu Rekord." www.faz.net, 26 February 2008.

28. Natural Gas: Aftermath in Canada (2007)

"BMO Financial hikes commodity-trading loss view." Reuters, May 2007.

"BMO says commodity-trading losses to dent profit." Reuters, April 2007.

"Ex-BMO trader gets fine." www.thestar.com, 7 November 2009.

"How did BMO's USD450M loss just materialize?" *Financial Post*, April 2007.

29. Platinum: All Lights Out in South Africa (2008)

Cotterill, J. "S Africa power monopoly too big to fail." *Financial Times*, 6 February 2019.

"Eskom says SA needs 'at least' 40 new coal mines." www.mg.co.za, 8 August 2009.

Johnson Matthey, www.matthey.com, 2009.

London Platinum and Palladium Market, www.lppm.org.uk, 2009.

"Stromausfall in Südafrika erreicht Rohstoffmärkte." www.fazfinance.net, 25 January 2008.

30. Rice: The Oracle (2008)

Müller, O. "Angst vor Hungersnot—Hoher Reispreis macht Asien nervös." www.handelsblatt.com, 9 April 2008.

"USA rechnen mit mehr als 100.000 Toten." www.focus.de, 7 May 2008.

31. Wheat: Working in Memphis (2008)

"Rohstoffmärkte sind spekulativ überhitzt." www.faz.net, 6 March 2008.

"Rogue trader rocks firm—Huge wheat futures loss stuns MF Global." www.chicagotribune.com, 29 February 2008.

32. Crude Oil: Contango in Texas (2009)

Baskin, B. "Oil stored at sea washes out rallies." http://online.wsj.com, 5 February 2009.

Bayer, T. "'Super-Contango'—Unternehmen bunkern Öl." www.ftd.de, 8 December 2008.

Hecking, C., and Bayer, T. "Abgeschmiert in der Prärie." www.ftd.de, 19 January 2009.

33. Sugar: Waiting for the Monsoon (2010)

Abraham, T. K. "World sugar shortage to extend a third year." Bloomberg, 29 January 2010.

Hein, C. "Indien betet für einen stärkeren Monsun." www.faz.net,
12 August 2009.

Kazim, H. "Dürre bedroht Indiens Wirtschaft." www.spiegel.de, 18 August 2009.

Lembke, J. "Der Zuckerpreis ist kaum zu stoppen." www.faz.net, 7 August 2009.

Mai, C. "Zuckerpreis erreicht 25-Jahres-Hoch." www.ftd.de, 3 August 2009.

Merkel, W. "In Indien und Australien wird die Dürre noch größer." www.welt.de,
24 September 2009.

Stern, N. "Ernteausfälle in Indien treiben Zuckerpreis." http://diepresse.com,
16 August 2009.

34. Chocolate Finger (2010)

"Kakao als Spielball der Spekulation." www.faz.net, 20 July 2010.

Marron, D. "The cocoa corner: Is Choc Finger down USD 150 million?"
http://seekingalpha.com, 26 July 2010.

Murugan, S. "What's driving cocoa?" http://seekingalpha.com, 4 August 2010.

"Sweet dreams. A hedge fund bets big on chocolate." www.economist.com/
finance-and-economics/2010/08/05/sweet-dreams, 7–13 August 2010.

Werdigier, J., and Creswell, J. "Trader's cocoa binge wraps up chocolate market."
www.nytimes.com, 24 July 2010.

35. Copper: King of the Congo (2010)

"Congo—Africa's disaster." www.independent.co.uk/voices/editorials/leading-
article-congo-africas-disaster-2013789.html, 30 June 2010. "Kongo will
mehr von eigenen Rohstoffen profitieren." www.gtai.de, 24 June 2010.

MacNamara, W., and Johnson, M. "Disquiet over ENRC's purchase of Congo
assets." www.ft.com/content/19fe6f94-b791-11df-8ef6-00144feabdc0,
3 September 2010.

MacNamara, W., and Thompson, C. "Congo seizes First Quantum Minerals'
assets." www.ft.com/content/27d6e104-b530-11df-9af8-00144feabdc0,
31 August 2010.

Thompson, C., and MacNamara, W. "ENRC buys into disputed Congo project."
www.ft.com/content/870a8b2a-acda-11df-8582-00144feabdc0,
21 August 2010.

36. Crude Oil: Deep Water Horizon and the Spill (2010)

"780 Millionen Liter—die bisher größte Ölpest aller Zeiten." www.zeit.de/
wissen/umwelt/2010-08/bp-oelloch-leck-verzoegerung, 3 August 2010.

Bethge, P., and Meyer, C. "Die Alptraum-Bohrung." www.spiegel.de/
spiegel/a-713063.html, 23 August 2010.

"Ölkatastrophe im Golf von Mexiko Alarm auf Bohrinsel war offenbar
abgeschaltet." www.spiegel.de/wissenschaft/natur/oelkatastrophe-im-golf-
von-mexiko-alarm-auf-bohrinsel-war-offenbar-abgeschaltet-a-708247.html,
24 July 2010.

"Ölpest im Golf von MexikoAuch BP macht die Katastrophe jetzt Angst." www.
stern.de/panorama/wissen/natur/oelpest-im-golf-von-mexiko-auch-bp-
macht-die-katastrophe-jetzt-angst-3284936.html, 30 May 2010.

"Ölpest im Golf von Mexiko BP-Experten durchtrennen leckendes Öl-Rohr."
www.spiegel.de/wissenschaft/natur/oelpest-im-golf-von-mexiko-bp-
experten-durchtrennen-leckendes-oel-rohr-a-698597.html, 3 June 2010.

"'Static Kill' erfolgreich. BP stopft Öl-Bohrloch." www.stern.de/panorama/
wissen/natur/-static-kill--erfolgreich-bp-stopft-oel-bohrloch-3537142.html,
4 August 2010.

37. Cotton: White Gold (2011)

Cancryn, A., and Cui, C. "Flashback to 1870 as cotton hits peak." www.wsj.com/
articles/SB10001424052748704300604575554210569885910,
16 October 2010.

Cui, C. "Chinese take a cotton to hoarding." www.wsj.com/articles/SB10001424
052748704680604576110423777349298, 29 January 2011.

Industrievereinigung Chemiefaser e.V. (IVC), www.ivc-ev.de.

National Cotton Council of America, www.cotton.org.

Pitzke, M. "Preisexplosion bei Baumwolle Das Ende der Billig-Jeans." http://
www.spiegel.de/wirtschaft/unternehmen/preisexplosion-bei-baumwolle-das-
ende-der-billig-jeans-a-696579.html, 25 May 2010.

United States Department of Agriculture, www.usda.gov.

White, G. "Cotton price causes 'panic buying' as nears 150-year high." www.
telegraph.co.uk/finance/markets/8301886/Cotton-price-causes-panic-
buying-as-nears-150-year-high.html, 4 February 2011.

Wollenschlaeger, U. "Baumwolle: Auf Rekordpreise folgt Rekordproduktion."
www.textilwirtschaft.de/business/unternehmen/Baumwolle-Auf-
Rekordpreise-folgt-Rekordproduktion-69081?crefresh=1, 9 March 2011.

38. Glencore: A Giant Steps into the Light (2011)

Ammann, D. "King of Oil." Orell Füssli Verlag, Zurich, 2010.

Ammann, D. "Marc Rich: Der mann, der seinen Namen verlor." www.
weltwoche.ch, 23 May 2007.

Honigsbaum, M. "The Rich list." In *The Observer*, www.guardian.co.uk,
13 May 2001.

"Rohstoffhändler Marc Rich gestorben." www.srf.ch/news/wirtschaft/
rohstoffhaendler-marc-rich-gestorben, 27 June 2013.

Schärer, A. "Die Erben des Marc Rich." www.woz.ch, 13 December 2001.

"Warum Marc Rich bei Madoff rechtzeitig ausstieg." www.tagesanzeiger.ch/
wirtschaft/unternehmen-und-konjunktur/Warum-Marc-Rich-bei-Madoff-
rechtzeitig-ausstieg/story/30815433, 27 January 2011.

39. Rare Earth Mania: Neodymium, Dysprosium, and Lanthanum (2011)

Quote from: J. Perkowski, *Behind China's Rare Earth Controversy.* http://www.
forbes.com/sites/jackperkowski/2012/06/21/behind-chinas-rare-earth-
controversy/#e5aaecd16b82, 21 June 2012.

Blank, G. "Wichtiger Rohstoff Seltene Erden. Knappheit made in China." www.
stern.de/digital/computer/wichtiger-rohstoff-seltene-erden-knappheit-made-
in-china-3874186.html, 29 December 2010.

"Chinas schwere Hand auf den seltenen Erden." www.nzz.ch/chinas_schwere_
hand_auf_den_seltenen_erden-1.8096711, 22 October 2010.

Geinitz, C. "Streit mit China um seltene Erden spitzt sich zu." www.faz.net/
aktuell/wirtschaft/rohstoffe-streit-mit-china-um-seltene-erden-spitzt-
sich-zu-13091.html, 25 October 2010.

Jung, A. "Rohstoffe. Wettlauf der Trüffelschweine," www.spiegel.de/spiegel/
print/d-75159727.html, 15 November 2010.

Liedtke, M., and Elsner, H. "Seltene Erden," Bundesanstalt für
Geowissenschaften und Rohstoffe." www.bgr.bund.de, 20 November 2009.

Lohmann, D. "Kampf um Seltene Erden. Hightech-Rohstoffe als Mangelware."
www.scinexx.de/dossier-540-1.html, 13 May 2011.

Mayer-Kuckuk, F. "Strategische Metalle China verknappt Molybdän-Förderung."
www.handelsblatt.com/finanzen/maerkte/devisen-rohstoffe/strategische-
metalle-china-verknappt-molybdaen-foerderung/3579078.html?ticket=ST-
1201086-huIl3W7cP5RSMLdwDNFj-ap3, 1 November 2010.

40. The End? Crude Oil Down the Drain (2016)

Cunningham, N. "OPEC: the oil glut is gone." https://oilprice.com/Energy/
Crude-Oil/OPEC-The-Oil-Glut-Is-Gone.html, 14 May 2018.

Cunningham, N. "The world is not running out of storage space for oil." https://oilprice.com/Energy/Energy-General/The-World-Is-Not-Running-Out-Of-Storage-Space-For-Oil.html, 21 January 2016.

Dennin, T. "The dawn of a new cycle in commodities." Research Paper, Tiberius Asset Management AG, April 2016.

EIA. "Crude oil prices to remain relatively low through 2016 and 2017." www.eia.gov/todayinenergy/detail.php?id=24532, 13 January 2016.

El Gamal, R., Lawler, A., and Ghaddar, A. "OPEC in first joint oil cut with Russia since 2001," Saudis take 'big hit.'" www.reuters.com/article/us-opec-meeting-idUSKBN13P0JA, 30 November 2016.

Raval, A. "'Oil market glut will persist through 2016,' says IEA." www.ft.com/content/e27ff724-717e-11e5-9b9e-690fdae72044, 13 October 2015.

Shenk, M. "WTI crude falls to 12-year low at $26.14 per barrel." www.bloomberg.com/news/articles/2016-02-10/oil-holds-losses-near-3-week-low-amid-record-cushing-supplies, 11 February 2016.

41. Electrification: The Evolution of Battery Metals (2017)

Autoverkäufe 2017. "Mercedes fährt BMW und Audi davon." cwww.abendblatt.de/wirtschaft/article213089441/BMW-verkauft-so-viele-Autos-wie-nie.html, 12 January 2018.

BNEF New Energy Outlook, https://about.bnef.com/new-energy-outlook, 16 August 2018.

Hull, D., and Recht, H. "Tesla doesn't burn fuel, it burns cash." www.bloomberg.com/graphics/2018-tesla-burns-cash, 3 May 2018.

Kraftfahrtbundesamt, www.kba.de.

42. Crypto Craze: Bitcoins and the Emergence of Cryptocurrencies (2018)

Akolkar, B. "China officially bans all crypto-related commercial activities." 22 August 2018, https://bitcoinist.com/china-officially-bans-crypto-activities/.

"Comparing 25 of the biggest cryptocurrencies." World Economic Forum, March 2018, www.weforum.org/agenda/2018/03/comparing-the-25-most-notable-cryptocurrencies.

"Cryptoprimer." www.investopedia.com/tech/crypto-primer-currencies-commodities-tokens/#ixzz5HfVcEWBS.

Kharif, O. "The bitcoin whales: 1,000 people who own 40 percent of the market." https://www.bloomberg.com/news/articles/2017-12-08/the-bitcoin-whales-1-000-people-who-own-40-percent-of-the-market, 8 December 2017.

Kharpal, A. (2017): "Founders of a cryptocurrency backed by Floyd Mayweather charged with fraud by SEC." www.cnbc.com, 3 April 2017.

Lee, J. "Mystery of the $2 billion bitcoin whale that fueled a selloff." https://www.bloomberg.com/news/articles/2018-09-13/mystery-of-the-2-billion-bitcoin-whale-that-fueled-a-selloff, 13 September 2018.

Meyer, D. "China enlists its 'great firewall' to block bitcoin websites." http://fortune.com/2018/02/05/bitcoin-china-website-ico-block-ban-firewall/, 5 February 2018.

Paul, A. "It's 1994 In cryptocurrency." www.forbes.com/sites/apaul/2017/11/27/its-1994-in-cryptocurrency/#7a81d58eb28a, 27 November 20017.

Potter, S., and White, T. "No end in sight for crypto sell-off as bitcoin breaches $4,250." www.bloomberg.com/news/articles/2018-11-20/no-end-in-sight-for-crypto-sell-off-as-tokens-take-fresh-hit.

Shiller, R. "Irrational exuberance." Crown Business, 9 May 2006.

About the Author

TORSTEN DENNIN is Professor of Economics and member of the Berlin Institute of Finance, Innovation and Digitalization.

For almost 20 years, Dr. Dennin has been a professional investment expert in commodity and equity markets. He is chief investment officer and a member of the Board of Asset Management Switzerland AG and founder of Lynkeus Capital LLC, an investment company focused on commodities and natural resources in Zug, Switzerland. Dr. Dennin started his professional career in asset and wealth management for Deutsche Bank AG in Frankfurt am Main, Germany, in 2003. There he was responsible for investment decisions for two commodity funds as well as several discretionary commodity strategies with combined assets under management of 500 million USD. From 2010 to 2013, he acted as co-head of natural resources for Altira AG / VCH Investments, which includes investment decisions for VCH Commodity Alpha and VCH Expert Natural Resources Equity Fund. From 2013 to 2017, Dr. Dennin took over as head of portfolio management and research at Tiberius Asset Management AG in Zug, Switzerland. Besides analyzing commodity markets as well as natural resources equities, he was responsible for all commodity investment strategies, including Tiberius Commodity Alpha and Tiberius Active Commodity Fund, totaling 800 million USD assets under management.

Dr. Dennin studied economics at the University of Cologne, Germany, and at Pennsylvania State University in the United States. In 2009, Dr. Dennin received his PhD in economics at the Schumpeter School of Business and Economics.

Dr. Dennin lives in Switzerland, is the author of several books, publishes regularly in industry journals, and is often invited by the media to comment on current market affairs. His latest book, *From Tulips to Bitcoins*, reached bestseller status on Amazon in the categories finance, commodities, and digital currencies and has been translated into six languages. The author can be contacted via LinkedIn.

www.ingramcontent.com/pod-product-compliance
Lightning Source LLC
Chambersburg PA
CBHW030452210326
41597CB00013B/634